5/02

D0350271

03
11

ILL ...

/02

VALUE INVESTING

with the

MASTERS

REVEALING INTERVIEWS
WITH 20 MARKET-BEATING
MANAGERS WHO HAVE
STOOD THE TEST OF TIME

VALUE INVESTING
with the
MASTERS

REVEALING INTERVIEWS

WITH 20 MARKET-BEATING

MANAGERS WHO HAVE

STOOD THE TEST OF TIME

KIRK KAZANJIAN
Author of **WIZARDS OF WALL STREET**

NYIF

NEW YORK INSTITUTE OF FINANCE

NEW YORK • TORONTO • SYDNEY • TOKYO • SINGAPORE

Library of Congress Cataloging-in-Publication Data

Kazanjian, Kirk.
  Value investing with the masters / Kirk Kazanjian.
    p. cm.
    ISBN 0-7352-0321-0 (case)
    1. Investment analysis.   2. Stocks.   I. Title.

  HG4529 .K39 2002
  332.63'22—dc21   2001058361

This publication is designed to provide accurate and authoritative information in regard to the subject matter covered. It is sold with the understanding that the publisher is not engaged in rendering legal, accounting, or other professional service. If legal advice or other expert assistance is required, the services of a competent professional person should be sought.

. . . From the Declaration of Principles jointly adopted by a Committee of the American Bar Association and a Committee of Publishers and Associations

Although the information and data in this book were obtained from sources believed to be reliable, neither the author nor the publisher assumes responsibility for its accuracy. Under no circumstances does the information in this book represent a recommendation to buy or sell stocks or funds.

ISBN 0-7352-0321-0

ATTENTION: CORPORATIONS AND SCHOOLS

Prentice Hall books are available at quantity discounts with bulk purchase for educational, business, or sales promotional use. For information, please write to: Prentice Hall Special Sales, 240 Frisch Court, Paramus, New Jersey 07652. Please supply: title of book, ISBN, quantity, how the book will be used, date needed.

 NEW YORK INSTITUTE OF FINANCE
An Imprint of Prentice Hall Press
Paramus, NJ 07652

http://www.phdirect.com

NYIF and NEW YORK INSTITUTE OF FINANCE are trademarks of Executive Tax Reports, Inc., used under license by Prentice Hall Direct, Inc.

*To all of the teachers and mentors
who have imparted their wisdom to me over the years,
including the many investment Masters
I have been privileged to know and work with
throughout my career.*

CONTENTS

PART TWO: INVESTING LIKE THE MASTERS

INTRODUCTION

When you think of the most celebrated investors of all time, Warren Buffett, John Templeton, and the late Benjamin Graham no doubt immediately come to mind. All three of these luminaries are consummate bargain hunters, on the prowl for good stocks that can be bought on the cheap. In other words, they are (or were) value investors.

Called by many the father of value investing, Graham, a former finance professor at Columbia University, first outlined his techniques for finding undervalued stocks and bonds in *Security Analysis*, an in-depth tome penned in 1934 with fellow Columbia professor David Dodd. Now considered to be the bible for value investors, *Security Analysis* illustrates a number of techniques for finding stocks and bonds "selling well below the levels apparently justified by a careful analysis of the relevant facts." Graham expanded on his value lessons in *The Intelligent Investor*, which was first published in 1949.

Warren Buffett was a student of Graham's at Columbia. They later became personal friends. And while neither specifically referred to himself as a "value investor," both clearly have become heroes and role models to those following this heralded investment discipline.

In its simplest form, value investing involves buying stocks selling below market prices as judged by a number of variables. Many value investors look for companies trading below so-called *intrinsic value,* a term Graham and Dodd introduced in *Security Analysis.* Intrinsic value is often in the eye of the beholder. In fact, Graham admitted that even though he coined the phrase, it was a rather "elusive concept." For most value investors, though, intrinsic value is what a rational investor would pay to buy out the entire business for cash.

Other value investors pay closer attention to traditional statistical measures, such as *price/earnings ratios* and *book value*. In all cases, value investors look to buy stocks at what they consider to be sale prices. Then, they hold on for what can be years before the value of their shares is realized, at which point they walk away with a profit.

By contrast, growth and momentum investors look for fast-growing companies, and are often willing to pay a premium for that growth. Price is much less of a consideration with them than with value investors. While this approach can lead to quick gains in a roaring bull market, momentum investing is especially vulnerable to market declines. We saw strong recent evidence of this. In 1999, a large handful of aggressive growth and momentum funds posted triple-digit gains, only to fall 50 to 80 percent in 2000, chalking up even more red ink in 2001. During this same time, value investors as a group posted positive returns and, in a number of cases, saw their portfolios rise even in the face of a vicious bear market for the overall market.

Ironically, this resurgence in value investing came at a time when a number of respected publications were questioning whether value, as an investment strategy, was dead. Some pundits proclaimed that stock prices no longer mattered since we were living in a new era. Techniques that called for buying stocks with ever-rising prices gained wide acceptance. But, in the end, value proved to be alive and well. We discovered that the new era was not new at all, and ever-rising prices are eventually subject to fall.

Without question, value investing has stood the test of time. It has survived several world wars, terrorist attacks, and numerous recessions. In fact, a number of academic studies show that the value approach has bested the growth approach over long periods of time across all types of stocks—large and small.

Still, the discipline isn't always in favor. In the late 1990s, although many value investors continued to post positive results, the majority looked out of step. Their undervalued securities were trampled by the fast-growing momentum stocks, which investors were all too eager to snap up. None of the high-flying Internet and technology stocks sold at bargain prices and therefore were absent from the portfolios of most value investors, except for those who bought such stocks at much lower levels. While this hurt performance in the short run, avoiding these pricey securities proved helpful once the bubble in these overpriced and over-hyped securities burst. What's more, as a result of the outrageous run-up in many momentum stocks and its aftermath, some experts predict that the value approach will remain in the spotlight for many years to come.

Without doubt, the world has changed since *Security Analysis* was published almost 70 years ago. So have the securities markets. At the same time, a new breed of value investors has emerged to carry on the tradition started by Graham, Templeton, and Buffett. They are the new value-investing Masters. In the pages that follow, you will meet these esteemed managers up close.

The 20 masters featured in this book are clearly at the head of their class. To be considered a Master, each manager had to be currently running a publicly available mutual fund with a demonstrated track record of outperforming his peers and, in many cases, the market overall. Why were only managers currently running funds included? Because many of you invest in stocks using mutual funds. As a result, I wanted to introduce you to some of the best value managers in the business whom you can actually hire to invest your money. If you don't own value funds run by at least some of these Masters, you may want to reconsider. This book will help you to identify which managers might be best for you.

Even if you don't invest in funds, this book is also for you. The sharpest value managers in the business will show you in clear detail how to find winning stocks. As you hear about their techniques in their own words, you'll learn from their mistakes and successes in the process. You can then apply these lessons to your own investment process.

Who are these value-investing Masters? They are traditional value investors such as Christopher Browne, David Dreman, Jean-Marie Eveillard, James Gipson, and Chuck Royce, all of whom have more than three decades of experience under their belts. They also include managers who are rewriting the rules of value investing—among them Bill Miller, Bill Fries, and even celebrated vulture investor Marty Whitman. In addition, I have included several members of the new generation of value investors—managers who haven't been in the business all that long, but have already proven their talent for making money. These young bucks include Bill Nygren, Jim Gilligan, Bret Stanley, and Kevin O'Boyle.

The Masters often mine different areas of the market for their investment ideas. Chuck Royce and Bob Perkins, for example, concentrate on small-company stocks. Bill Nygren and Dick Weiss are most interested in mid-caps. Many of the rest will buy just about anything.

Part One of *Value Investing with the Masters* is divided into 20 chapters, each one an interview with a different Master. The interviews are presented in alphabetical order and follow a similar pattern. We start off talking about the Master's background and how he initially got into the business. We then discuss his investment process and describe in specific detail how he finds value in the market. Along the way we uncover specific examples to illustrate his process. In many cases, we also chat about the recent bear market, what can be learned from the market bubble that burst in early 2000, and what the future holds for value investing.

In Part Two, I have synthesized the key traits shared by most of the managers in a chapter called "What the Masters Have in Common." Taking this one step further, I then collected the most frequently mentioned lessons learned from these Masters and put them together in the chapter entitled "The 10 Keys to Successful Value Investing." This chapter contains a number of rules you can use when selecting individual stocks on your own.

At the end of the book, you'll find a glossary of selected terms frequently used by value investors. Therefore, as you're reading these interviews, if you run across a word you're not familiar with, flip to this section and chances are you'll find a definition for it here.

Keep in mind that not all of your portfolio has to be invested using a value style; but most experts would argue that value should be a part of it. There are other legitimate approaches to stock picking as well. To learn more about these other disciplines, you might want to read the predecessor to this book, *Wizards of Wall Street,* which features one-on-one interviews with 18 top mutual fund managers who have successfully employed a variety of stock picking techniques over the years.

In closing, I'd like to thank all of the Masters and their trusted assistants for their help in making this book possible. They were most generous with their time, and for that I am grateful. I'd also like to acknowledge my expert assistant and transcriber, Darla McDavid, for her continued excellent work, along with my editor, Ellen Schneid Coleman, and the staff at Prentice Hall Press, who always do a top-notch job.

Now, let's learn more about value investing from the true Masters of this discipline. I trust you will find these conversations to be as enjoyable and enlightening as I did.

—Kirk Kazanjian

PART ONE

THE MASTERS OF VALUE INVESTING

CHRISTOPHER BROWNE

TWEEDY, BROWNE COMPANY

While almost every Master featured in this book extols the virtues of Benjamin Graham, only Chris Browne can claim that Graham was a former client of his firm. Tweedy, Browne was originally founded some 80 years ago. It began as a brokerage firm and then became a securities dealer, before evolving into a premier value money manager. Although Forrest Berwind Tweedy started the firm, Browne's father was an early partner. In the 1950s, the firm rented space to a noted investor who introduced Tweedy, Browne to Warren Buffett. Buffett wound up buying the bulk of his Berkshire Hathaway shares through the company.

Chris Browne never planned to join the family business. He took a job at the firm during a summer break in college to earn some extra money, and has been there ever since. His brother Will joined Tweedy, Browne a few years later. Today, Chris, Will, and their partners run more than $8 billion using many of the value techniques pioneered by Graham. They are most noted for running the Tweedy, Browne American and Global Value funds. Ironically, although the firm's roots are embedded deeply in domestic stocks, Morningstar crowned them international managers of the year in 2000 for their excellent work on the Global Value Fund.

The 54-year-old Browne begins his stock selection process by using financial databases to screen more than 20,000 U.S. and international publicly traded companies, looking for those meeting his absolute value criteria. He doesn't pay much attention to the market and insists that, even though he's a devoted follower of both Graham and Buffett, what he's really looking for is growth.

Kazanjian: *Your firm has a fascinating history. Give us a few of the highlights.*

Browne: The firm was founded in 1920 by Forrest Berwind ("Bill") Tweedy. He tried to find a niche in the brokerage business. He discovered that there were a number of companies out there with 50 to 150 minority stockholders and some large major shareholders, but little or no market for the stock. As a result, these shareholders had no way to sell their shares. He went to the annual meetings of these companies, got shareholder lists, and sent the stockowners postcards asking if anyone wanted to buy or sell their shares. In this way, he then became a specialist in trading closely held securities. In the 1930s, Ben Graham ran across Tweedy as he was looking for some cheap stocks. A number of these closely held securities, many of which traded on the pink sheets, sold at big discounts. In 1945, my father, Howard Browne, and an associate left another firm where they were bond traders to go into business with Tweedy. They expanded the business to service some money managers. Graham was one of them. They even moved their offices next door to Ben Graham in 1945. Around 1957, Graham retired and offered his business to Warren Buffett. Buffett declined for a variety of reasons. At one point, Warren Buffett also became a brokerage client. In fact, I think my father bought nearly all of the original Berkshire Hathaway stock for him. Bill Tweedy retired that same year. About this time, they were introduced to Tom Knapp, who went to the Columbia Business School and worked with Graham in the 1950s. Tom helped the firm make the transition from brokerage firm to value money manager.

Kazanjian: *How did you get involved in the business?*

Browne: In the summer of 1968, after finishing my junior year at the University of Pennsylvania as a Russian major, I joined an Army reserve unit. After getting out of the Army, I took the subway down to my father's office in New York to borrow $5 for the train ticket back home to New Jersey. Ed Anderson, another partner at the firm, started talking to me about investing. I was polite and listened. After about two hours, Ed asked what I was doing for the summer. I had no idea. He suggested that I work at the firm, and I agreed. That's how I got started.

Kazanjian: *Since your dad was in the business, you must have thought about getting into investing at some point.*

Browne: Not at all. Dad almost never discussed work at home. My older brother, Tony, went to Harvard Business School. He went to work for one of the then hot hedge funds called City Associates. I actually picked up more from Tony than from my father, in terms of the stock market.

Kazanjian: *What did you do at the firm initially?*

Browne: The first thing I did in the morning was post all the trades. This was the painful part. I was also in charge of the lunch list. Then Ed would give me the Standard & Poor's book and have me compute net current assets per share for various stocks. If something was trading at two-thirds of net current assets, I'd fill out an IBM punch card with a bid price and send it to the National Quotation Bureau. He also made me the bank analyst, which consisted of going through Polk's Bank Directory, arranging each bank alphabetically and geographically, cross referencing it to its stock, and computing the stock's book value. If the bid price was two-thirds or less than book value, I would write it down and fill out a card. Basically I did the legwork, which freed Ed up to do other stuff. No one worked really hard in this organization. It was strictly a 9-to-5 job. But they had plenty of business.

Kazanjian: *When did you learn about managing money and the whole value approach?*

Browne: There wasn't a lot to learn. It basically involved calculating net current assets per share. This is one of Ben Graham's basics. We'd look for stocks selling at two-thirds of current assets. If we found them, we'd buy the stock. Once the price reached the current asset level, we'd sell.

Kazanjian: *Moving up to the present time, your firm has grown to become one of the country's premier value investment management shops. How much do you manage altogether now?*

Browne: Around $8.2 billion. Half of that is in our funds, and the rest is in separate accounts.

Kazanjian: *You sold part of your firm to Affiliated Managers Group (AMG) in 1997. What was the reason for that?*

Browne: It was really an estate planning decision. We explored different alternatives. I even wrote to Warren Buffett and suggested that our company fit the criteria he looked for in the businesses he purchased at Berkshire Hathaway. The investment management business has a low capital requirement, high return on investment, a fairly steady earnings stream, and a reasonably predictable growth rate. I suggested that to solve our inheritance problem, he buy half of the firm. He wrote back a nice letter and said that Charlie Munger and he had thought about this, but always felt it would be a conflict of interest for them to own an investment management firm. We looked at some other potential acquirers and decided that AMG was the right one for us. They were preparing to go public and didn't own a brand-name firm. To our surprise, they considered Tweedy, Browne to be a brand-name firm. It was a $300 million deal that went well, and everybody has been happy ever since. We're still totally autonomous.

Kazanjian: *Let's talk about your investment process.*

Browne: There are 10 characteristics we look for in stocks, which has helped us to beat the index over time. First, we look for stocks with price/earnings or price/book ratios that are cheaper than 80 to 90 percent of all stocks. These stocks have, on average, outperformed most indexes in the past. Our stocks generally fall within this extreme 10 to 20 percent "value layer." They also often enjoy strong insider buying and company share repurchases. Second, we do not segment stocks by market capitalization. We buy stocks of all sizes, large and small. Third, we do careful research on each company, including interviews with management. This gives us forward-looking information and insights that aren't available through traditional Wall Street research. Fourth, we don't try to mimic the indexes. We focus on selecting stocks that are likely to generate above-market returns. Fifth, we stay as fully invested as possible. Research shows that 80 to 90 percent of investment returns occur during just 2 to 7 percent of your total holding time. Sixth, we keep turnover low, which reduces commission costs and produces higher after-tax returns. Seventh, we keep transaction costs as low as possible. Eighth, like Warren Buffett, we think of ourselves as owners of businesses and act like owners. As a result, from time to time, we encourage value-enhancing actions on the part of companies we own. Ninth, we focus on our investment style. All of our money is invested using a value approach. And last, but not least, we are avid students of investing who are constantly trying to improve the way we do things.

Kazanjian: *It sounds like both a quantitative and qualitative process.*

Browne: Yes. It's quantitative in the first cut, when we're looking at the valuation. Then it becomes qualitative.

Kazanjian: *Give me an example of your process in motion.*

Browne: We are often attracted to companies and sectors that are out of favor. In 1993, for example, when Hillary and Bill were going to rewrite healthcare in this country, all of the pharmaceutical stocks were trading at low double-digit PEs [price/earnings ratios]. Johnson & Johnson sold at 12.5 times earnings. If you took out the pharmaceutical business altogether, you were paying a fair price for Tylenol, Band-Aids, Johnson's Baby Oil, and all of the other products. In essence, you got the pharmaceutical business for free. So from a quantitative perspective, it looked good. Then we saw that the demographics of the pharmaceutical business were terrific. Within 10 to 15 years, the baby boomers are going to start taking more and more pills. And the company had solid management with long-term growth and profitability. It was a great business. We still love it today.

Kazanjian: *How about another example?*

Browne: MBIA is a good one. This insurance company first popped up on our screens when we saw strong insider buying in the mid-1990s. The stock was fairly reasonable, trading at around 12 times earnings, with reasonable growth. People have a perception that growth stocks all grow at 25 percent a year. But if you look at the vast majority of stocks, most are able to grow at a rate of the cost of capital plus inflation [in other words, if the company pays 6 percent to borrow money, with 4 percent inflation, it should be growing at more than 10 percent a year]. When we got to the qualitative aspects of MBIA, we saw it had the largest market share and was the lowest-cost producer. There was no way that the competition could wipe it out.

Kazanjian: *In 1993, you started the Tweedy, Browne Global Value fund. What made you go international?*

Browne: John Spears, my partner and fellow portfolio manager, began looking at some insurance stocks in Japan in 1982 that were selling at a third of book value. After doing some research, we bought six or seven of these stocks. All of them doubled or tripled. In the mid-1980s, we found an insurance broker and travel agency in the United Kingdom trading at six times earnings. We bought that. We then began managing money for a client in the United Kingdom who was an investment banker. He said that we should start buying stocks in Europe because they were so cheap. So we started dabbling there. Long story short, we eventually started an offshore fund of foreign investments. Then we decided we wanted to let all of our clients participate in this growth overseas. Given the number of clients we had, our only choice was to start a mutual fund.

Kazanjian: *Do you evaluate foreign companies any differently than U.S. companies?*

Browne: No. Initially, we had a couple of things to overcome. One was accounting. We had to make sure we were making apples-to-apples comparisons. We found that Europeans only had one set of books. They pay their taxes and shareholders out of the same set of books. Two, there was really an attitude on the part of Europeans that shareholders were a necessary nuisance. Also, management didn't have an incentive to see the stock price appreciate because they didn't have stock options. In fact, they did things to try to depress earnings. As an example, we looked at Roche Holdings in the early 1990s. Analysis 101 says you take beginning book value plus earnings less dividends to come up with present book value. But it never came out that way with Roche. If Roche had a really good year, it would set up an egregious reserve for some remote contingency that could take place. These were after-tax reserves, mind you. They would wipe out 200 million Swiss francs of reported profits to shareholders by taking this bogus reserve. Then they would reverse it a few years later. In the U.S. when you reverse your reserve in a way that previously hit earnings, you float it back through the earnings. Not in Europe. You had a situation where book value increased by 200 million Swiss francs, but it didn't show up in the earnings statement. It was sort of fun finding these things.

Kazanjian: *You hedge the currencies in your global fund. What's the reason for that and what impact does that have on your returns?*

Browne: The impact is that it eliminates currency fluctuations and gives us the return we would have earned in the local currency. That was a major issue we had to deal with when we went international, because if you looked at the chart of any of the major European currencies versus the dollar in the 1980s, you saw a high degree of volatility.

Kazanjian: *Do you favor or avoid any particular countries, or do you look for companies on a stock-by-stock basis?*

Browne: We only invest in developed countries. My brother, Will, has sort of a jaundiced view of Latin America, since he served there in the Peace Corps. He really doesn't trust them.

Kazanjian: *Do you ever say something like, "The Japanese market is undervalued so let's overweight Japan?"*

Browne: We don't do that. It's a function of where we find the cheapest stocks. When we first started the Global Value fund, we had 24 percent in Switzerland.

Kazanjian: *How many stocks do you typically own in a portfolio?*

Browne: The international portfolio is pretty broad with around 190 names. A typical domestic account has maybe 80 stocks.

Kazanjian: *Still pretty well diversified.*

Browne: It is, but half of the money is in market caps $5 billion and above, and half is in market caps $5 billion and below. Around 20 percent of the total is in market caps below $1 billion. Obviously as you go down the market cap spectrum, the number of names increases because you have small positions in the tinier names.

Kazanjian: *What makes you sell a stock?*

Browne: If it gets too expensive, is a nongrower, or is a "bobber." By that I mean if it bobs up to 90 percent of what a private value player would pay for it, we get rid of it. If it's a company that continues to grow while we own it, we'll hang on longer. It usually has to be trading at a premium to the private market valuation before we get rid of it.

Kazanjian: *Are you trying to buy these stocks at a certain percentage below intrinsic value?*

Browne: There's not a hard and fast number, but we like to wait until they get bombed for some reason so we get something of a double dip.

Kazanjian: *Are you pretty patient?*

Browne: The turnover rate for the portfolio has averaged about 15 percent for the past five or six years. It's pretty low.

Kazanjian: *You, like most value investors, had a tough time in the late 1990s when growth was in favor. Do you think the tide has turned so that value is back for a sustained run?*

Browne: I think it depends on your definition of value. A lot of people think of value simply as low PE stocks. Some stocks should have a low PE because they're lousy businesses. Who is the greatest living value investor in the world today? It's Warren Buffett. If you apply traditional measures to the stocks in his portfolio, hardly any of them will fit into the value quadrant. He doesn't buy junk. He buys good businesses. That's value. And that will always be in favor.

Kazanjian: *Given that, to what do you attribute that period of under-performance?*

Browne: We looked up that data, because we wondered about that, too. Through August of 1999, something on the order of $120 billion was redeemed from value funds, while $180 billion was invested in growth funds. During that time, you saw Johnson & Johnson go from $95 to $69, even though it didn't miss a single earnings projection. There was just a mass liquidation going on. People were jumping on the bandwagon. This mania actually peaked in March 2000, which was the absolute peak of the Nasdaq, too. What happened was you had a classic bubble. The bubble burst and now we're back to normal investing. If you look up a group of top money managers with 20-year records, you'll find a disproportionate number of those managers are value guys. The concept of growth investing is basically a myth. Most people who are categorized as being growth today are momentum traders. Why do growth funds have twice the turnover rate of value funds? Think about it. The idea is supposed to be that you can buy a growth stock because it's growing. Therefore, you should be able to hold on to it for 20 years. The managers are supposedly making earnings estimates 5 and 10 years out on these stocks. But many of them can't even get the next quarter right, and wind up trading in and out of them. One account we have has owned American Express for 10 years. Not including dividends, that stock has compounded at 22 percent for 10 years. That's growth stock investing. The company grew while you owned it and gave you a great rate of return.

One of my biggest complaints about most fund managers is that they give shareholders limited amounts of materials describing their investment techniques and current impressions of the market. Tweedy, Browne certainly can't be faulted for that. The firm's annual reports are full of essays and other material to better educate shareholders on what Chris Browne and his fellow portfolio managers are thinking. They also send new shareholders a plethora of booklets on value investing and the proven strategies the firm follows. It's a refreshing change from the boring prospectus that most fund firms send out when you call to request more information about the fund. I guess that—like their former client Ben Graham— Tweedy, Browne takes pride in having educated shareholders. ■

DAVID DREMAN

DREMAN VALUE MANAGEMENT

David Dreman always seems to be going against the crowd. He has long been at odds with the academic community, disputing almost every major study taken as gospel by die-hard believers of the efficient market. He criticizes most Wall Street research as worthless. And he was buying old-line companies and yelling that we were in the biggest bubble in history when everyone else was out loading up on high-priced tech and Internet stocks.

As it turns out, Dreman is usually proved right. That's why he's considered one of today's premier contrarian investors—a label he enjoys. (He fittingly sails around the world on a yacht christened *The Contrarian*.)

Dreman was born and raised in Canada. His dad was a trader on the Canadian stock exchange, so he grew up speaking the language of investing. In 1965, Dreman came to the United States, whose markets he thought were more exciting. He began as an analyst and editor at Value Line, before moving on to research positions at J&W Seligman and Rauscher Pierce Refsnes Securities. He started his own firm, Dreman Value Management, in 1977.

Today, the 65-year-old manager runs two mutual funds, including the top-ranked Scudder Dreman High Return Equity Fund, and two annuity products through a sub-advisory agreement with Scudder Kemper Investments. He's the author of several widely acclaimed books and a regular columnist for *Forbes*. In addition, several years ago he funded a foundation to study the area of behavioral finance, which, he says, explains a lot about why investors do what they do. Of course, he insists that buying stocks selling at the bottom 20 percent of the barrel—in terms of valuation—is a strategy that almost always produces superior results over time.

Kazanjian: *I know your dad was pretty influential in shaping your contrarian thinking.*

Dreman: He was a natural contrarian. He passed away in 2000. He began working on the trading floor in Canada in 1929. He finally stopped going there only a couple of years before his death. He was always a believer that most experts were wrong. He went against the grain. But it was more than that. He did a lot of his own research. I guess that's where I picked up my questioning attitude. If you go to business school or graduate school, you almost automatically take anything an expert tells you as fact. You don't question it much. I tended to question a lot of things that didn't appear to be right. That probably comes from my contrarian background.

Kazanjian: *What part of Canada did you grow up in?*

Dreman: Western Canada, in Winnipeg. I was on the trading floor for the first time when I was four or five.

Kazanjian; *Were you instantly hooked on stock market investing?*

Dreman: It was part of my life. I grew up with it. When I went through business school, I got even more interested in it.

Kazanjian: *When did you buy your first stock?*

Dreman: When I was in college. I bought General Motors, but my reason for buying it was contrarian.

Kazanjian: *Which was?*

Dreman: The company's workers were on strike. Some said the strike would go on forever. I didn't think anything like that would happen.

Kazanjian: *You turned out to be right.*

Dreman: Yes. Most strikes end in a matter of at most a month, and that's how it turned out.

Kazanjian: *Where did you go to college?*

Dreman: Originally at the University of Manitoba. I also did some graduate work in the U.S. at Columbia.

Kazanjian: *What was your first job in the investment business?*

Dreman: My father didn't have an investment side at his firm, so I set that up after college. That was in the late 1950s, early 1960s. Then I came to New York. The American markets were much more volatile and interesting because there were so many more industries to cover and a lot of technology. I came here in 1965 and worked for Value Line for a few years, before moving to J&W Seligman.

Kazanjian: *Were you an analyst at Value Line?*

Dreman: An editor analyst. I had a group of people working with me.

Kazanjian: *What did you do at Seligman?*

Dreman: I was a researcher there as well. After that I went out and started my own firm in the late 1970s.

Kazanjian: *Is that the firm you have today?*

Dreman: Pretty much. We sold the original firm, but the record is something I've still got.

Kazanjian: *How much do you manage altogether now?*

Dreman: About $5.5 billion. Roughly $4 billion of that is in mutual funds. The rest is in institutional and high-net-worth individual accounts.

Kazanjian: *How do you define contrarian investing?*

Dreman: There are all sorts of definitions. Ours is taken from the idea that certain investment strategies—such as buying low price/book, low PE, or low price/cash-flow stocks—have outperformed the markets in studies spanning 50 years or more by around 2 to 3 percent annually. On the other side of the coin, stocks that have been in favor have underperformed. Even when we look at this incredible era of technology growth, value stocks have outperformed for a long time, while growth and technology stocks on the whole have underperformed.

Kazanjian: *Even counting those huge gains growth stocks enjoyed in the late 1990s?*

Dreman: Yes. The interesting thing is that over the last 10 years our strategy has beaten the S&P, even though this was a period where technology rode high. The S&P was comprised of about 38 percent technology and telecommunications stocks a few years ago.

Our strategy doesn't work every year, and there are years where you look horrible, but it has worked very well over time. One example of when it didn't work was 1999. We had a technology bubble and anybody who was in value or contrarian stocks did poorly. Our funds were down some 12 percent. But the following year they were up 42 percent when the market was down 11 percent.

Kazanjian: *Why were you down so much in 1999? Was it because when your stocks were out of favor, people were indiscriminately selling them off?*

Dreman: Exactly. We were in a mania. I don't think people realize how much of a mania it was. They say bubble, but I don't think they'll realize the extent of the bubble for another 5 or 10 years. We were in a mania much bigger than the South Sea bubble and every bit as big as Tulip mania. It was probably the largest mania in American history, maybe even world history. There were stocks selling at 5,000 to 10,000 percent of their real value based on our earnings discount models. We took the most enthusiastic estimates that analysts had and blew up the growth rates to the fastest growth rates in history. In some cases, we estimated the fair value of some of these stocks to be one-tenth the price the stocks were trading for. Our growth assumptions were ridiculously optimistic, yet the stocks traded 10 to 20 times higher than our wildly optimistic forecasts.

Kazanjian: *What do you think caused the bubble?*

Dreman: It goes to investor psychology, which is a relatively new area. We're supposed to be schooled in security analysis to spot stocks when they're 30 to 40 percent out of whack with their real value, and yet here we had stocks that were 5,000 to 10,000 percent overpriced. There are a number of psychological theories that address the question. Cognitive psychology is one. Social psychology, or how you interact with groups, is another. Peer pressure is a third. Analysts are under pressure to come up with winners, and sometimes they throw away the fundamentals in the process. In my opinion, Mary Meeker, Henry Blodget, and dozens of others made ridiculous calls. I'm sure they didn't base their numbers on any rational models.

Kazanjian: *How did they come up with those crazy numbers?*

Dreman: I think they threw papers up against the stairs and the highest paper got it. Quite seriously, it was a little like trying to be Babe Ruth and pointing at the fence. In this market, people believed anything. When Merrill Lynch said that Amazon.com would go to $400, it was almost a self-fulfilling prophecy. You've got to remember that during this period, the average Internet stock IPO [initial public offering] went up about 120 percent on its first day of trading. It was reckless on the part of the analysts who worked for the major firms that were making hundreds of millions, if not billions, of dollars underwriting these new issues.

Kazanjian: *Do you think individual investors are also to blame?*

Dreman: I think in any bubble, individual investors follow the crowd. They always follow the experts and the experts are horrendously wrong. Expert opinion is wrong much more often than it is right. It tends to go in line with the popular thinking of the time, which also means it tends to go in line with where the stock prices are. People get mesmerized by short-term stock movements and they forget that, like a casino, the odds change very suddenly and dramatically. We've had four or five of these bubbles since World War II and each one has disintegrated.

Kazanjian: *You do a lot of work in the whole area of behavioral finance.*

Dreman: I set up a foundation to study it, and before that wrote a book on behavioral finance, *Psychology in the Stock Market,* in 1977. I locked horns with the efficient market long before there was a field of behavioral finance.

Kazanjian: *Why is it that investors tend to react in exactly the opposite direction of how they should?*

Dreman: People aren't totally rational. That's not to say they're mad, but they're erratic. Cognitive psychologists have done some work on what they call the base rate versus the case rate. The base rate might be the long-term return of common stock, and the case rate is how stocks have done in the last 5 or 10 years. People always look at the more recent results and project them forever. Stocks have returned around 10 percent annually since the 1920s. There are major periods where you had higher returns and others where stocks returned nothing or virtually nothing. That's how you arrive at an overall 10 percent return. When stocks were red hot in the 1990s, people looked back and projected that the enormous returns the bull market had produced since 1992 would continue forever. We did a study in April 2001 and found that investors in our survey were looking for annual returns going forward of 15 to 20 percent, which is about 50 to 100 percent more than the historic rate of return.

Kazanjian: *What does that tell you?*

Dreman: People have adjusted to the idea that common stocks provide superior returns over time, which is true, but they've gone overboard with it. Bonds have provided inflation-adjusted returns of around 1 percent a year since World War II. Stocks have provided inflation-adjusted returns of around 7 percent. Stocks are good investment vehicles, but not as good as investors in our survey think. To answer your question more specifically, if returns aren't good for another year or two, I suspect these expectations will go down significantly.

Kazanjian: *Do you view most Wall Street research as a contrarian indicator? For example, when analysts come out and say it's time to buy a given stock, do you normally take that as a sell signal?*

Dreman: This is being a little unkind to analysts, but we've done a lot of studies on analyst estimates. In fact, we had a sample of 750,000 consensus estimates going back to 1970. We found the average error rate in any one year was something like 43 percent. When you remember that a 1 or 2 percent miss can knock a stock down 20 percent, that's big. We also found that you need 5 or 10 years of precise earnings to rationalize a price. We found that the odds of getting within 5 percent of the actual earnings for 20 consecutive quarters were 1 in 14 billion. Nobody is able to estimate as finely as we think we can. Therefore, we always tend to pay too much for the calendar girls and too little for good companies that are just temporarily out of favor. That's the essence of the contrarian strategy as we practice it.

Kazanjian: *If you can't rely on Wall Street, what can you rely on when it comes to choosing your stocks?*

Dreman: Wall Street analysts know their companies. You should cut a research report in two. The first part, the information about the company and its prospects, is probably pretty good. The second part, the recommendation, should be used as kindling. We use analyst information, but we don't use the recommendations very often. If you buy a diversified portfolio of low PE, low cash-flow, or low price-to-book stocks even randomly, like most of these academic studies, you'll outperform the market pretty significantly. This means that people consistently pay too much for favorites and too little for out-of-favor stocks.

Kazanjian: *Why don't the other strategies hold up over time?*

Dreman: Again, one of the main reasons is that we think we can precisely fine-tune earnings. If you pay a lot trying to fine-tune earnings, and have an average error of 43 or 44 percent annually, you'll have some nasty surprises. Conversely, if you can fine-tune earnings for an out-of-favor stock, you'll probably have some positive surprises. In one study, we found that of the 1,500 largest stocks, the bottom 20 percent (in terms of valuation) had negative earnings surprises. They were hurt only modestly in the quarter the surprise came in. Conversely, people who owned higher-priced growth stocks were significantly hurt by negative surprises more and more as the year progressed. It always came back to the same fact. People tend to put a lot of faith in being able to determine who the future winners and losers will be. They're attracted to what's popular at the time, but by then it's usually ready to go out of style. They come in right at the end of the fashion trend, just before next year's fashions come out.

Kazanjian: *In 1999, when the market was going up and growth stocks were skyrocketing, you were negative for the year. How did you remain true to your discipline without being tempted to join the crowd?*

Dreman: I've been through this three or four times before. It's tough because other value managers are doing better than you and some consultants and clients are unhappy. They point to other value firms and say, "Why are they doing so much better?" When you look at their portfolios, it's because they've got about 30 percent in growth and tech stocks. We didn't have any tech stocks in the portfolio in 1999. The value managers who bought tech stocks in 1999 blew up in 2000. We were up 42 percent that year. One of the major problems with any discipline, whether it's contrarian or growth, is that people tend to abandon it when it doesn't seem to work. You really have to stay with your discipline to get good results over time.

Kazanjian: *Do you believe people should own elements of growth and value in their portfolio, or should they put it all in value?*

Dreman: The majority should be in value or an index fund. I don't see the idea of owning both value and growth when you can get them both in an index fund.

Kazanjian: *So you're a proponent of index funds?*

Dreman: I think you can do better in a contrarian fund over time than in an index fund and I think we've shown that. Some of the studies we've done going back to the early 1970s show that had you been in a contrarian fund, defined as buying the bottom 20 percent of stocks by any measure, you would have outperformed the market by about 150 percent. That is certainly much better than the index fund. On the other hand, if you take the top 20 percent of stocks over the same period, not one of them beat the market.

Kazanjian: *Getting back to index funds, do you believe in the efficient market theory?*

Dreman: Not at all. I think it's nonsense. That statement needs some support. Basically, nothing proposed by the efficient market hypothesis has stood the test of time. All the major studies have been refuted. There have been Nobel prizes won for work that's now totally worthless. Some academics did a study showing that companies that split their stock shares didn't do better over time. Therefore, the academics concluded, the market is efficient. When I looked at their study, I found it was full of hocus-pocus. They did not measure the splits on the date of announcement. They measured from the date of issue, which is 90 days later. So all the news was already in the stock. In reality, the stocks went up pretty significantly during the period after the split was announced. The academics also did the same thing with risk and beta, which every consultant uses today. Higher risk is supposed to give you a higher return. Risk was measured by beta. The higher the beta, the greater the risk. The lower the beta, the lower the risk, according to the academics. What we found was there's no correlation between risk and beta. High beta sometimes results in lower returns and low beta results in higher returns. Even the academics have pretty much refuted everything they have said.

Kazanjian: *If you don't buy the efficient market theory, then by default wouldn't you also not buy the idea of indexing?*

Dreman: Indexing simply shows that most people can't pick stocks accurately. If you have a wide enough index that's properly weighted, you should get an average return.

Kazanjian: *Speaking of academic theory, what do you think of asset allocation?*

Dreman: It sounds good until you look at the facts. Take international investing. In 1998 I measured the EAFE [Europe, Australasia, and the Far East] international index against the S&P 500 for the last 10 years. The S&P beat it handily. Again, it's a wonderful theoretical idea that if you own a bit of everything, you'll do better. It doesn't work that way though.

Kazanjian: *A lot of people take as conventional wisdom that small-cap stocks do better than large-cap stocks over time. It's one of the prime tenets of the asset allocation argument.*

Dreman: Once again, that's not true. We looked at a major study showing that small-caps outperformed all other categories. It turns out the researcher never used small-cap stocks for his study. The study covered two major periods when small-caps did well: 1931–35 and 1940–45. I got interested in this study because the 1931–35 period was during the Great Depression. How could small companies possibly do better during that time? It turns out he was looking at large companies on the verge of Chapter 11 that were selling at small prices. Not only that, there was basically no trading going on then. The bid–offer spread on some of these stocks was more than 100 percent. The academics take the middle price and assume you could get the middle price if you bought 100 shares. In real life, it's hard to do that. I think the notion of small-cap outperformance has been thoroughly refuted.

Kazanjian: *Yet you have a small-cap fund, right?*

Dreman: It's a value small-cap fund. We looked at the Russell 2000 going back to when it started in 1980 and found that value or contrarian small stocks did significantly better than the growth part of the Russell. In fact, they did better than the large-cap contrarian stocks by a couple of percentage points.

Kazanjian: *Thus proving there is a small-cap effect.*

Dreman: But it's a contrarian small-cap effect. When we took the index itself, it really didn't do that well. I guess all of this gets back to the fact that these efficient market studies were poorly done.

Kazanjian: *Given all that we've just talked about, what should investors put their money in?*

Dreman: Being a little subjective on the subject, I'd say contrarian stocks. What you're really buying are good blue-chip stocks, which, on the whole, are growth stocks. We buy these stocks when they have low PEs. A low PE for us is defined as a PE that's less than the overall market. These stocks should also be growing at 10 to 15 percent a year, whereas most stocks in the S&P are only growing at 7 percent a year.

Kazanjian: *How do you find these stocks?*

Dreman: Oh, it's easy. Any computer screen or Value Line will give you the 100 lowest PE stocks by market cap or any other measure.

Kazanjian: *So in terms of finding and evaluating companies, you start out by running a screen for low PE stocks.*

Dreman: Low PE, low price-to-book. You can find all of this in the *Value Line Investment Survey* every week, or you can run a computer screen to find the 100 stocks with the lowest PE or price-to-book ratios. You can also look for stocks with high yields and other signs of financial strength.

Kazanjian: *Such as?*

Dreman: We start with low PE, low price-to-book, or low price-to-cash-flow. Then we want to have a solid balance sheet and above-average dividends, because dividends can still make a major difference over time.

Kazanjian: *What kind of PE are you looking for?*

Dreman: We use a relative PE. Benjamin Graham used absolute PEs from the Great Depression as his margin of safety. He missed a lot of the bull market because his PEs were too low. He kept raising them in the *Intelligent Investor* from edition to edition. I think it's better to have a relative PE. All of the research studies are done in both bull and bear markets, so you're always using a relative PE.

Kazanjian: *How much lower would you like the PE to be relative to the market?*

Dreman: You want it below the market. We don't limit ourselves, but we're often near the bottom 10 to 12 percent. We also want to see above-average earnings growth relative to the S&P. We're not looking for the highest dividend yield, but a yield higher than the S&P and a payout ratio or dividend growth rate that's rising faster than the S&P. This sounds hard to get, and you don't get all of these things in one stock, but it's surprising how often you'll get most of them. Freddie Mac and Fannie Mae are two stocks we've owned since the late 1980s. They've gone up 15-fold for us, and they've grown at 15 percent-plus for three decades. They still trade for around 17 times earnings, while the S&P trades for around 25 times earnings.

Kazanjian: *Why such a huge disparity?*

Dreman: It's a market anomaly. People have never given these companies the PEs they deserve.

Kazanjian: *What digging do you do beyond the numbers?*

Dreman: We look at management. If management is bad, we'll stay away from the company. We look at all kinds of qualitative factors, too. People get too excited about some of the qualitative factors and lose the overall perspective on the companies. Some low PE companies will always stay that way. That's something you have to watch out for.

Kazanjian: *I trust this means you look to see whether the stock is cheap for a good reason and may be on the verge of getting cheaper.*

Dreman: Right. We use an earnings forecast, but not in the way that most analysts and money managers do. We use it to get a sense of the general direction. If we think that earnings are going to turn down, we probably won't buy the stock now. Usually if the estimates show earnings will be down 10 percent, they might actually be down 30 percent.

Kazanjian: *How do you evaluate technology stocks? After all, even when they're down, tech stocks tend to sell at above-market PEs and earnings can be erratic.*

Dreman: Not always. We had a few chances in the 1990s to buy tech really cheap. Compaq was trading for almost nothing back in the early 1990s. It was getting a lot of competition and lower-price models were coming out. The stock really got knocked down. Intel was trading at 15 times earnings in 1995. We owned that. We've owned Hewlett-Packard and Apple at least four or five times. We bought Texas Instruments and Motorola at pretty depressed levels.

When these stocks come down, we can really buy growth at a major discount. We did that with pharmaceuticals in the early 1990s when Hillary Clinton was attacking the drug industry as being unethical. The PE in Bristol-Myers went from 40 to about 15, with a 6 percent yield. I love to buy growth at a price.

Kazanjian: *How long do you tend to hold on to your positions?*

Dreman: We used to sell stocks when they reached a market multiple, and often still do. We've found that because tech stocks tend to get a somewhat higher multiple, as you suggested, you can hold them longer.

Kazanjian: *What are some other reasons that you sell?*

Dreman: When there's a change in the fundamentals strong enough that the outlook isn't as promising, we'll sell immediately. We found that it pays to sell, not if there's a bad quarter, but if there is a major fundamental change in the longer-term outlook. Because we have a fairly concentrated portfolio with roughly 50 to 55 names, we won't hold a stock for more than two or three years if it doesn't outperform the market.

Kazanjian: *You own a lot of tobacco stocks. Tobacco is obviously a controversial area, yet it attracts many value investors. Why do you have so much faith in it?*

Dreman: There's no question that you have the risk of litigation. What people forget is that the major cases are probably behind these companies now. They have enormous pricing power, probably more than any other industry anywhere today. When big tobacco settled with the states for $275 billion a few years back, it only cost them 20 cents a pack to make this up in 25 years. Sure, they might lose a $100 million lawsuit. But it's almost nothing because by the time it gets to court and is cut down, it will be $30 million, and it will be appealed for years. We've seen that these companies have been able to raise prices after the state settlements, and they are raising them every year. Although tobacco usage is going down somewhat in the United States, pricing is going up faster. I think that this is an area where stocks are still tremendously undervalued.

Kazanjian: *Do you think that some institutions stay away from these stocks because they fear a backlash from shareholders who don't want to be in tobacco?*

Dreman: I think that's quite possible. In our mind, it's not a moral judgment. These are legitimate companies. Our job is to get the best rate of return for our shareholders.

Kazanjian: *Dividend yields have been falling for some time now. Many companies have either stopped paying or reduced them over the past few years. Will dividends ever come back into style?*

Dreman: It's hard to say. I think we may be moving back to a more fundamental market. If so, dividends will probably go up. The current yield of 1 percent is ridiculously low. In the past, dividends have been a big contributor to contrarian returns.

Kazanjian: *Do you time the market at all?*

Dreman: I don't think anybody can do a good job of that. We try to stay away from market timing.

Kazanjian: *On a somewhat related note, do you raise cash when you're cautious?*

Dreman: Rarely. We'll only raise cash in a market that's in free-fall. I've seen too many good money managers get hurt trying to outsmart the market. They wind up missing the rallies. Volatility has always been helpful for us. We are very opportunistic in the sense that we always look for stocks that are knocked down. We don't run away from bear markets or volatility. We love it. These periods allow us to get 15, 20, or 30 percent growers at much lower prices. Back in the early 1990s, we did well for five years by positioning the portfolio during a semipanic in financial stocks. Right now we're in a similar situation where any bad news knocks stocks apart and should allow us to build a strong portfolio for the years ahead.

Kazanjian: *What about bonds? Do they play a role in an investor's portfolio?*

Dreman: It depends on the age of the investor. No matter what your age, you should have some cash reserves, either in short-term bonds or money market funds. The older the investor, the larger the portion of a portfolio that should be in bonds. The larger the portfolio, the more you can keep in stocks and still have a comfortable income. Older investors should always have enough income coming from bonds that they aren't forced to draw on their stocks.

Kazanjian: *For individual investors, what are your thoughts on whether they should buy individual stocks or funds?*

Dreman: They probably should buy funds. The problem is most individual investors don't have enough experience to assemble a really diversified portfolio. Very often they'll buy one or two hot stocks and have lousy performance as a result. I would look for two things: a fund with a good 5-to-10–year record and a manager who has run the fund the whole time. Otherwise the strategies and performance going forward could be very different from the past.

In 1999, when Dreman's deep value strategy was out of sync with the overall market, he dubbed himself T-Rex, since some people were calling him a dinosaur for not joining the new-era bandwagon. Dreman believes that while we'll have more market manias as time goes on, the next one might take awhile to get here, since people were so badly burned during the most recent one.

Dreman divides his time between Aspen, New Jersey, and his yacht *The Contrarian,* which sails the Caribbean in the winter and Nantucket in the summer. The yacht is fully equipped with communications equipment, so Dreman can keep a constant pulse on his investments while at sea. ■

JEAN-MARIE EVEILLARD

FIRST EAGLE SoGEN FUNDS

Jean-Marie Eveillard is arguably the most respected international value investor in the business today. But he admits he didn't look so smart in the late 1990s, when aggressive growth funds made his performance seem pretty measly by comparison. One reason is that Eveillard abhors risk. He says his investment priority is to avoid losing money, as opposed to making big returns as quickly as possible. That flies in the face of the extraordinary risk taking that paid off for some momentum-oriented investors during what Eveillard describes as his own period of wandering in the desert.

Eveillard got into the business some 40 years ago. After graduating from École des Hautes Études Commerciales, a major French graduate school for business studies, he took a job as an analyst with the French bank Société Générale. Although the bank practiced growth investing, which was trendy at the time, Eveillard always felt more comfortable as a value guy. In 1979, the native of France was offered a chance to manage one of the bank's small global mutual funds out of New York. Eveillard took the job and has been there ever since. The fund became what is now known as First Eagle SoGen Global. (In late 1999, Société Générale sold its domestic funds to Arnhold and S. Bleichroeder Advisors, which owns the First Eagle family of funds.) First Eagle SoGen Global, as its name implies, invests in securities from around the world. Eveillard also runs the newer First Eagle SoGen Overseas and Gold Funds.

The 60-year-old manager scours the globe for what he describes as "original, obscure, oddball, and out-of-the-way" stocks. Why? Because they are the most likely to be undervalued. As a result, he buys a fair number of small companies that most people have never heard of, although he loves out-of-favor big blue chips even more.

Eveillard is unquestionably a patient man. His average holding period is five years, and he's willing to sit out the occasional droughts that inevitably come from following an investment style as disciplined as his.

Kazanjian: *Is stock market investing as much of a pastime in France as it is here in the U.S.?*

Eveillard: No, and I don't think it ever will be. Nevertheless, there is greater interest in the stock market today in France than there was 30 or 40 years ago when I started out.

Kazanjian: *How did you develop an interest in investing?*

Eveillard: In 1962, I graduated from a French business school. One of the requirements was to spend a month with a business company. I ended up being assigned to a French financial magazine, somewhat of a cross between *Business Week* and *Barron's*. I developed an interest in the stock market. That September, when I started looking for a job, Société Générale, the French bank, had an opening doing securities analysis and I took it.

Kazanjian: *What did your job at the bank entail?*

Eveillard: It was the early 1960s and the dawn of securities analysis in France, Germany, and elsewhere in continental Europe. Up until then, one invested based on tips from brokers. Whatever securities analysis existed—and very little did at the time—was more along the lines of Ben Graham. It had a lot to do with such things as trying to figure out the value of real estate. In other words, if a company had headquarters in a fancy area in Paris, the building must be worth a lot. But in the late 1950s in the U.S. under the leadership of Donaldson Lufkin and other so-called institutional brokerage firms, you saw the start of the growth school. Naturally, in the early 1960s, those trying to introduce securities analysis in continental Europe adopted the latest school of investing, which was the growth school.

Kazanjian: *Were European companies pretty accommodating to securities analysts such as yourself?*

Eveillard: When I spent my month at that financial magazine, one of my duties was to get on my scooter and crisscross Paris, picking up annual reports at annual meetings. I would call from my office at the magazine and say I'd like them to send me an annual report. There was such hostility to outsiders. They would say, "No! If you want an annual report, pick it up at the annual meeting. We're not gonna send you one." I remember the French companies had such leeway that they reported as earnings the exact number they intended to distribute as dividends and no more. They were afraid the unions would go after them for making too much money. And they didn't report less because they didn't want shareholders to accuse them of distributing capital.

Kazanjian: *Were you only analyzing French companies at that time?*

Eveillard: Yes. That was in the fall of 1962. For five years I did securities analysis according to the new mantra at the time, which was basically growth.

Kazanjian: *So you really started out as a growth investor. What did growth mean at the time?*

Eveillard: It meant well-established companies that everybody was talking about a lot. Glamour and growth went together. In the late 1960s, I also began managing portfolios for wealthy individuals who were clients of the bank. That's when I began to understand that the great majority of individuals, if left to their own devices in terms of investing, will do the wrong thing at the wrong time. I think that's still true today.

Kazanjian: *Why is that?*

Eveillard: What works against the great majority of individuals is that they don't have a basic understanding of the rules of investing. A great number who invest cannot read a balance sheet, but it's less a lack of technical knowledge, because that's not very difficult to acquire. It's more a failure of character or intellect or both. People act in a sheepish manner. It's warmer inside the herd. They tend to want to be among the stocks that already have gone up. It makes them feel successful themselves.

Kazanjian: *Don't you think professional investors are guilty of that, too?*

Eveillard: They are, but less so. Even when they are, they know deep down that they're behaving like sheep and probably shouldn't. Many individuals don't realize what they're doing is wrong. They just extrapolate mindlessly.

Kazanjian: *You eventually wound up in the U.S. How did that happen?*

Eveillard: After five years, I was getting a little tired of the bank. A French bank in the 1960s was not a fun place to be. I was considering leaving when all of a sudden there was an opening in Société Générale's commercial banking operation in New York City on Wall Street. I was single at the time and agreed to take the position when they offered it to me. I was supposed to be there for a year or two and wound up staying for six years. I was supposed to be the liaison in New York for Paris headquarters. A few months after arriving there, I came across Ben Graham's books. His theories appealed to me a lot more than what I had been practicing in France. It always seemed to me that Ben Graham spoke to three things: humility, caution, and order. One of the problems with the growth school is that people appear to deny that the future is uncertain. But it *is* uncertain. Let's be humble about it. Therefore, caution is required, so Graham always insisted on what he called the margin of safety, the cushion. He also spoke to the idea of order. In other words, securities are more than just pieces of paper to be traded in and out of on the basis of market psychology. Indeed, there is such a thing as intrinsic value. That's the company's true value. Mr. Market, as Graham called it, can have the price move at times substantially away from true value in either direction. That gives you an opportunity to sell when Mr. Market becomes too optimistic and the stock is trading way above intrinsic value, and it gives you a chance to buy when it trades way below.

Kazanjian: *When did you first get to put Graham's teachings into practice?*

Eveillard: It took another 10 years. Until 1974, I did securities analysis as it was done at our headquarters in Paris. They were believers in the growth school, so willy-nilly I had to look at it that way. In early 1975, I made the mistake of going back to Paris and spent three miserable years there professionally. The bank had a small fund called SoGen International with about $15 million in assets. They could tell I wasn't happy and in January 1979 suggested I go back to New York to manage that fund. That's the first time I had an opportunity to run a mutual fund on a value basis.

Kazanjian: *Is that the fund now known as the First Eagle SoGen Global Fund?*

Eveillard: Yes, although it's always been a global fund, which was challenging in the beginning, since I ran the fund all alone until 1986. I had complete freedom. I was far away from Paris and the fund was so tiny that they really didn't bother me. I could do exactly what I wanted to do.

Kazanjian: *Which was?*

Eveillard: I tried to run it on a value basis and owned both domestic and foreign securities. I looked at foreign securities exactly the same way I looked at domestic securities. People wondered how I could figure out what all the foreign markets would do. I was not involved in trying to find out what the markets would do. I tried to find securities I thought were selling 30 to 40 percent below what I thought their intrinsic value was. That's what I still do today.

Kazanjian: *So when you put your portfolio together, you're not trying to determine which countries look best. You're strictly looking for attractively priced securities, regardless of what country they're in?*

Eveillard: That's right. There is never a concern about any countries or sectors being underweighted. In mid-1988, 18 months and 30 percent too soon, we completely left the Tokyo stock market. I had nothing invested in Japanese securities. At that time, Tokyo's stock market was the second largest in the world on its way to briefly becoming the largest, and we owned zip. Is there a concern in terms of overweighting a particular country? Only to the extent that we wouldn't want to have 25 percent of the assets in a developing market such as Indonesia. But if we had 30 percent of the assets in Germany and 5 percent in the U.S., so be it.

Kazanjian: *What about macro considerations? Some people argue the Japanese market is overvalued. Others say it's cheap. The same thing can be said for Europe and the U.S. Does the overall market valuation or economic outlook for a particular country factor into your decision-making process?*

Eveillard: The top-down outlook cannot be completely ignored, although I would argue that in developed countries it almost can be. In fact, we own a lot of Japanese equities today that were selected from the bottom up, taking advantage of the fact that the Tokyo stock market is mired in a more than 10-year-long bear market. Every now and then I say to myself that Japan might go into a financial crisis. But even if it does, it will find a way out. Look at what happened in England in the mid-1970s. All of their postwar mistakes caught up with them and they had their back against the wall. It was a financial crisis. The International Monetary Fund had to be called in. All of a sudden, there were major reforms put in place because the British understood that they were facing a financial crisis, and that what had been going on for 30 years simply could not go on any longer.

Kazanjian: *What do you think of some of the other major markets, including the U.S. and Europe?*

Eveillard: In the U.S., it seems to me there are emerging problems associated with the fact that the speculative bubble that finally burst in 2000 has negative economic and financial consequences associated with it. The bursting of a bubble always does. I also think the productivity miracle in the U.S. was, to some extent, a mirage. When I look at Europe, it doesn't have the longstanding problems of Japan, but it had its own speculative bubble, although to a much lesser extent than the U.S. The old knock on Europe was always that taxes are too high. Well, the Germans are reducing taxes and, because of the European Union, the others will have to tag along. Unless I'm missing something big, which I may be, Europe looks good.

Kazanjian: *How about Southeast Asia and the emerging markets?*

Eveillard: We do something every now and then in those areas because sometimes we cannot resist the extraordinarily attractive valuations. We've never looked at emerging markets from the point of view of emerging growth. These countries are rife with political, economic, and financial instability. It's one thing to invest in Switzerland. The Swiss are not about to start a revolution tomorrow. It's another thing to invest in Southeast Asia. Still, sometimes the values are extraordinary. Two of my associates over the past few years have traveled to South Korea because we found a number of small- and medium-sized corporations there that are quite profitable, family controlled, with no debt to speak of and that sell for a song because nobody is interested. The foreigners don't know about them, and the locals—as is often the case in Asia—are day traders.

Kazanjian: *You mentioned earlier that accounting in Europe was historically suspect. Is that still true today?*

Eveillard: Nowadays I believe that American accounting is among the worst. Most American companies have vastly overstated their earnings over the past few years. Under the pressure of the bull market, once your stock sells at 30 to 40 times earnings, you cannot afford to have a down year or even a year that's only up modestly. As a result, all sorts of accounting tricks have been played to the point where the SEC has had to come in. Warren Buffett himself has repeatedly complained about the fact that stock options are a cost of doing business, and as such should be reflected in the income statement, which they are not.

Kazanjian: *Given that you have the whole world to choose from, which means literally tens of thousands of potential securities, how do you go about choosing the stocks that eventually make it into your portfolio?*

Eveillard: We don't run screens, as many value investors do, because we don't like to rely on reported numbers. We're always looking for hidden assets. The best example is if you look at the balance sheets of some forest products companies in the U.S., you'll see that some of them acquired their timberland at the turn of the century. They're still carrying it on the balance sheet at $1 per acre, yet today it's worth $1,000 or $2,000 an acre. When we look at an American company, we don't take the reported earnings for granted. We look at the footnotes to see whether or not they are overreporting. We don't want to be taken.

Also, we are aware that some companies—most notably in Europe-underreport earnings for various reasons. For instance, the corporate tax rate in Germany is high. This is an incentive to underreport. The trade-off is that the taxing authorities there let you take all sorts of deductions to offset the high rates.

Another thing we look at in continental Europe is that until a couple of years ago, stock buybacks were authorized, but there were all sorts of tax penalties associated with them. Only recently have those penalties been eliminated. Up until then, companies let cash pile up on the balance sheet, bought real estate, or took minority stakes in other companies. In other words, in Europe you often had the basic business with so-called peripheral assets on the side. As a value investor, you try to figure out a reasonable price to pay for the entire company. If you take that attitude, obviously the peripheral assets are relevant because they're worth something. If you don't like them, you can sell them off once you own the company.

Kazanjian: *Do you get leads on these companies from outside research?*

Eveillard: We look at outside research, but we don't trust anybody. There is a conflict of interest associated with investment banking and research. Most of the research is done for growth investors who are looking for securities to move into today and out of in six or nine months. That's not the approach we take. We have a turnover ratio of 20 percent, which means that on average, we hold securities for five years. We have always done a bit of business with a great number of research sources throughout the entire world, so we're inundated with ideas. Sometimes we only spend 15 seconds on a report or maybe no time at all. But every now and then we stop and decide to investigate something further.

Usually we have to completely redo the numbers. For instance, to make international comparisons, sometimes you have to look at enterprise value to EBITDA [earnings before interest, taxes, depreciation, and amortization] because depreciation accounting standards may vary. As one example, we found out that the Copenhagen Airport, which is privatized, depreciates its runways over 20 years. British Airport runways are depreciated over 100 years. A runway is a runway, but if you try to apply the same price/earnings ratio to both Copenhagen and British airports, it doesn't work. Maybe one idea out of 20 will catch our eye or cause us to investigate further. Sometimes after that we lose interest. Other times we dig deeper before getting to the point where we decide to buy it.

Kazanjian: *How do you come up with intrinsic value?*

Eveillard: Intrinsic value is what we think we would pay, expecting a reasonable return, if we were to buy the entire company. It is a number that takes into account current interest rates. One of the reasons Buffett is such a genius is because he has figured out that there are only a tiny number of companies that you can have reasonable confidence will be as successful 10 years from now as they are today. One absurdity of the multiples that were applied to technology companies up until 2000 was that 95 percent or more had absolutely no visibility for where they would be 10 years down the road because technology is a fast-changing field. Value is a big tent. It accommodates old value, which is basically Ben Graham. It accommodates new value, which is Warren Buffett. It even accommodates new new value, which is Bill Miller of Legg Mason [who is featured elsewhere in this book].

We are involved with both old and new value. To use Buffett's words, that means we tend to own both questionable businesses at comfortable prices and comfortable businesses at questionable prices. As I said, intrinsic value takes into account current interest rates. Then, given our own assessment of the business, we determine how much of a multiple of free cash flow or enterprise value to EBIT [earnings before interest and taxes] in absolute terms we're willing to apply. We never think in terms of, if Company X is in the same business as Company Y, Company Y should sell at the same value as Company X, because Company X's stock may be vastly overvalued. In Japan in the late 1980s, people called to tell me the market was selling at 75 times earnings and they had something for me at 55 times earnings. I said, "What's the big deal? That's no bargain."

Kazanjian: *Are you looking to buy the stock at a certain discount to intrinsic value?*

Eveillard: Ideally we try to buy it at a 30 to 40 percent discount to our estimated intrinsic value. But if we think we have a genuine understanding of the business, and it is a genuinely good company, we may be interested in buying at a 25 percent discount. Sometimes we have much less confidence in the intrinsic value number to where even a 45 percent discount would not be cheap enough.

Kazanjian: *Once you have the numbers down, what additional digging do you do?*

Eveillard: The numbers are the end result of looking at public information, trying to understand the business, talking with two or three securities analysts who follow the industry, and such. We don't spend a lot of time with company management. Investors generally use company management for one of two things: One is to figure out how the current quarter looks. Since the intrinsic value of a business has almost nothing to do with how the quarter ends up, that's of no interest. The second purpose of contact with management is to have management tell you their long-term strategy. Most of the time it's a bunch of nonsense. Running any business is mostly a matter of trying to see and seize opportunities. It's not a matter of having a long-term plan. If it were a matter of having a long-term plan, the Soviet Union would not have dissolved.

Kazanjian: *Do you sell once a stock reaches intrinsic value?*

Eveillard: Yes, although we acknowledge that there are companies that continue to create value. That's what Buffett himself is after. In other words, there are companies that can be bought for $75 or $80 today where the intrinsic value is $100. If they continue to create value, next year intrinsic value may be $115, and two years down the line it could go up to $125, etc. The value investor is looking for a business that's not only understandable, but also one with stability. One of our biggest holdings is a German manufacturer of residential boilers. Most people think that's dull, which it is. But it's mostly an appliance. As such, it is a fairly stable replacement business.

Kazanjian: *What are some other reasons you'll sell a stock?*

Eveillard: Maybe we think the business is worth $25 today and when we take another look 18 months later, we find out we made the wrong assessment. Our new assessment may show the value is only $15. Usually by that time the stock has declined, so we have to take a loss upon accepting our mistake.

Kazanjian: *Do you hedge currencies when buying foreign stocks?*

Eveillard: For a long time we didn't. We started to hedge about 10 years ago. Our basic attitude is we understand the intellectual rationale of people who are fully hedged at all times. We also understand the opposite extreme of people who are unhedged. We worry, though, that there may be extreme circumstances where being fully hedged or completely unhedged could become extremely troublesome. Our basic attitude is to be 50 percent hedged. We split it down the middle unless we think that a currency is terribly out of whack, which is what we currently believe about the Euro.

Kazanjian: *Traditional asset allocation wisdom is that you need to have part of your portfolio invested overseas because of the diversification benefits from international investing. However, some recent studies have refuted that, and a few contend that the real international effect is solely related to currency fluctuations. Where do you weigh in on that?*

Eveillard: Those same people make the argument that statistically what happens to a specific security has a lot to do with the industry or country it's in. That may be true over a 6-to-12–month period, but not over the long term. The Tokyo and U.S. stock markets have been like night and day over the past decade. If you were a Japanese citizen and made room for American securities in your portfolio, you would have done a lot better than if you had stayed exclusively with your own domestic securities.

Kazanjian: *Therefore, you do believe in the importance of international diversification?*

Eveillard: Yes. I believe there are tremendous differences among the various stock markets over time. If you want to be on the side of caution, you must be diversified. I think the most attractive side of buying foreign securities, though, is very simply that it's a big world out there beyond the borders of the United States. There are bound to be investment opportunities in other countries, so why not expose yourself to them?

Kazanjian: *You often say your goal is to keep risk down as low as possible. As a result, you think of how much money you can lose, more than how much you can make off of an investment.*

Eveillard: That's because I have my entire savings invested in the funds. I think like a shareholder. To me, it is serious money—not play money, which is the case for many mutual fund investors. It's a savings that is supposed to finance retirement. At the end of the year, if a fund manager comes to you and says his fund was down 15 percent last year but his benchmark was down 20 percent, I say that's nonsense. You had $100 at the beginning of the year; now you have $85. That's terrible.

We, together with many value investors, suffered considerably between the spring of 1995 and the spring of 2000. In 1995–96, the idea seemed to develop among investors that all you needed to own was big multinational growth stocks, which is hogwash. Then came the technology revolution and, even worse, the Internet stocks. It was what I call my own period of wandering in the desert. For a full five years, we continued to make money for shareholders, but not as much as the aggressive momentum types of funds. Between the fall of 1997 and the fall of 2000, we managed to lose 7 out of 10 of our shareholders in the SoGen Global Fund, not because we lost money for them, but because we made less than the others. It was what one of my friends calls the mother-in-law syndrome: A shareholder in my fund gets a call from his mother-in-law, who announces that her fund was up 45 percent last year. The poor fellow has to acknowledge that his fund was only up 15 percent, and the next morning rushes into his broker's office and tells him to redeem and throw the bums out of his portfolio. That's what happened.

Kazanjian: *Don't periods like that cause you to reconsider how you do things?*

Eveillard: There is extraordinary pressure to change from shareholders, brokers, financial planners, and even myself. It was to the point, as always happens toward the end of a drama, where a number of value investors left the investment business altogether. But we held firm and it wound up paying off.

Kazanjian: *You've also had a gold fund for several years. Gold really hasn't done much for more than a decade. Several years ago, you told me that if the performance didn't pick up, you planned to close the fund. The performance has remained awful, but the fund is still open.*

Eveillard: My basic assumption for starting the fund in 1993 proved to be wrong. We correctly predicted there would continue to be an imbalance between supply and demand of between 500 and 1,000 tons a year. Where things went awry is that the gap was filled. Because of central bank selling and lending, there proved to be a downside to the investment. Five years later, in the fall of 1998, I said to be patient is good, but to be stubborn is not so good. Then came the Russian crisis and the Fed having to organize a bailout of the Long Term Capital Management hedge fund. I figured if the Fed had to step in on something like this, I wanted to hold on to the gold fund.

Then I figured that eventually the price would stabilize or go up, which would cause the central banks to stop some of their selling.

Kazanjian: *It sounds like hope springs eternal.*

Eveillard: Like they say, anything can happen, good or bad. I think gold is a cheap insurance policy today. But, yes, hope springs eternal.

Kazanjian: *The median market cap for your stock fund is under $1 billion. Does that mean you generally buy small-cap stocks?*

Eveillard: To a large extent. It's based upon the simple idea that the smaller and more obscure a security is, the more likely it is to be ignored, neglected, or mispriced by the market.

Kazanjian: *But you can buy anything?*

Eveillard: Absolutely. In a way there is nothing we like better than identifying what we perceive to be an unduly depressed big stock. We have always owned some big stocks.

Kazanjian: *Is buying foreign stocks pretty difficult and expensive to do for the average individual investor?*

Eveillard: It's not very expensive. Commission rates even in Japan have been negotiated and are no longer fixed. I think that for an individual, it's more a matter of whether they have the time, the skill, and the desire to investigate foreign securities. It's a little more complicated to rate a German balance sheet than an American balance sheet if you're an American. That's why most investors are better off in funds. But individual stock investing can be done if you're willing to put the right amount of time into it.

Several years ago, Eveillard told me that he would consider retiring in 2000 because of the inherent stress that comes with a job like his. He apparently had a change of heart. Eveillard has signed a contract that will keep him at the funds through at least the end of 2004, up through his 65th birthday. He also just launched a new fund—First Eagle U.S. Value—that invests exclusively in companies based in America.

Although you can tell that Eveillard is a bit critical of momentum investors, he insists that many forms of growth investing are legitimate. They just don't suit him. As he puts it, different investors have different skills. "If a basketball coach asks someone who's been playing small guard to play power forward, the poor fellow doesn't have a chance to begin with," Eveillard says. "By the same token, if someone asked me to all of a sudden become a growth investor, I'd probably be the worst of them. It's not my natural talent." ■

WILLIAM FRIES

THORNBURG INVESTMENT MANAGEMENT

Bill Fries works 7,000 feet above sea level in an office some 2,000 miles from Wall Street. A native of New Jersey, Fries now lives in Santa Fe, New Mexico, where he's run the Thornburg Value Fund since 1995. A few years back, he also started Thornburg Global Value, which hunts for similar companies overseas.

Fries, 62, follows an admittedly eclectic approach to investing, filling his portfolio with three types of "value" stocks: basic value, consistent growers, and emerging franchises. Basic value stocks have many of the traditional value characteristics, such as low PE ratios and prices near book value. Consistent growers are generally blue-chip companies with predictable, steady earnings that may be a little pricier, but generally are worth it. And emerging franchises are younger companies on the leading edge of change, which may be undervalued based on future growth potential, as opposed to the current market price.

Because of this flexibility, a company such as Caterpillar might sit next to Pepsico, E-Trade, or AOL Time Warner in Fries's portfolio. Fries maintains that his approach gives investors a smoother ride over time by producing consistent results in a variety of markets.

Before joining Thornburg, Fries spent almost two decades as an analyst and running money at USAA Investment Management. During that time, he oversaw such funds as USAA Growth, Income Stock, and Aggressive Growth. And while overall he's encouraged about the prospects for the U.S. market over the next few years, he's even more optimistic about some of the foreign countries he's currently investing in.

Kazanjian: *Your hometown of Santa Fe seems like it's a long way from Wall Street.*

Fries: It is a long way from Wall Street. Our tag line about value is that we're value investors from a different place, and that means more than just being from Santa Fe.

Kazanjian: *We'll get into that more in a minute. Did you grow up in New Mexico?*

Fries: No. I grew up in Sussex, New Jersey, about 57 miles from New York City.

Kazanjian: *Did you have ambitions of getting into the investment field as a young man?*

Fries: I did. I had an eighth-grade teacher who was influential, and my family was always interested in the stock market and investments. It was kind of natural for me to be interested as well.

Kazanjian: *Did you major in business in college?*

Fries: I majored in finance at Penn State. After getting my undergraduate degree, I spent four years in the Marine Corps as a communications officer. Then I worked in Philadelphia at Girard Trust Bank as a securities analyst. During my time there, I attended graduate school at Temple, where I ultimately earned my MBA.

Kazanjian: *When you first started out at Girard, what kinds of securities were you analyzing?*

Fries: Initially companies in the Philadelphia area, such as Alanwood Steel, office equipment companies such as Burroughs and Philco, and some consumer companies such as American Home Products. I became indoctrinated in an approach that we identified as central value. It focused on cash flow and cash flow returns on gross assets. This approach to measuring profitability helps to neutralize some of the accounting variances when evaluating companies. Back in those days there really weren't uniform rules on how to calculate earnings per share or fully diluted earnings per share [EPS]. Part of an analyst's job was standardizing the EPS calculation among companies.

Of course, the standard has been changed a number of times since then. Accounting has always been important to me—I think, in part, because it's not static. For example, recently we've gone through a whole iteration of new accounting rules that apply to companies making acquisitions in the technology area.

Kazanjian: *How long were you at Girard?*

Fries: About 3½ years. Among my jobs there was backup analyst for tax-exempt bonds. I learned the bond business. At some point the bank across the street needed somebody in the bond area. They gave me an attractive offer, so I traded municipal bonds for Fidelity Bank for about a year and a half. But I missed equities, so I decided to get back into the stock research area. I joined a brokerage firm in Philadelphia where I was one of three analysts. We followed companies and industries across the waterfront. This was in the late 1960s, early 1970s. This job gave me good experience because the whole thesis for our research department was to provide useable and well-documented investment ideas for partners and brokers.

Kazanjian: *Were you doing this through the 1973–74 period?*

Fries: I was indeed.

Kazanjian: *What was that experience like?*

Fries: It probably seems worse now, but it was like Chinese water torture. There were an awful lot of stocks that were very overvalued. They would just dribble off every day for almost an entire year. There were a few rallies, but not many. We were just beginning to recognize the nation's energy problems. We had a war going on that had to be funded. Inflation was rampant and potentially more devastating than it is today, partly because a large segment of society was pretty much in denial about it.

Kazanjian: *So you think the down market that began in 2000 is different from 1973–74's?*

Fries: Yes. The problems we have today are largely isolated to capital spending in the technology area. In 1974, the economy was much more dependent on heavy industry. We also have much lower interest rates now. I can remember in 1974 thinking about how serious the economic imbalance from escalating energy prices was going to be. It was like a significant tax on the consumer. Oil was about $2.50 a barrel at the beginning of the 1970s. By the end of the decade, it had jumped to more than $30 a barrel. There was no way around the economic impact.

Kazanjian: *By the late 1970s you wound up at the USAA?*

Fries: Yes. I went to USAA as an analyst in 1974. By that time I had been an analyst for about 10 years. USAA is an insurance company in San Antonio, Texas. USAA had started a fund management company a couple of years earlier and was moving management of its insurance investments in-house. I was hired to help support those efforts.

Kazanjian: *Isn't USAA Investment Management primarily a growth shop?*

Fries: At that time it only had two funds. Most of the mutual fund assets ($60 million) were in the USAA Capital Growth Fund. The insurance company's assets were managed using a value philosophy. The Income Fund was tiny at that time. The overall philosophy was conservative. I think it still is.

Kazanjian: *Were you using your basic value criteria to choose investments at that time?*

Fries: It's interesting that you ask that. At that time the division or dichotomy between investment approaches did not exist, at least not to the point where what was value and what was growth was clearly identified. That's been a phenomenon of the last decade, in part because there have been some pretty compelling academic papers on the merits of value investing. A lower-risk approach to equity investing is appealing and there is some evidence of long-term success with this approach.

Frankly, I'm not sure that studies of past performance are not heavily influenced by periods over which performance is measured. As you can imagine, if you measure a string of three- or five-year periods ending in 1998 or 1999, you'd get quite a different result than if you measured that period up to 2000. There is pretty good evidence that investors have been rewarded for avoiding the highest-priced stocks, or what I view as the clear distinction between "value" and "momentum" investing. To me, the distinction between "growth" and "value" is not nearly as clear as the distinction between "value" and "momentum." In reality, growth is embedded in why people buy equity investments. Capital appreciation is the primary motivation for people to own equities. Implicit in that term, at least for long-run investors, is the idea of having your capital grow. I think that somehow gets lost in the philosophical debates involving value and growth investing. I don't think there really is an exclusionary aspect of value investing that says you don't want to consider a company's growth aspects when you buy value.

Kazanjian: *In 1995, you wound up at Thornburg Investment Management, where you are today. Wasn't Thornburg primarily a fixed-income shop at that point?*

Fries: In terms of public money, yes, but it had managed an equity portfolio in-house since 1990.

Kazanjian: *Did you start the Thornburg Value Fund, or did you take it over from someone?*

Fries: The partners of Thornburg managed a private portfolio from 1990 to 1995 using a similar philosophy. That philosophy incorporated some of the experiences that I had at USAA in managing a number of different portfolios, from very aggressive to very conservative. One of the things I learned at USAA was that there is no one answer to the investment challenge. Good stock selection across a number of risks delivers consistent performance over time. With that in mind, we put some labels on what we saw as the different aspects of value. We identified basic value stocks, consistent earners, and what we called emerging franchises. The fund today gives participation in all three of these different approaches to value.

Kazanjian: *Let's talk about those categories one by one. What is a basic value stock?*

Fries: Most people identify measures of value relating earnings, cash flow, or book value to the price of the stock. They also look for higher yields. This typically leads you to certain industries, often with cyclical characteristics. A PE ratio is nothing more than an earnings yield turned upside down for convenience because it's easier to calculate. Stocks with low PEs (or high earnings yields) represent a solid and fundamentally sound way of measuring basic value. This is a core part of our concept of value. The most rewarding basic value type of investment comes into play when a stock sells off because a company has a problem. If the problem is temporary, this creates a value investment opportunity. When the turnaround comes, the result can be very good investment performance.

Kazanjian: *What numbers do you look at when determining basic value?*

Fries: Reference to historical levels of price-to-book value and balance-sheet strength are important. Each company is a unique situation. Earnings power potential and the PE using normalized earnings are important as well. Banks, financial services, and insurance companies tend to have low valuation characteristics. Price-to-book value is particularly useful as a value reference for these companies. The electric utilities traditionally have been regulated to where the rate of growth and the return are not going to be particularly high. As a result, they tend to sell at low multiples. You see lots of value investors with significant holdings in these industries.

Kazanjian: *By definition, do these stocks often stay in the value category for long?*

Fries: Indeed they do. But they can also provide big opportunities. For example, financial service companies and banks were poor performers in the 1980s because of nonperforming assets, particularly assets related to real estate. Many ultimately sold down to book value or below. This turned out to be a fabulous opportunity. You had banks going from less than book value to three or four times book value. It's a clear case of where buying low price-to-book-value ratios was great for value investors.

Kazanjian: *What percentage do you keep in this, the deepest value part of your portfolio?*

Fries: At the present time it's about 40 percent, which is pretty normal. But it can vary. We don't allocate by portfolio segment. We invest where the market creates value.

Kazanjian: *Are the allocations merely a result of where your research leads you?*

Fries: Yes. We may be looking at a basic value stock versus a consistent grower versus an emerging franchise. With the risk-averse market we have today, there's real appeal in basic value. In fact, some of the technology companies thought of as growth companies are now basic value stocks. This is not unique to this market cycle. In the past, there have been promising companies that traded down to below book value in the depths of the cycle.

Kazanjian: *Let's move on to consistent earners. What are those?*

Fries: Those are typically blue-chip companies with a couple of characteristics investors find admirable and are willing to pay premium prices for. Procter & Gamble is a great example. You have consistency of revenues, so there's not a lot of cyclical volatility. The company makes a consumable item that gets used every day, and is purchased at millions of places by millions of people at a fairly low price. Granted, there is some competition, but the company's branding is well established. When people go to buy Tide, they don't even think of Procter & Gamble. Consistent earners generate high returns on equity. They are market share leaders and pretty much own the shelf space in stores where their products are sold. They may not grow particularly fast, but the revenue stream is perceived to be an annuity.

Kazanjian: *But are they cheap?*

Fries: The common denominator for us in all three of these categories is to buy these companies when they're out of favor. We think there are times when even though a stock such as Procter & Gamble may be selling at twice the multiple of a basic value stock, there is value in the franchise. We're prepared to buy those stocks when they're out of favor. That may mean paying an average price for an exceptional company.

Kazanjian: *Is there a certain benchmark you look at to compare relative value?*

Fries: We relate relative value to the market multiple. If you can get a distinctly above-average company at a market multiple or a discount to the market multiple, that's appealing, especially if the stock is usually not available at a discount. You have to look at the business and management's ability to reinvest free cash flow effectively. Gillette is an example of this. It's currently down significantly from its historical levels. The problem is that the company dominates the razor blade business. It has had so much success, it generates a lot of cash. Gillette has to figure out whether to distribute, buy back stock, or create a new business with that cash. As has happened to lots of companies, Gillette's reinvestment in new business has not been as successful as its original business. This is a problem that many of these blue-chip consistent earners have to contend with. Just being out of favor isn't enough. You still have to analyze the company and make judgments about the future. That's what value investing and investing in general are all about. If you perceive the future correctly, you usually can make pretty decent investment returns.

Kazanjian: *How do you make those kinds of predictions?*

Fries: It's mostly a judgment call, but it's predicated on a thorough understanding of what's going on in the world and evidence of management's ability to execute a plan.

Kazanjian: *Do you meet with management before making an investment?*

Fries: We often do. Sometimes you meet with management today and you might not make an investment for a year. You keep building your base of knowledge by taking advantage of access to management, either by going to their premises or by seeing them at conferences. We think meeting with management is an important part of making a judgment about a company's future. Companies effectively are a team of people creating a culture in which they hope to thrive.

Kazanjian: *The third and final category is emerging franchises.*

Fries: Emerging franchises are typically younger companies. They may not necessarily be small, but they are younger and on the leading edge of change. The best example I can give you from our current portfolio would be something as large as AOL Time Warner or as small as Advent Software. Both companies are agents of change. Think of your own lifestyle. Ten years ago the Internet was probably not part of your everyday life as it is today. Here's a company that identified characteristics of a technical capability, turned it into an annuity-type subscription business, recognized the power of easy use, and became the dominant industry player. Now it has added a rich suite of content to that.

Kazanjian: *AOL Time Warner is not a name you would expect to see in a value portfolio.*

Fries: No, you wouldn't. But our idea of value is more than financial measures related to price. There is value in market share leadership; value in the company's 30 million subscribers. AOL Time Warner has 200 million magazine subscribers. I see value there. These aspects of value may not be conventionally related to the stock price. They represent value nonetheless and are especially important in judging the promise of emerging franchises.

Kazanjian: *Tell me about your sell discipline.*

Fries: We establish a target price when we buy a stock using a time horizon of 12 to 18 months. This target is based on the developments that we think will take place over that time.

Kazanjian: *Is that also what you consider to be intrinsic value?*

Fries: Intrinsic value is based on a quantification of various value measures. Using a PE ratio, for instance, we put a target price on the earnings level out a year at the multiple we think is fair for the stock. This would be one measure we would use to establish a target price.

Kazanjian: *Do you always sell when it reaches your target?*

Fries: No. This is especially true in the emerging-franchise arena. We may change the target price as our thesis on a company develops as expected or better. As a stock approaches a target price, we look out for the next 12 to 18 months to see what's changed. If the company has done everything it was supposed to do, earnings are higher, and the multiple is still at a reasonable level, we may end up hanging on to the stock and establishing a new price target. Despite recent experience, one of the biggest mistakes investors make over the long run is selling emerging-franchise–type stocks too early. I can look back over my career and identify a number of stocks I've sold too early. Despite the fact that they have some massive volatility along the way, sale of the really great companies can be a big opportunity lost.

Kazanjian: *Of 10 ideas, how many work out?*

Fries: I'd like to think that better than six work out. They say if you're right half the time, you're doing better than average. Part of our success has been not having many stocks that worked in a negative way. In other words, we've protected the downside. I remember a couple of years where we looked back and found most of our success came from having not owned stocks that sold off much. A stock may have been sterile, meaning it didn't make any money, but it didn't go down much. The risk for value managers is that you become too complacent with the values you have locked up. The train leaves the station again and you've got a portfolio that's not really diversified, doesn't have comprehensive value, and may not participate.

Kazanjian: *Do the emerging franchises tend to be the riskiest holdings in your portfolio?*

Fries: By far.

Kazanjian: *What percentage is that?*

Fries: We generally keep that under 50 percent.

Kazanjian: *What percentage do you keep in the consistent growers?*

Fries: About 40 percent currently, but, again, we don't allocate a fixed percentage.

Kazanjian: *That's roughly an equal split between the consistent growers and basic value.*

Fries: Consistent growers can get overpriced, though. For instance, in 1999 when drug stocks were in favor, they were in the consistent-grower camp. We essentially didn't own any because of their pricing. Our basic value component has been as high as 55 percent.

Kazanjian: *How diversified is your portfolio?*

Fries: It's focused, but diversified. We have about 50 names. That's not too many when you consider that we run over $2 billion in assets.

Kazanjian: *How much will you put into a single holding?*

Fries: Some holdings will get over 4 percent. A typical holding might be 3 to 4 percent. The emerging-franchise holdings typically start at less than 2 percent, especially if they're smaller companies.

Kazanjian: *Do you try to diversify across industry sectors?*

Fries: I'm very cognizant of industry concentration. Our biggest industry holding might be 15 percent. I look at risk a bit differently. I consider classic technology to be electronics companies, semiconductors, semiconductor capital equipment companies, and component suppliers. I would include in that software and telecommunications equipment companies. When I'm judging how much risk I have in the portfolio, that's the way I categorize things. For instance, in financial services, I put brokers together with mutual fund managers and recognize that banks have some of the same risks. While I may have two categories—institutional banking and financial services—I recognize that there's a relationship between them.

Kazanjian: *You have a fairly large concentration in investment management companies, which is something of a contrarian play given the tough times in the market as we speak.*

Fries: We try to buy what is out of favor. I think some of these stocks are out of favor. Certainly the online brokers are very much out of favor currently. But online trading and banking are going to be part of the future landscape.

Kazanjian: *You're long-term positive on the whole investment management industry?*

Fries: Very much so. Many of these companies are systems companies. If you take Bank of New York or Charles Schwab, the systems investment they have is huge. They're not easily replicatable. The assets under their care and the investments they've made to gather those assets represent real value.

Kazanjian: *Given what's happened with the tech wreck, are you evaluating technology companies differently than you used to?*

Fries: I think we've all been forced to take a fresh look at technology. We look at those companies more skeptically than ever because investors went through a period of time when the absence of a business model that incorporated visible profitability or even positive cash flow was tolerated. From here on, I think people are going to be more demanding. Some of these companies will succeed, but a high percentage have been what I call "pretenders," companies that look like they have promise but are more motion than available business. Most of these pretenders will never come back. As analysts, we have to be careful to make sure we understand the business plan and the business model. That's more than just having a spreadsheet that happens to generate a bunch of numbers that may be feasible, but may not be practical or rational.

Kazanjian: *Where do most of your investment ideas come from?*

Fries: Ideas can come from a variety of places. Our process uses screens as a place to start. Stocks that are down in price are always of interest. We sort out companies with dangerous financial leverage. Like most investors, we prefer high returns on equity and earnings visibility, so we incorporate criteria to identify these measures of value.

Kazanjian: *You also manage a global fund.*

Fries: It's really an international fund. We call it global because we want to be able to own a few American companies, but it's more than 85 percent foreign.

Kazanjian: *Do you evaluate foreign companies differently from American companies?*

Fries: No. We use the exact same philosophy and the same three types of value categories. The value parameters have to be a bit different because the accounting policies are different. There is certainly more political risk. We do hedge the currencies, so we tend to take out the currency risk exposure. This is something we typically don't have to worry about with domestic companies.

Kazanjian: *Looking out three to five years, do you think there is going to be more opportunity in the international markets or in the U.S.?*

Fries: There are certain economies that, if the political tranquility prevails, will have the opportunity to grow at much faster rates than the U.S.

Kazanjian: *Such as?*

Fries: China, for one, has an enormous opportunity. I've visited China twice in the last couple of years. I'm very impressed with the progress they've made. Beijing looks more like Dallas than you might expect. China is not a country of ox carts and straw hats. This is a country that is quickly modernizing. It's been growing at better than 6 percent a year. I view it as a place that's the equivalent of where Japan was in 1960. China has a few things going against it. One is politics. Nonetheless, they are trying to develop a market economy with some measure of control and organization. Both the technology and energy areas look like areas of opportunity.

Kazanjian: *You list all of the companies you own in your portfolios on your website, along with a brief overview of why you like them. Many mutual fund firms have been criticized for not disclosing enough information about portfolio holdings. Do you feel funds should be more open with shareholders?*

Fries: We think that investors are more likely to be content with their investments if they know what they own. We believe in full disclosure. We also are big believers in using technology. We use the Internet extensively. Computers have made it possible to run an organization like this from a place such as Santa Fe. We have the same electronic feeds that people in New York have.

Kazanjian: *Technology is the great equalizer.*

Fries: Plus, I think we have some advantages because we are away from the madding crowd and all of the other extraneous influences. I don't run into five or six other portfolio managers every day at lunch who can distract our focus. That gives us independent judgment. I think there's some value in that. I think there are some advantages to being here in Santa Fe away from the typical Wall Street noise.

Another advantage to being in Santa Fe is that Bill can enjoy some of his favorite distractions, such as playing golf, hiking, fly fishing, and playing tennis, year round. He credits much of his success to the team of analysts he works with, who help him come up with ideas for the fund. They work together in an open area, where they talk freely throughout the day. As Fries likes to say, the investment committee is always in session.

While some have criticized him for holding so many names that would more typically be found in growth portfolios, Fries respectfully disagrees. He figures that within the next 10 years, the whole idea of bifurcating managers by value and growth will undergo scrutiny. In the meantime, he'll continue to deploy the steady winning ways that have propelled his portfolios to impressive returns. ■

JAMES GILLIGAN

VAN KAMPEN INVESTMENTS

Jim Gilligan has been making money all of his life. As a young boy, he had a number of businesses going, including a paper route that he eventually hired others to service so he could move on to other ventures. He even made loans to his five brothers and sisters, and profited from the interest. In his high school economics class, he was introduced to the stock market, and was instantly attracted. That fascination has stayed with him ever since.

In the early 1980s, Gilligan began his career as an auditor and analyst with Gulf Oil Corporation, largely because he couldn't find a job in investments out of college. It was a time when many airlines were going bankrupt, and Gilligan often had to decide whether to extend them enough credit to fuel their jets. After about four years at Gulf, tired of ongoing contraction in the oil business and determined to get into the investment field, Gilligan landed a job at American Capital, which later merged with Van Kampen Investments.

Today, Gilligan is senior portfolio manager of the Van Kampen Equity Income and Van Kampen Growth and Income funds. Gilligan generally looks for what he calls value with a catalyst. The catalyst is something he believes will lead to increased growth in earnings for the company. In determining whether a stock is a value, he looks at such factors as its market value compared to various benchmarks. As a result of his process, the 43-year-old manager often buys companies that aren't very sexy, but operate in strong industries and have promising futures.

Kazanjian: *You were quite the entrepreneur as a young boy in Pittsburgh. I guess it's not surprising that you wound up in the money management business.*

Gilligan: My family wasn't poor, but there were six kids and there wasn't a lot of money. From the time I could walk, I had a paper route. I kept it going through my senior year of high school. Eventually, I paid other people to deliver the route for me, and I moved on to other things. I saved all the money I made, probably because of the influence my parents had on me. They didn't spend their money either.

Kazanjian: *In other words, you were value-oriented even back then.*

Gilligan: I was a hoarder, if nothing else. I'm the youngest of the six children, yet I financed cars for a couple of my brothers and sisters. I really didn't get interested in stocks until high school. I took an economics class that had a stock-picking contest. It was fun to look every day to see how your stocks did. At the end of the term, I took third place in the contest.

Kazanjian: *What other businesses did you have as a boy?*

Gilligan: I mowed lawns and shoveled driveways. I was always doing something.

Kazanjian: *Did you go to college with a career goal in mind?*

Gilligan: I knew I liked business and finance. I went to Miami University in Oxford, Ohio. I double-majored in economics and finance, which I found was fairly worthless when I got out of school in 1980. The job market was pretty sour. We were in a recession. I went to Atlanta looking for work and got a couple of job offers for almost minimum wage. My parents had forced me to fill out an application for graduate school. I didn't want to go back to school because I didn't like it that much, but, in the interest of pleasing them, I sent an application to the University of Pittsburgh and was accepted. I discovered during the whole job search process that I lacked a good fundamental basis in accounting. When I went back to school, I loaded up on accounting. I got an MBA with an emphasis in accounting.

Kazanjian: *Did you find that your economics degree helped you as an investor?*

Gilligan: As an investor, yes. For almost any entry-level job, an economics degree has very little meaning because it encompasses everything. Entry-level jobs are usually very defined and narrow. In terms of what I do today, understanding the economy and the factors that influence it is very useful.

Kazanjian: *I take it that graduate school was a more enlightening experience than college had been.*

Gilligan: It was 1981. I went into a one-year accelerated program. That's about the only way you'd get me in. I really enjoyed it. As I took more accounting courses, I began to appreciate the science of it. I also found my behavioral science courses to be very interesting. The psychology classes I took as an undergraduate always seemed like a waste of time, but the courses in graduate school helped me see the dynamics of individual and group behavior, which has helped me in analyzing behavior in the stock market.

Kazanjian: *Did you learn much else about investing in college?*

Gilligan: Yes. I took investment courses, but the spark for my interest in stocks came before that. When I got out of college, I put on my resume that I wanted a job in investments. The trouble was that such jobs were almost nonexistent without connections. I came close to a job offer with a bank in Atlanta, but it wound up going to the vice president's son. In graduate school I was most concerned with getting an accounting background. Everyone I talked to in the investment field said you really need more accounting, which is funny because I don't think investment management programs at graduate schools emphasize accounting enough. They teach a lot of portfolio theory, which is all well and good, but students lack the basic fundamentals of how to analyze securities.

Kazanjian: *What was your first job out of graduate school?*

Gilligan: I was hired by Gulf Oil in Houston as an accounting intern. I was in a management-training program where you spent a couple of years rotating through different areas every three months. I joined the oil industry in 1981, which was almost at the peak. I stayed there for four years and every year the company downsized. That not only prevented my upward movement, but also caused a lot of people to lose their jobs. Then a guy named T. Boone Pickens showed up at Gulf's door. [Pickens is a Texas entrepreneur who founded Mesa Petroleum and gained fame for acquiring many companies, some through hostile means.] He took a run at Gulf Oil. It was very interesting to see that, from inside the company. Gulf Oil, at the time, was one of the worst-run oil companies. These people were very entrenched. They laughed Pickens off at first, but then they got scared. He was my hero because he was shaking things up. As all this progressed, Chevron ended up buying Gulf. Chevron offered me a job in Houston and in San Francisco, but at that point in my life I decided that I wanted to make a career change that would put me into the investment field.

Kazanjian: *What did you wind up doing after completing the management program?*

Gilligan: I went into wholesale credit for a little less than two years. It wasn't really what I wanted, but it taught me a lot about extending credit and looking at company risk. I had to determine whether these companies should get credit. At the time, the airlines were all going bankrupt. We were extending credit to them. There was a point where fuelers would have to call and get approval before they'd load an Eastern Airlines jet with gas. One day I went in and, because of a hurricane, was the only one in the office. The phone was ringing off the hook with the airlines wanting fuel. I was approving the requests, even if they weren't under my control. I decided I better leave and not get in any more trouble. It was a tough period and you had to work with customers and really know what their financials were to prevent taking any big losses. After that position I went into the internal audit department. Again, this was not a career that I wanted to pursue long-term, but it gave me invaluable experience in corporate accounting and particularly the importance of controls in assuring the reliability of financial information.

Kazanjian: *You left without another job?*

Gilligan: I told the company I was leaving without a job, but I was already pursuing other options. I looked at a number of different ways to get into investments. I happened to have a friend who worked for a fixed-income portfolio manager in Houston. I sent him a resume, which he circulated to the chief investment officer. I think the investment officer liked me because he enjoyed hiring people who didn't have industry experience. He also liked my accounting and economics background.

Kazanjian: *Is this the same firm you're at today?*

Gilligan: It was a predecessor company called American Capital, which has had a long and storied history. It merged with Van Kampen in 1994.

Kazanjian: *At the time you came in, were you working on the fixed-income side?*

Gilligan: No. As it turned out, I was on the equity side.

Kazanjian: *What did you do?*

Gilligan: I struggled. I didn't have any experience. I was only four years into my career. I had saved a little bit of money and most of that was in the Gulf Oil 401(k) plan. This was in 1985. I had limited exposure to mutual funds. The firm sat me in an office and told me to follow the trucking and chemical industries. For about three months, I struggled quite a bit. I wasn't sleeping because my mind was going 200 miles per hour. Everything I did or saw was somehow related to the stock market. I'd be driving home and wind up lost. The lack of sleep started to get to me. I made a decision to give it a few more weeks. If I still wasn't able to sleep, I'd have to cut this career short. Fortunately, I started sleeping.

Kazanjian: *Did the firm at that time have any particular investment bent?*

Gilligan: Almost all of the portfolios were growth-oriented. The person I latched on to as a mentor managed the funds that I took over after he left the company. He was value-oriented and very good at directing the other analysts and me.

Kazanjian: *Up to that point you were learning by experiment?*

Gilligan: Yes. Very much so.

Kazanjian: *It sounds like you began to find there was a particular approach that made sense to you.*

Gilligan: Because of my educational background, I originally focused on cash flow. Back then, there were a flurry of takeovers and that approach worked well. The raiders were going after companies generating cash and investing it poorly. Some of the instruction this portfolio manager gave me is still part of what I do today. It involves looking at companies each quarter and trying to pick up inflection points [opportune moments to buy the stock] by examining revenues, earnings, and margins to see where the trend is broken. For example, in the previous quarter, the company's sales may have been down 10 percent, yet in the most recent quarter, they're only down 2 percent. The deceleration of the sales decline may indicate that an inflection point is near and that would warrant a closer look at the company. A big part of my philosophy, which has developed over the years, is that the market sets prices based on what it knows. What it knows is almost exclusively what it's seen in the past. If I can anticipate a change in a trend by looking at quarterly results and finding those companies where something positive is happening, I may be able to capture the increased expectations, and the resulting stock price appreciation that comes as the market finally takes notice [when the absolute results show positive comparisons]. I've found that the market generally doesn't like things unless they look pretty good.

Kazanjian: *When did you get your first shot at managing money?*

Gilligan: I ran a small fund called the American Capital Growth Fund that consisted mostly of employee assets in 1988. This was more of a growth-oriented product with about $12 million.

Kazanjian: *Do you still run that fund today?*

Gilligan: No. It was merged out of existence. Provident Fund for Income is now known as Van Kampen Equity Income. Fund of America is now Van Kampen Growth and Income. I manage both. The chief investment officer initially just gave me responsibility for the Provident Fund. I remember analyzing the portfolio at home that night and scribbling how I planned to restructure it. The fund probably had 80 percent turnover the next day, but since it only had $100 million in assets, it was easy to make that kind of dramatic shift.

Kazanjian: *What was it like the first time you were making such big decisions about how to invest other people's money? It's one thing* *to scribble your plans on paper. It's another to actually implement the trades.*

Gilligan: It's always intimidating. The first trade I ever did was for that portfolio manager who was a mentor to me. One time when he went on vacation, he asked me to look over the fund. I bought 5,000 shares of Boeing while he was gone. I agonized over that for the longest time because it was a lot of money.

Kazanjian: *How much do you manage all together now?*

Gilligan: A little over $6 billion.

Kazanjian: *Funds today have all kinds of labels. What's the difference between the Growth and Income and Equity Income funds?*

Gilligan: Originally Provident Fund for Income, which is now Equity Income, was a balanced fund. Balanced funds didn't have much of a following at that time and really still don't. We decided to change the fund's orientation and categorize it as an equity income fund. As such, we use fixed-income bonds and Treasuries, but we also use convertible securities. At any given time, 20 to 40 percent of the fund is in convertibles and bonds.

Growth and Income is almost totally invested in stocks. Early on, we used some convertibles, but the market was so strong in the early 1990s that the convertibles were holding back performance. As a result, we decided to forgo that strategy and become almost exclusively a stock portfolio.

Kazanjian: *Equity Income sounds like a more conservative fund.*

Gilligan: Yes, it is.

Kazanjian: *Given the conservative nature of your funds, whom would you say your portfolios are most appropriate for?*

Gilligan: Really, anybody. If you go back in history, the returns on these kinds of products over the long run are, in most cases, better than returns on the average growth fund, while the volatility and risk are much less. At certain points, such as the late 1990s, you couldn't make that case because the rewards and returns of the very hot growth stocks were just so outside the box.

Kazanjian: *Why do more conservative funds tend to do better over time than the more aggressive funds?*

Gilligan: I have a theory, but I can't prove it. I think anyone with a valid discipline for growth or value will outperform over the long run. Value people, by their very nature, have a discipline. Some growth managers seem to have no discipline other than looking at relative strength or chasing the hottest thing. We had a period back in the late 1990s where that strategy worked for a number of years. You had one group dominating, so everyone piled on to it. A lot of people without discipline did very well because you could invest in technology and not worry about it. But, I believe that's the exception rather than the rule. This has all unwound now. I think it points out the flaws of those undisciplined strategies.

Kazanjian: *We often hear that if you have a long time horizon, you should be an aggressive investor and buy aggressive growth funds. What you're saying is that if you're a long-term investor, you may want to own conservative funds.*

Gilligan: I'll give the growth people some credit. If you can find a disciplined growth player, I think you can do as well as and possibly better over the long run if they are truly investing in growth. The trouble is that such disciplined investors can be hard to find.

Kazanjian: *Don't you think part of the reason aggressive funds struggle over time is because they tend to have huge up and down years, making upward progress difficult? By contrast, the more conservative funds take a more steady approach. Plus, people tend to buy into aggressive funds right at the top, and then sell out as soon as they fall.*

Gilligan: Exactly. A few years ago, someone looked at investor returns in load versus no-load funds. It seemed that because of surrender charges and by working with an advisor, load fund shareholders tended to stay in the funds longer. Therefore, they were less likely to get in at the peak and sell at the bottom. Investors by nature tend to buy the wrong thing at the wrong time.

Kazanjian: *Do you feel that investors pay too much attention to performance?*

Gilligan: Absolutely. The media's performance rankings are at fault because every quarter, they show not only the top stocks for that quarter, but also the top funds for the quarter. A quarter may not be significant, yet an individual with limited experience and knowledge of the marketplace could focus on it and make some very bad decisions.

Kazanjian: *What do you think of index fund investing?*

Gilligan: I think it's a valid way to invest. Some managers make a big deal of pointing out how there are so many undisciplined portfolio managers out there who underperform. When you compare the index funds to that universe, the index funds look good. But when you compare disciplined investors to the indexes, the disciplined investors may look better. The trouble with indexing, just like everything else, is that it's popular when it's working. It worked for a good number of years. Now that it has not been as successful, people are becoming interested in active management again. You have to be consistent with your investments. If you choose the course of indexing, you've got to be in it for the long haul.

Kazanjian: *How do you know if your fund manager is a disciplined investor?*

Gilligan: The same way you can tell it in the management of the companies I buy. I look at what they're trying to accomplish and how well they do at meeting these benchmarks. If you're looking at a value manager, you want to see a defined value style and a portfolio that looks like a value fund. Then you measure the portfolio against the appropriate benchmarks. You also want to see tenure and nothing suspicious or out of the ordinary.

Kazanjian: *When you say* tenure, *you mean the ability to judge performance over a long period of time?*

Gilligan: Yes.

Kazanjian: *Yet looking at your portfolio, I see some names such as AOL Time Warner and Microsoft that people might say go against your discipline.*

Gilligan: That goes back to your definition of value. We don't use a strict PE measure. We look at the potential relative to the price. For example, we bought AOL right after the accounting problems surfaced in 1996. It was a value stock then, even though it didn't have earnings. The potential for earnings was clearly there. Every once in a while we see an opportunity like that. As for Microsoft, that company's return on capital is large and it has difficulty finding a use for all the cash it produces. The best investments you can make are in growth companies that are being overly penalized by the market for a short-term problem or because their potential is not recognized by the market. It's not a matter of buying dogs, but rather buying good companies that have gone astray or have fallen out of favor with the market. That's where the huge opportunities lie. In the purely cyclical companies, it's more of a trading game. But if you can find growth, your holding period may get extended dramatically.

Kazanjian: *What's the first thing you look at in terms of finding securities?*

Gilligan: We try to find good stocks by observing, listening, and running screens based on value criteria. We're also trying to determine what is happening in the economy and try to isolate any trend that we can exploit in the investments we make.

Kazanjian: *When you take a look at where the world's going, what types of things are you paying attention to?*

Gilligan: Our basis of investing is "value with a catalyst." At times, the catalyst is hard to find. A catalyst generally involves something that will bring about a return of earnings growth. Once you find the catalyst, your expectations are that earnings will come through fairly quickly. In an economic downturn or recession, it's hard to get any visibility in the catalyst other than a belief that the economy will recover at some point. We use history and what we know of the markets to try and find our catalyst in situations such as this.

Kazanjian: *Do you make investment decisions based on this broad world view?*

Gilligan: We're still going stock by stock, but if I'm screening a stock that looks cheap, yet I know it's economically sensitive, I might not buy it if I don't expect the economy to be strong enough to bring about a recovery in the company's earnings.

Kazanjian: *When you run a computer screen, what are you searching for?*

Gilligan: My favorite measures are enterprise-value-to-sales and enterprise-value-to-EBITDA.

Kazanjian: *What is enterprise value?*

Gilligan: The market value of the stock plus debt. We look at PE ratios, but that's secondary. We use enterprise-value-to-sales more because sales are a more steady measure. Earnings can go away, but sales, while they fluctuate, don't change greatly. We use enterprise value rather than price-to-sales to incorporate the debt of companies. A simple price-to-sales comparison, by ignoring debt, will make highly leveraged companies relatively more attractive than they should be and well-capitalized companies relatively less attractive. That doesn't make much sense.

Kazanjian: *What types of numbers are you looking for?*

Gilligan: It all depends. We look at these value measures relative to what the return on capital is or could be. In the case of a cyclical company with normal margins, usually any time you can get below one times enterprise-value-to-sales, you may start to become interested. In higher-growth areas, such as pharmaceuticals and technology, you have to go higher. What we're looking for is not always absolute, but sometimes relative to where these stocks have traded in the past. If we can find a pharmaceutical company with a 20 to 30 percent return on capital, even if its enterprise-value-to-sales is three or higher, it could be extremely attractive. Those sales are more valuable than the sales of an industrial machinery company.

Kazanjian: *Once you've got an idea on the table, how do you decide whether it's selling at a value worthy of being purchased?*

Gilligan: We look at those measures relative to the history of the company. We really pay attention to the return on capital and the margins over time. We are particularly interested in how the company is getting to profitability. In order to determine this, you have to go beyond the net and even operating margins and look at the trends in gross margin; sales, general, and administrative expenses; research and development; and the tax rate. Then we see how these ratios stack up against the competition and finally what we believe the realistic profitability levels should be.

In many cyclical companies, we try to estimate a normalized earnings level, which is ultimately the basis for your valuation. To determine normalized earnings we predict what sales should be, and then put a margin that the company has been able to generate over time on those sales. This assumes that history is a valid guide in determining margins—and for many companies, it is. For years, you could put an eight times multiple on peak earnings for any cyclical company to determine the price target, and it almost always worked. If the current earnings estimate is higher than the normalized earnings, we generally don't have a lot of interest in the stock. If we can find a situation where normalized earnings are higher than current estimates, in all probability the stock market price is based on a depressed level of earnings and there is likely some upside, especially if we have confidence in the company's ability to achieve a turnaround.

Kazanjian: *Do you put much emphasis on PE ratios?*

Gilligan: We do because, ultimately, we want to put a PE ratio on the normalized earnings that we have calculated. We look at what PE ratio has been valid for the company over time. Depending on what we're looking at, we can use either a relative or an absolute PE. We've been using more and more absolute ratios as valuations in the market have returned to more normal levels. In the latter part of the 1990s, in order to even play the game, you had to at least step up to relative PEs. Otherwise you never bought anything.

Kazanjian: *From a valuation and growth perspective, what would an ideal company look like?*

Gilligan: There are no absolutes, but my best company grows somewhere between 8 and 15 percent. Any time it gets over 15 percent, growth people are generally so attracted to it that they bid the stock up too high. If I can find an 8 to 15 percent growth on the top and bottom line, I'm interested. I definitely want to see top-line growth, and a return on capital that exceeds the company's cost of capital. The nirvana company has a return on capital that's at least in the teens. It generates free cash flow, spends no more than depreciation on capital spending, has a fairly clean balance sheet, and at the end of the day sells at what looks like a reasonable valuation. If you can buy a company like that at a discount to the market, it could be a good opportunity.

Kazanjian: Discount *meaning a discounted PE?*

Gilligan: That or where the enterprise-value-to-cash-flow is at a discount.

Kazanjian: *Both of your funds have the word "income" in the title. Does that mean that you're also looking for dividends?*

Gilligan: As history has progressed, the income component of the market has dwindled. We don't focus on yield in the securities we select. Because we are generally looking at large-value companies, we find companies that are more mature and more likely to pay an above-average dividend because they may not have as good a use for their capital as more growth-oriented companies.

Kazanjian: *In addition to the numbers, what else are you looking at to make sure the company is something you want to own?*

Gilligan: That's where the catalyst comes in. If it's really a value stock, the trends in revenues and margins probably look pretty bad for the most recent few quarters. Sales growth is probably anemic and maybe margins are suffering. I want to see that deterioration, at a minimum, winding down. I don't want to catch a falling sword.

Kazanjian: *Do you want the numbers to be trending up?*

Gilligan: Not necessarily trending up. I just don't want them going down anymore. That includes earnings, but particularly includes sales. If sales are down 10 percent in one quarter, 5 percent in the next, and 3 percent in the next, I want to see the next number be 3 or less, to indicate that we've reached an inflection point. It's not that big of a delta that most investors will pay attention to. But if we can see the value in the company and the potential to ramp those numbers up even higher, that's what generally attracts us. We also look at what the average analyst recommendation on the stock is. In general, we want stocks that are ranked low and/or undiscovered by the Street. We are also constantly monitoring the portfolio for stocks that are highly ranked. There's a large risk in stocks that are highly ranked because if sell-side analysts are recommending a strong buy, there's nothing higher than that but there is much downgrading that could be done.

Kazanjian: *With so many managers looking for those undiscovered stocks, it seems amazing that they remain that way for so long.*

Gilligan: I don't think all that many people are trying to discover them. In the recent past, it's been mostly a momentum market where people followed each other and really didn't try to discover anything new.

Kazanjian: *Give me an example of a company you found through this process.*

Gilligan: In early 1999, our screening process turned up 3M. We hadn't owned 3M in a number of years. The company's businesses were weak and currency devaluations were impacting it greatly. But we saw that the trend had reversed. The top line grew 3 percent in one quarter and 4 percent in the next. When we started looking at it, we found a company that was selling at a substantial discount to the market with a return on capital above 20 percent. It had good businesses and generated good cash flow. We started digging into it further by calling sell-side analysts to get a feel for what they thought. No one was recommending it. They all hated it. They said the company was dead and gone. Nevertheless, we started accumulating a position, at which point I went to meet with management. In doing the analysis, we also found out that the CEO planned to retire within two years, and the CFO planned to retire within a year and a half. The board had brought in a consultant to look at the organization and make recommendations because they were frustrated with the company's performance. All of those things were the catalysts for change we were looking for.

Kazanjian: *For many individual investors, the only real research they're able to do on a company, other than reading publicly available research, is to get a company's annual report. Are those documents valuable? If so, what do you look for in them?*

Gilligan: Annual reports are very valuable. Any time you're looking at a financial report, you want to focus on change, year over year, and quarter over quarter. You're trying to find out what the trends are in terms of gross margins; selling, general, and administrative expenses; research and development; the tax rate; and the number of shares outstanding. On the balance sheet, look at the receivables, days of sales outstanding, inventory turns, and any outsized growth in assets or liabilities. You want to see that cash is coming in and that it's growing at least on par with income. If you find that income growth is heavier than the growth in cash flow, something is going on.

Kazanjian: *How diversified are your funds?*

Gilligan: Over the past 10 years, the funds I manage have anywhere from 80 to 120 stocks. In terms of sector weightings, I've never been known to overweight sectors. I also tend to have a lower concentration in my top holdings because, even though I know which ones are my favorites, I don't know with certainty which ones will work.

Kazanjian: *A number of managers I've interviewed for this book hold concentrated portfolios.*

Gilligan: I know. Over a long enough period of time, that will work as long as you're disciplined. However, on any given day, you can take some enormous hits. If your investors are patient and understanding, that's fine. But I don't know too many of those.

Kazanjian: *What makes you sell a stock?*

Gilligan: We sell a stock either because it turns out the story was wrong, because things aren't improving as we thought, or because a negative event has cropped up that overwhelms all of the company's positives. The best reason to sell a stock is because we find something better with as much upside and less downside potential. I've learned that you can have all the confidence in the world on your upside, but sometimes it's more important to have confidence in your downside because those stocks can really detract from your performance.

Kazanjian: *Do you set sell targets on the upside?*

Gilligan: We set targets. When we buy something, we envision a fair price, but we don't use that as an automatic trigger. The market moves and you have to move your target accordingly. We find that when you pick a stock that works, you often grossly underestimate how well it will do. Conversely, on the downside, when something unravels, you are usually surprised by how bad it can get. Also, if a position grows to more than 3 percent of the portfolio, we'll likely trim it back.

Kazanjian: *When an investment doesn't perform as you expected, what is the most frequent cause?*

Gilligan: Most of the time, the company doesn't deliver on mutually agreed upon benchmarks.

Kazanjian: *What would you say is the most interesting part of your job?*

Gilligan: For me, the market is a drug. Things are changing by the second. Just keeping up with it is a fierce competition. The amount of information you are exposed to is mind numbing. The challenge is to use your knowledge and instincts to try to get in front of what's going to happen so you can try to profit from it. But this business can be frustrating at times, especially when things such as the technology bubble go on for extended periods of time. You see people throw billions of dollars around without any fundamental analysis.

Some of them are kids who have expectations of companies that are totally unrealistic. But, at the end of the day, it's a great business. I can't imagine a better way to make a living.

Given how hard it was for Gilligan to break into the investment business, I asked what advice he had for young people trying to do the same today. His counsel: Be an active investor if you have the resources to do so, and get an MBA. A graduate degree, he says, is essentially a requirement at most firms today. Then, get in the door at an investment company any way you can—even if it's not the exact job you want—and work your way up. As Gilligan puts it, once you're in, it's like a fraternity. Most people try to get in through the front door, but often it's better to sneak in from the back. And finally, don't be intimidated by the lofty credentials others in the profession may have. Common sense goes a lot further in determining success than the universities or graduate schools one attends. ■

JAMES GIPSON

In naming Jim Gipson domestic stock fund manager of the year for 2000, Morningstar described his approach as "a bit unusual, but quite effective." Gipson leaves no stone unturned in searching for companies for his Clipper and PBHG Clipper Focus funds. He looks for strong franchises trading at a 30 percent discount to intrinsic value. And when he finds a company he likes, he buys it in bulk. That's why it's not surprising to find up to half of a portfolio's total assets in his top 10 names.

Gipson has lived in southern California most of his life. A soft-spoken and matter-of-fact manager, Gipson started his own firm—Pacific Financial Research—in 1981. Clipper Fund was launched shortly thereafter. After years of outperforming the market, Clipper ran into strong head waves in the late 1990s, as Gipson's favorite stocks were pushed out of the spotlight by the sexier tech names he eschewed. Gipson admits it was the toughest time he had been through since getting into the business in 1973. Friends who knew nothing about the market were making more money in stocks than he was. Stocks he shorted in his personal account kept shooting higher and higher. Disgruntled shareholders wrote to tell the 59-year-old former naval officer that he had lost his mind. But Gipson's patience and stubbornness helped him to weather the storm. Longtime holdings Philip Morris, Fannie Mae, and Freddie Mac came back to life in 2000 and helped his fund to more than make up for the gains deferred in previous years.

Gipson thinks patience is a virtue most investors lack. He believes the pursuit of getting rich quick leads mostly to inferior returns. He's also patient when it comes to putting his money to work, and isn't afraid to keep up to a third of the portfolio in cash if he can't find enough attractive ideas to buy.

Kazanjian: *Where did you grow up?*

Gipson: I was born and raised in Los Angeles. I got my bachelor's and master's degrees in economics at UCLA.

Kazanjian: *I should warn you that I'm a University of Southern California graduate.*

Gipson: As a matter of fact, we've actually dared to employ a few USC grads here.

Kazanjian: *Did you have any interest in the stock market when you were growing up?*

Gipson: Well, I was on a television quiz show when I was 15 years old and won a couple of thousand dollars. I invested that money in the stock market. I suppose that's when my interest in investing started.

Kazanjian: *What did you buy?*

Gipson: That's a sore topic. I wanted to buy IBM and DuPont. My mother, in consultation with our lawyer, decided that was too risky, so they put me in a mutual fund. A few years later when I redeemed the money for college, I had barely broken even. Needless to say, IBM and DuPont did exceptionally well during that period. I should also add that I didn't know what I was doing at that time.

Kazanjian: *When you went to college, what career were you thinking of?*

Gipson: I knew I wanted to be in business at some point. I didn't know precisely where. I eventually wound up at the Harvard Business School. When I graduated in 1973, virtually no one had an interest in going into investment management. The placement office at that point had 17 general categories, and investment management was not one of them.

Kazanjian: *I wonder whether graduates over the next few years will be less interested in Wall Street, given what's been happening with the market.*

Gipson: I'm not sure. There's a tendency for graduates to go into whatever area is hot or popular at the time, as opposed to what they personally find interesting and fascinating. I went into something that was fascinating to me but very unpopular with my friends.

Kazanjian: *Why was the market so fascinating to you?*

Gipson: I just found the game fascinating and enjoyable, then and now. There is a lot to be said for looking forward to what you're going to be doing in the morning when you wake up. A number of people go into jobs for reasons other than doing what they enjoy. Of course, there's a positive correlation between people who like what they do and people who do it well.

Kazanjian: *Before Harvard, weren't you a consultant at McKinsey?*

Gipson: Yes. I was with McKinsey for two years after the Navy. I was primarily involved in marketing, which I didn't like and frankly was not suited for.

Kazanjian: *What did you do after Harvard?*

Gipson: I went to work for a closed-end mutual fund called Source Capital in Los Angeles. Source, like many other funds in the 1973–74 bear market, took its share of nicks. Fortunately, the publicly traded securities portfolio, which I was involved in, did a good job of preserving its capital. At the beginning of my career, I adopted the concept of value investing. I define that generously to recognize that growth is one component of value. It doesn't automatically mean never buying quality growth companies. Warren Buffett made the observation that at the beginning of your career as an investment manager, you either grasp the idea of buying a dollar's worth of value for less than a dollar or you don't. It also helps that when I joined Source in 1973, there were two relatively unknown people who had just taken major positions in the common stock: Warren Buffett and Charlie Munger [Buffett's business partner and right-hand man]. I observed them at the time. I still keep in contact with Charlie occasionally. The value orientation that I had before even going into the business was reinforced by my exposure to them.

Kazanjian: *That must have been a great experience. Where did you go next?*

Gipson: I spent a couple of years at Batterymarch Financial in Boston. At that point, it was not only a hot firm but also probably the most computerized investment firm in the country.

Kazanjian: *What did you do there?*

Gipson: I was a portfolio manager.

Kazanjian: *Using a value style?*

Gipson: More specifically, translating a value orientation into terms that would be recognized by the firm's computers.

Kazanjian: *How did that work?*

Gipson: I took various valuation techniques and applied them on a quantitative basis. If you actually read what Benjamin Graham wrote in *The Intelligent Investor,* he took various valuation screens, such as companies selling at a discount to net working capital, and bought a collection of them. I did something similar and still do today.

Kazanjian: *You opened your own firm, Pacific Financial Research, after leaving Batterymarch?*

Gipson: I did. I began managing money here on January 1, 1981.

Kazanjian: *Did you start out with any assets?*

Gipson: At the very beginning, no. I was in a one-room office hoping to persuade someone to let me doodle with his portfolio. The first client, FMC, is still an existing client. I knew the company from my days at Batterymarch. One thing that was particularly memorable is how we played the loser's game to avoid buying overvalued assets. In 1981, oil stocks were hot. We avoided oil stocks entirely. We sold expensive stocks and bought bonds in a meaningful way. By late 1981, we were 70 percent in bonds. Keep in mind that in October 1981, long-term Treasuries hit 15 percent, the highest rate in the 200-year history of this country. This was the greatest opportunity in two centuries to buy bonds. They were much cheaper than stocks. No brains were required to see this. I would go to investment meetings where you had analysts saying bonds are much cheaper than stocks, but bonds have been in a 30-year bear market. The opportunity was there, but few acted on it. Throughout the 1980s, we sold expensive stocks and bought cheap bonds. Going into the crash of 1987, 40 percent of the portfolio was in zero-coupon Treasuries. They went up. Stocks went down. This strategy is now known as tactical asset allocation. Essentially an entire cottage industry of asset allocators grew up after the Crash of 1987, making stocks and bonds more fairly valued in relation to each other. We have largely stopped this strategy because the opportunities aren't there. We saw something similar in 2000. Once again, it took no brains to see that the cash-burning dot.com stocks, along with many of the larger tech names, were vastly overvalued. Still, they went up for so long that it became difficult for people to avoid them.

Kazanjian: *Today it seems like everyone has a desire to get rich quick. You, on the other hand, are more interested in building wealth slowly.*

Gipson: I can understand the desire to get rich quick. I don't know how to do it and I don't think anybody else does either. Some think they do. From my perspective, there is a large virtue to being a rational, disciplined investor. I will be the first to admit that in late 1999 and early 2000 it was difficult to remain patient. Patience is a virtue that is easy to preach and more difficult to practice.

Kazanjian: *It's normally when you get impatient that you get into trouble.*

Gipson: Right. Your readers should realize that whatever investment style they select, periods of superior performance generally come in unpredictable lumps. This is one of the things that frustrates people who are trying to get rich quick or making long-term judgments about the deployment of capital based on short-term performance.

Kazanjian: *When you go through a period such as 1999, when your fund's performance and many Nasdaq-oriented funds are up 100, 200, or even 300 percent, how do you keep your cool and maintain your discipline?*

Gipson: It's a fair question and I understand from consultants that there's no shortage of managers who did stray during that time. To be honest, we didn't like the criticism. From a psychological standpoint, many people have "avoiding criticism" as their major goal in life. One way to avoid criticism is to do what everyone else is doing. The real essence of what you're asking comes down to character. Do you have the patience to persist in doing what you believe is the rational thing, even though you're not being rewarded for it and, in fact, you're being criticized for it? This is an element of character that has nothing to do with where you went to school or how smart you are. I can't explain it much better than that. It goes back to what I said a moment ago. Brain power is a necessary but not sufficient condition for success as an investor. There are times, late 1999 being a good example, where no brain power was required to see the right thing to do, but you did have to have the patience and gumption to continue doing it, face whatever criticism you were getting, and, in some cases, lose clients as well.

Kazanjian: *What do you think was going on in the market back then?*

Gipson: It was the greatest financial mania in American history in terms of valuation excess. You had the highest price/earnings ratios, lowest dividend ratios, and highest price-to-book ratios in history. If you're a physician, you try to make a diagnosis based on not just one symptom, but a cluster of them. By every valuation measure known to economic man, the stock market was extremely overvalued in 1999–2000. This was no secret. Everyone in the business saw it. The question was whether you drew the obvious conclusions, as we did.

It was also the longest-lasting financial mania. If you arbitrarily start it from Alan Greenspan's observation about irrational exuberance in the fall of 1996, the mania went on for 3½ years. Furthermore, it was amazing to see the number of people sucked in. In 1900, about 1 percent of the nation's households owned stocks. In 1929, it was about 10 percent. Now, courtesy of 401(k)s and the like, it's up to about 50 percent. That's virtually every household with financial assets. As a result, you don't have a new wave of investors itching to come in and push stocks up as you once did.

Kazanjian: *What do you think is the biggest lesson people will take from this?*

Gipson: Be rational and value-oriented, and avoid participating in manias where you're buying stocks you really don't understand.

Kazanjian: *Do you think we'll have another market mania like this again, or will the pain from this one be strong enough to keep people more rational for a while?*

Gipson: I don't think they're more rational yet, but I think by the time it's all sorted out, it will be at least another generation before we have another major speculative market.

Kazanjian: *In the meantime, will people return to value or will they just get out of the market?*

Gipson: Probably a combination of both. I recall about a year ago *The New York Times* had an article featuring a young woman who was about 30. The quote under her picture was "My generation has no fear of the stock market." I remember saying to myself, Yes, young lady, and at some point you'll own nothing other than a certificate of deposit.

Kazanjian: *Your prediction may have come true sooner than you thought.*

Gipson: If you look at the quantitative aspects of investor behavior, people haven't given up yet. People have been conditioned for so long that stocks are the only place to be and that you buy on the dips. There is a legion of investors out there who are waiting to replay the glory days of the late 1990s.

Kazanjian: *Let's talk about the investment process you use to manage your $7.5 billion in assets under management.*

Gipson: First, what we try to do is take the perspective that if the New York Stock Exchange closed tomorrow for the next 10 years, what companies would you buy that (a) you understand, (b) are in good businesses, and (c) sell at a sizable discount to what a rational private buyer would pay to be a partner in the business. This is in direct contrast to what people trying to get rich quick do. Our perspective is to really understand the business. There are some businesses, particularly in the tech area, that no one understands. We simply won't buy them.

Kazanjian: *What do you mean by "understand"?*

Gipson: We must have a reasonable understanding of how the company works and what its prospects are likely to be. I think there is a large misperception on the part not just of investors, but also of corporate managers as to how predictably understandable their companies are. Six months before announcing massive layoffs, Cisco CEO John Chambers was bragging that his business was accelerating. It turned out the business wasn't as predictable as many thought. By contrast, Freddie Mac will be doing the same things it's doing right now in 10 years. It's a company we can easily understand.

Kazanjian: *In some sense an understandable company is a simple company in terms of what it does.*

Gipson: In the best of all possible worlds, it's simple, but generally it's something that you can understand well enough to make a reasonable projection of its future operating model.

Kazanjian: *You said the second criterion is a good business. How do you define a good business?*

Gipson: In general, a good business is one that has a competitive advantage, generates superior returns on capital or on equity, and generates cash apart from accounting earnings.

Kazanjian: *Do you have specific numbers you're looking for?*

Gipson: We build a large number of customized valuation models to match the nature of the business with the idea of coming up with a value for what a rational private buyer would pay for the business if he or she were to buy the whole thing. I'll compare this to a tailor. If you're a lazy tailor, you've got a rack of garments that all have low PEs on the front of them. As a tall man, a short man, and a fat man walk into your tailor shop, you plunk this tentlike garment over their heads and they all walk out clothed with one PE or another. We try to be a more diligent tailor by taking a good look at the nature of the company and its assets, and then tailoring them into a valuation to meet the nature of that business.

For example, price-to-book is a meaningful number for an insurance company, but totally useless for a media company. We continually build special-purpose valuation models to replicate the way rational private buyers either do value companies or probably would value companies if they were traded. The better we value them, the better chance we'll have of recognizing them when they're cheap enough to buy.

Kazanjian: *That speaks to the point of selling at the discount, which is your third criterion.*

Gipson: Having established the value, we will only buy when it drops to at least a 30 percent discount to our estimate of intrinsic value. That is, if the value is $100, we'll buy it at $70 or less.

Kazanjian: *To show how this criterion works, give me an example of a specific company you bought using it.*

Gipson: I'll use an older example because it takes your question one step further. We bought Merrill Lynch in 1994. It was selling at 1½ times book value, which we thought was cheap for the kind of franchise it had. When the Orange County crisis hit in 1995, we noted that Merrill's market capitalization declined by more than the after-tax value of the entire Orange County loss. We stepped up and bought more shares. This is a good test of a value investor's strength, compared to a momentum player. If a momentum player buys something at $70 and it goes to $60, he'll sell because he's afraid it'll go to $50. If you're a value investor and you thought it was cheap at $70, it's even cheaper at $60. The rational thing is to buy more.

Kazanjian: *One stock you've held for a long time is Philip Morris, which is obviously a controversial name. Take me through what led you to that company and why you held on with such conviction even while the stock was under so much pressure.*

Gipson: Philip Morris [which at press time announced plans to change its name to Altria] is a good example of buying more on weakness. It is a very well-managed, extremely profitable cash-generating company. If you just look at the financial side, it is one of the most profitable large companies in the world. It does a remarkably good job of earning big money on shareholder's equity and often uses a good deal of the cash generated to buy back shares cheaply. Philip Morris is a lot more than domestic tobacco, although that is what people are primarily concerned about. The international tobacco business is worth more than the domestic tobacco business. It also owns most of Kraft General Foods, which is a very profitable food company. When the concern over tobacco litigation hit a peak, Philip Morris spent a few days under $20 and we bought more. You were getting a nearly 10 percent current yield on a company growing twice as fast as the S&P 500. That seemed to us to be an extraordinarily good bargain.

Kazanjian: *Were you concerned about the tobacco litigation?*

Gipson: Yes, we were. I want to make this clear. We tried to be realistic about the risks involved. That is a definite risk, but we thought the market had vastly overblown the situation. If the legal process essentially wiped out all value for domestic tobacco—if Marlboro cigarettes disappeared from this country tomorrow—Philip Morris was still worth a whole lot more than the current price of the stock.

Kazanjian: *How about a stock that didn't work for you and what you learned from that?*

Gipson: In the late 1980s we bought some savings and loans companies. If it had been a once-in-a-generation loan loss problem, we would have made a lot of money. Unfortunately, it was a once-in-a-lifetime problem for many of them.

Kazanjian: *You tend to hold on to your positions for quite some time.*

Gipson: You're right. We are low-turnover managers. That is a function of a few things. First, it's our temperament. Many investors like a lot of action and turn over their portfolios quickly. We don't. Second, we are aware that our professional mission in life is to make our clients rich, not to make our brokers wealthy. Third, if you view yourself as a long-term partner of the business, you're happy to stay put.

Kazanjian: *And you tend to concentrate on your favorite ideas.*

Gipson: Your best ideas, one through 20, are a whole lot more likely to do well than your worst ideas, 101 through 120. It makes sense to concentrate to a reasonable degree. Mathematically, you get about 95 percent of the maximum theoretical benefits of diversification with 13 stocks. The majority of institutional portfolios are far too diversified. Why? The reason is seldom spoken, but it's the deeply felt idea that I could be wrong on this so I better not make it a major position.

Kazanjian: *How many stocks do you typically own?*

Gipson: Somewhere between 20 and 35. That is probably a little more than we need to, but we occasionally run into market capitalization constraints.

Kazanjian: *Such concentration sounds risky.*

Gipson: If you look at the risk in our portfolio, you will find it to be exceptionally low.

Kazanjian: *What do you attribute that to?*

Gipson: We start by thinking about preventing losses. We also have a devil's advocate stock-selection process. This is a concept shamelessly stolen from the Roman Catholic Church. The decision about whether or not a company has value—which is what drives everything in the process—is made by a small team consisting of a proponent, a devil's advocate, and me. The whole logic for the approach is that, from the Catholic Church's standpoint, before they canonize someone as a saint, they want to make sure that they have done their due diligence to ensure there are no skeletons in the closet. We've put that in a structural framework. If you like a stock, there's a tendency to talk only to people who share your positive view. We, on the other hand, look at what can go wrong.

Kazanjian: *That devil's advocate approach is intriguing. I take it you have someone making the case of why you should buy it, and another who argues why you shouldn't buy it. Then you decide which one makes the most sense.*

Gipson: Exactly. I'm essentially the referee and the three of us collectively come to what seems like a reasonable and defensible position. This is not decision making by a committee. In this business, the larger the committee, the systematically worse the decision.

Kazanjian: *What makes you sell a stock?*

Gipson: It's very simple. We will sell a stock when it reaches intrinsic value. It can do that in two ways. Either the price can go up, or the value can go down. The vast majority of times when we sell a stock, it's because the price has gone up in excess of our estimate of intrinsic value. From an intellectual standpoint, it's the reverse of the buy decision. We buy at a sizable discount to intrinsic value. We sell at intrinsic value, though we continually update our estimate of intrinsic value as the facts unfold.

Kazanjian: *I suppose Philip Morris is a testament to your patience. Is there a point where a stock price doesn't appreciate over a certain period to the point where you lose patience, sell out, and deploy your money elsewhere?*

Gipson: That hasn't happened yet. One of the great weaknesses of a value investor is addressing when the market will recognize the value of a stock. The honest answer is that no one knows, so you need a reasonably diversified portfolio. As long as the value is there, as long as the company's operations are good, and as long as the value of the company is growing, we are content to be a long-term partner of that business.

Kazanjian: *You keep a fair amount of cash in the Clipper Fund.*

Gipson: That's been true during this period of irrational exuberance. We have been fully invested in the past. We look forward to spending our cash, but we'll only do that when the market gives us the opportunity to do so.

Kazanjian: *Why not just add more to the names in the portfolio that you do like?*

Gipson: As a matter of fact, we give shareholders the option. Several years ago, a number of our institutional clients decided that they wanted to make the asset allocation decision and wanted to use us basically as stock pickers. We decided to start a second fund, now called PBHG Clipper Focus, that is at least 95 percent invested at all times.

Kazanjian: *Do you ever sell stocks short?*

Gipson: In my personal portfolio, yes. I will make one small confession. A couple of years ago I shorted Yahoo! at 300 times earnings on its way to 900 times earnings. The little dents in the wall of my office are from my banging my head against it saying, I don't believe it, I don't believe it. The stock went to well over $400. I closed out my position at $14. This is just another illustration of how insane prices were during the irrational exuberance that lasted until March 2000. People will look back on this time and think of how there were millions of otherwise sensible people who were just plain nuts.

Kazanjian: *Many of those people were new to investing and now are probably reexamining what they believe about how to invest. What would you tell them to convince them to consider a value approach?*

Gipson: Part of this goes back to what I said at the beginning. The value approach is something that either appeals to you right at the beginning or probably never does. The idea of buying a dollar's worth of assets for less than a dollar, and doing so on a consistent and patient basis, is very powerful.

Gipson has surrounded himself with a remarkably stable group of analysts and operations people. Of the firm's five investment principals, the newest one joined in 1987. Gipson sold his firm to United Asset Management in 1997, which in turn was acquired by Old Mutual, a South African financial services concern. But his contract gives him complete autonomy over the firm's continued operations.

Gipson keeps most of the money in his funds invested in large companies. Still, he believes small-cap stocks will do better over the next few years, primarily because they are cheaper. And, to emphasize a point Gipson raised, he feels that before buying any stock or fund, investors should ask themselves how much they could lose by owning it. If the answer is more than you can stomach, it's a good sign that the investment might not be right for you. Gipson is convinced that if investors had asked themselves this question during the tech bubble, fewer people would have been so devastated by the subsequent collapse. ■

JOHN GOODE

SMITH BARNEY ASSET MANAGEMENT

How did a farmer from California's Central Valley end up in the investment business? Chalk it up to a concerned father, a case of hepatitis, and a bit of luck along the way. John Goode still has roots in the valley and continues to own the 40-acre farm south of Fresno where he was raised. He grows Thompson Seedless grapes on his farm, but produces a bounty of profits for shareholders of his Smith Barney Fundamental Value Fund.

The 56-year-old Goode is president of Davis Skaggs Investment Management, which is now owned by Citigroup, parent of Salomon Smith Barney. Goode looks for companies with leading franchises whose share prices are temporarily depressed but likely to return to investor favor. He wants to buy these stocks at attractive prices relative to their future earnings potential. He seeks out what he calls "rubber balls," as opposed to "broken eggs," the distinction being that the latter remain depressed in price.

While he picks stocks one at a time, Goode has a knack for spotting trends before the rest of the crowd. He was on record warning about California's energy problems months before they became a reality. He also had the foresight to get out of technology stocks almost at their highs in March 2000.

Goode is a patient investor who keeps a highly diversified portfolio, because, he says, he never knows which of his holdings will turn out to be the big winners. He learned an important lesson about investing from his 100-year-old cousin Gladwyn (who, it turns out, used to walk to elementary school with my late aunt): There have been numerous "new economies" over the past century, and most end the exact same way—with the realization that there's nothing new going on after all.

Kazanjian: *We have something in common. We both grew up in California's Central Valley.*

Goode: It's a small world, Kirk. I'm constantly amazed by how many people come from there.

Kazanjian: *It's obviously a big farming area. Were you raised on a farm?*

Goode: Yes, in Fowler, California. I still own the farm and the 105-year-old farmhouse where I was raised. I get down there as often as I can.

Kazanjian: *How did you wind up in the investment business?*

Goode: My father died when I was 13. He and my mother both graduated from the University of California, Berkeley. One day before dad passed away, we were out in the fields and he said, "John, this is a great place, and I know you love it, but you're going to college." I have never forgotten that talk. A few years later, I was accepted at Berkeley, but decided to go to Stanford instead. I was an economics major. After graduation I went to the Stanford Business School. During the summer between my first and second years in business school, I got a job with Capital Research in Los Angeles. One thing led to another.

Kazanjian: *You weren't investing in stocks before that?*

Goode: I was certainly familiar with the stock market growing up, because my father and mother had small positions in a few stocks such as Safeway and Union Oil. I was always intrigued by the stock market. When I got to college, many of the students came from families with significant holdings in the market. I found that banter about the stock market took place fairly regularly.

Kazanjian: *What did you like most about the stock market?*

Goode: It was a never-ending education. I never liked the idea that you had to commit to working in one segment of the economy. The stock market allows you to avoid that trap. One year there's a certain bias or leadership in the market. Two or three years later you adjust because there are different realities in place. It's both frustrating and exhilarating at the same time because, if you're successful in the business, you get a chance to evolve with what's going on in the economy and, you hope, do the right thing for your clients as well. Trying to find a good investment requires one to be a little like Sherlock Holmes. I was a research analyst for my first 15 years in the business. It's really the spirit of the chase. You have to deal with uncertainty. It really was my research roots that eventually led to me being a portfolio manager here at Smith Barney.

Kazanjian: *What happened after getting your MBA?*

Goode: My draft deferment ended and I was going in the military during the Vietnam War. I came down with, of all things, serum hepatitis. I guess I got a bad needle at the draft physical. I went home to Fowler and recovered. Then, in September 1969, I joined Davis Skaggs, which was a small regional brokerage firm.

Kazanjian: *That's the same firm you're with now. I assume it was independent at the time, before being taken over by Smith Barney. What were you doing in the beginning?*

Goode: I was a research analyst covering a wide range of industries and investments. About a year after I joined, the firm lost its research director and I was given the chance to take over. In 1982, I became chairman of the board and negotiated the sale of Davis Skaggs to Shearson/American Express the next year. I suspected the days were numbered for most regional brokerage firms because of the major industry changes taking place in the early 1980s. I was able to convince our partners that the value of the Davis Skaggs franchise might decline in the coming years if we didn't merge with another larger firm. In 1988, I took over as president and CEO of Davis Skaggs Investment Management. It had about $100 million of assets at that time. Since taking over, we have been able to increase our assets under management to about $10 billion. We manage five mutual funds for Smith Barney/Citigroup Asset Management.

Kazanjian: *Is your firm now owned by Citigroup, the parent of Smith Barney?*

Goode: It is.

Kazanjian: *When did you actually start managing money?*

Goode: In 1988. I had a few accounts when I was in research at Davis
Skaggs, so I knew something about the process. I had a real advantage when I got into managing money full time. When I was an analyst, I covered everything. I looked at technology, natural resources,
financial services, healthcare, and anything that looked attractive. I
was a generalist. That's not the way it's done today. I had a different
kind of education than most when I became a portfolio manager. I
had a very broad-based look at the stock market over a period of
time through some interesting cycles, especially 1973–74 and 1987.

Kazanjian: *What's your investment philosophy?*

Goode: We try to buy "rubber balls" rather than "broken eggs." We
want to own good franchises, but on our own terms. Most people
think a good franchise is a growth stock that never misses quarterly
earnings estimates. That's totally unrealistic. You find, from time to
time, good companies that experience near-term problems that
cause many investors to abandon ship. That's when you get a
chance to buy some interesting companies at attractive prices. Expectations generally are lower at these times, yet those companies
may be very attractive 5- or 10-year plays. That's the rubber ball.
It's a company that's going to rebound and come back into investor
favor. By contrast, the broken egg is a stock that's just cheap and de-
serves to remain so.

Kazanjian: *How do you know the difference between the two?*

Goode: That's the art of the business. For example, at present we've
been buying Carnival Corporation, which is the leading company in
the cruise ship business. The problem is that the industry has been
adding capacity. When you buy a new cruise ship, you have to purchase the entire vessel, not an eighth or a quarter of one. Therefore,
you wind up with pricing and capacity problems from time to time.
Two years ago, the stock was $55. It went down below $25. The
cruise ship business has some solid growth characteristics. It's a relatively small industry, with only four principal players, and it should
grow by at least 10 percent annually over the next few years. There
are considerable barriers to entry with new cruise ships costing $400
million or more. We think Carnival is a good example of a rubber
ball. Current examples of broken eggs would include most Internet

stocks. Their share prices might be off 80 or 90 percent, but the majority don't have a business plan that ever will allow them to make any money. Most Internet companies will be out of business by this time next year.

Kazanjian: *Why was everyone so excited about those stocks a couple of years ago?*

Goode: Occasionally business conditions and the media combine to generate unusual investor optimism, and this results in many stocks reaching unrealistic valuations. These periods often are referred to as "bubbles." In the middle of the 19th century, the book *Popular Delusions and the Madness of Crowds* detailed a number of investment bubbles over the past 400 years. What we went through in 1999 and early 2000 makes Tulip Mania in Holland a few centuries ago look like a minor psychological aberration. The democratization of the stock market in the 1990s brought many first-time players into the market. These players—or should I say investors—did not have the perspective that comes from experiencing several full market cycles. Many people and investors in the past decade felt that we were living in a "new economy" unlike any before it. They bid stocks up without any serious attention to valuation or the risks inherent in new business enterprises. You get periods like this every few decades, but this one was a real beauty. I doubt that we will see anything like this again in our lifetimes.

Kazanjian: *Speaking of the new economy, I heard you speak before about your 100-year-old cousin, Gladwyn, who also experienced a number of so-called new economies in her time.*

Goode: Gladwyn was born in 1899 and just passed away in 2000. She talked about the introduction of the telephone, electricity, refrigeration, and the automobile early in the 20th century. When you look at all of the "new economies" over the past 100 years, they've all developed and corrected in much the same way. Take the auto industry, for example. There were 400 auto companies in 1915. There was great enthusiasm for and speculation in automobile manufacturers. After all, automobiles represented a major departure from the past. The horse was being retired after 10,000 years of providing a principal means of transportation and work. Even with a change as profound as the automobile, there wasn't room for 400 successful business plans in the automobile industry. The dirty little secret of capitalism is that in order to make sure a new technology survives, far more investors are invited to the "dance" than seem to be necessary with 20/20 hindsight. Once roots are put down by the successful companies, the unnecessary participants are killed off. It has happened time after time. There were a number of television manufacturers in the early 1950s. A few years later only a few survivors remained.

Kazanjian: *Is the lesson that, in a mania, one must get in early and get out at the peak?*

Goode: There are two ways to look at the apparent opportunities in a new economy. The first follows along the lines you've suggested. In a new-economy mania, investors need to understand that they're in a high-risk environment where true long-term investing may not be possible. It's a highly dangerous environment and one almost needs a trading mentality to survive. The second approach is to wait for the speculative frenzy to end and allow the values to return to much more reasonable levels. The lesson of the past century is that investing in the second round makes much more sense and carries with it far less risk.

I saw this pattern firsthand 20 years ago in the biotechnology industry. When Genentech and other biotech companies came public, there were valuation questions raised in the early speculative phase. The response was along the lines that "You can't put a value on a cure for cancer." In fact, it was going to take a long time before anybody came up with a commercial product, let alone a cure for cancer. Eighteen months after the speculative frenzy for biotech shares ended in the early 1980s, I visited Amgen. The stock had declined 80 percent from its highs, was trading at $4, and had $4 per share in cash on the balance sheet. By this time it was also easier to determine which companies would be some of the survivors in biotechnology. The risks associated with the industry, which were still significant, were much reduced once the speculative phase had passed.

Kazanjian: *You must be finding many rubber balls among technology stocks. You've owned a fair amount of tech over the past few years, especially for a value guy.*

Goode: We think technology is a three-to-four-year play because of the nature of the companies themselves and the capital expenditure cycle. Arguably there's a positive long-term trend line for technology stocks, but there is exceedingly high volatility around that trend. You want to purchase positions near the cycle trough when the bloom is off the rose. We did that in 1996–97. We didn't buy the Oracles and Ciscos of the world. We thought they were grossly overpriced, even though they went up dramatically in the next few years. Instead, we bought companies such as Adobe Systems. The stock promptly went down 25 percent! It was perceived as a broken growth stock and not even its investment banker wanted to say kind things about its prospects back then. It had a terrific balance sheet, but it was primarily a supplier of software to the Apple platform. We thought it would develop products for Windows applications, which would broaden its markets. What we didn't see is that it would also develop products for the Internet. This stock went from $8 a share in 1996–97 to $80 by the first quarter of 2000. That's when we harvested our profits. We bought the stock when nobody liked it. When everybody was singing its praises four years later, we were sellers of the stock.

Kazanjian: *Did you analyze Cisco and Oracle incorrectly back then, or was the market simply overoptimistic about those stocks?*

Goode: I think what we did was correct. We felt Cisco was a great company but more than fully priced in 1996–97. What we did not foresee was the speculative heights that the market would reach, especially among the largest technology companies. The market was increasing its future growth rate projections for these stocks as they increased in size, which made no sense at all. A 40-percent growth rate over 10 years means a dollar of earnings today has to become $29 in year 10. This might happen with a small company, even a mid-cap company, but it still would be a heroic result. It's highly unlikely that this could occur for much larger companies such as Cisco, Microsoft, and Oracle, yet they were trading at PE ratios above 100 in some cases. The only way this would make any sense was if these companies could, in fact, compound earnings at 40 percent-plus, which we thought was very unlikely. As value managers, we purchased stocks such as Adobe, Scientific Atlanta, and Cypress Semiconductor. We also owned Texas Instruments, which we bought a few years earlier when it still had an aerospace division and produced DRAMS. Our first purchases were at four times depreciation. Clearly, these weren't the companies on everybody's lips in the latter part of the 1990s. Because of this, we underperformed the S&P 500 from 1996 to 1998. But between mid-1998 and the early part of 2000, the technology stocks we owned not only caught up with but also roared ahead of the larger, better known technology names. We came out better, and I think our approach involved assuming considerably less risk. I might add, we banked considerable technology profits in early 2000, thus avoiding what is termed a "round trip."

Kazanjian: *In fact, you seem to have gone on a tech-free diet at almost the perfect time in the first quarter of 2000. What do you attribute that to, besides good luck?*

Goode: There are several factors that caused us to make a large reduction in our technology holdings. I've been in the investment business for 32 years and the lessons learned in previous speculative cycles certainly helped. The closest thing to what happened in 1999 and early 2000 came in 1972–74. Many of the same arguments were being made in that earlier period. The original Nifty Fifty were so-named because institutions felt they were such great companies it didn't much matter what price you paid, in terms of the PE ratio. They were one-decision stocks destined to outperform all other stocks forever, according to leading institutional investors. Twenty-five years later, the investment music had a similar sound to it. I also heeded the lessons I learned from my cousin Gladwyn about new eras over the past 100 years. As I said, most new eras produce investment bubbles that burst and cause large losses for many investors. With an investment bubble the question is not if but when something goes wrong.

In addition, there was a specific piece of information in early 2000 that told me a major correction in the Nasdaq was imminent. Sanford Bernstein, the brokerage firm, had calculated the amount of lock-up stock eligible to come to market between March and June 2000. Lock-up stock are those shares that venture capitalists and insiders can sell six months after an IPO. Depending on the average price you placed on these shares, the potential selling was between $100 and $150 billion. It seemed inevitable to us that the tsunami of supply would shortly overwhelm the demand for Internet and other technology shares, which appeared to have been sated in any case. Excess supply was about to end one of the great speculative frenzies of all time. In terms of relative values, technology was pinned to the ceiling.

At the same time, the price of oil was $12 a barrel, and only 4 to 8 percent of investors were bullish on energy stocks. You had located, in effect, the last bear on energy. Therefore, the probabilities were that all the bad news was priced into energy shares. I also saw some problems developing in California's energy picture. When you looked forward into the summer and talked to energy wholesalers, it was clear that prices, especially those for natural gas, were going up dramatically. If you knew that natural gas was the fuel of choice, and that nobody was paying attention to these stocks, it stood to reason this might not be a bad place to put some money. So we took money out of technology and invested some of it in natural gas and other energy shares. Similar arguments could be made at the same time for many healthcare and financial stocks, which had been in their own personal bear markets for several years. The allocation of assets away from technology and into these sectors of the market was consistent with our investment disciplines.

Kazanjian: *You almost sound like a trend follower.*

Goode: For best results, you need to anticipate trends and inflection points in the market. Opportunities to do this don't appear every day. However, if you can get in front of the future, that is, if you can be early in spotting a developing trend, the investment rewards can be tremendous. At the same time, there was another piece of anecdotal evidence that was very important. Warren Buffett, one of the greatest investors of all time, was being ridiculed in early 2000 for being out of step with reality. Then I saw that Julian Robertson was calling it quits at Tiger Management. And at Fidelity a value portfolio manager with an impressive long-term record hung up his cleats. I thought that was the closest thing I had ever heard to a positive bell ringing for the value approach. I live for times like this. Portfolio managers distinguish themselves in times of market turbulence by making tough calls that go against the prevailing wisdom of the moment.

Kazanjian: *Let's get back to your overall investment approach. Tell me more about how you find those rubber balls.*

Goode: Earlier I indicated that we try to spot trends or inflection points early. This is one leg of the investment stool. A second leg includes our computer screening capabilities. This quantitative effort can identify companies with good long-term characteristics such as return on capital versus their inflation-adjusted cost of capital, free cash-flow generation, and a variety of other factors. The objective of our quantitative approach is to identify a population of companies that represent good business franchises. They may not be attractively valued today, but we want to know businesses that consistently earn a premium to their cost of capital. When circumstances cause the shares of these companies to reach levels we believe are attractive, we are prepared to move.

The third leg of our investment stool is fundamental research. We have six analysts responsible for companies in the 11 S&P sectors. They are also responsible for ferreting out interesting smaller and mid-cap ideas. Our analysts further refine the stocks identified by our quantitative efforts. The analysts themselves also are looking for stocks that may not have been uncovered by our computer screens. Every company has various transitions going on over time. Sometimes it is in management, other times it may be a new product or a major capital expenditure cycle. Mergers and acquisitions play a role, as do divestitures. Our analysts' responsibility is to understand their companies in ways that can't be determined by looking at just income statements and balance sheets. Their efforts need to be understood within the context of my earlier comments. The goal of our investment process is to produce portfolios made up of companies and sectors with good risk/reward characteristics. Risk control is the starting point for us in the selection process.

The fourth and final leg in our investment process is technical analysis. Decisions aren't made on the basis of this alone, but technical analysis can add to the weight of evidence for or against an investment decision. For example, we look at insider buying and selling activity. Large increases in one or another may be an important investment clue. We also use a simple mathematical tool to quantify the enthusiasm or pessimism associated with a stock. The percentage difference between the stock price and its 90-day moving average often measures the degree of investor sentiment. At extremes, it suggests that our fundamental research efforts should be increased to determine whether a particular stock should be bought or sold.

Kazanjian: *In some ways, it sounds like looking for fallen growth stocks.*

Goode: We're looking for good long-term value whether the wrapper says value or growth. For example, we own stocks such as Alcoa, Chevron, and Dow Chemical. These are all considered to be classic value stocks. We also own American Express, which I bought in the early 1990s. That company didn't make any money for investors for 10 years prior to our purchases. Warren Buffett invested at about the same time. I bought Intel when the chip recall problem in 1996 caused many investors to sell the stock. I bought Texas Instruments when it had an aerospace division and was still producing DRAMS. We bought our first shares at four times depreciation. I would argue that value and growth stocks are not separate and distinct. What you're really trying to do is find something that's cheap relative to its future prospects. It may be a value stock or it may be a former growth stock darling that just somehow has fallen from investor favor for reasons that will not persist long term.

Kazanjian: *Do you use any traditional value criteria for evaluating these companies?*

Goode: Companies take so many write-offs today that I'm not sure such things as price-to-book, PE, or dividend yield are as useful as they once were. We do look at enterprise-value-to-cash-flow as a measure of value. We are always looking for companies that can produce excess cash flow over time. For us, this is one of the critical factors that define a good business franchise. We do use price-to-sales ratios to some extent, although it's not a primary decision tool. We spend considerable time evaluating balance sheets and often try to understand the interplay between a company's income statement and its balance sheet.

Kazanjian: *A lot of managers I've interviewed look for companies selling at a deep discount to intrinsic value. I haven't heard you mention those words. Do you pay attention to this?*

Goode: It depends on the stock. Intrinsic value to me says there's some sort of asset base that you can put your hands on, which is not always the case. We do take a look at free cash flow, and free cash flow is one of the ways you can determine discounted value from some sort of central or intrinsic value. But we don't get too enamored with that concept. I've found that many value managers derive intrinsic values for their companies that are far too high.

Kazanjian: *What's the single most important determinant for you in deciding whether to buy a stock?*

Goode: I want to see that I'm buying a stock that, based on reasonable numbers, can outperform the market meaningfully over the next five years. As I indicated earlier, there are various factors that go into the investment decision. With each decision, the mix is different. However, the interplay between fundamental, quantitative, and technical considerations, in combination with a catalyst or trend, provides the necessary confidence level to commit client assets. It helps if we are excited about management because, in the final analysis, this is often the difference.

Kazanjian: *What else do you look at before making a buy decision?*

Goode: We visit companies and have them come through our office. The annual report and numbers are only a small part of the equation. I like to talk directly with and get to know the companies I own as well as I can. I think you always learn something from direct contact with a company. I especially like to meet the top management to learn whether they're serious moneymakers.

Kazanjian: *How do you judge management?*

Goode: That also gets into the art of the investment business. You look for somebody who has been through a business cycle or two, and has come through it with some degree of success. I look for somebody whose life primarily revolves around the business rather than his or her golf handicap or some other consuming passion. For example, one company on the New York Stock Exchange recently had its top management try to buy up most of a particular town. This had nothing to do with operating the business and clearly consumed valuable time. It may have been an interesting challenge for the people involved, but did nothing for shareholders. We want top management's passion to be focused on managing the company. The common stock price for our favorite managers is their report card. You also want someone who has a vested interest in the sense that he or she owns a significant amount of stock actually in a portfolio. We are not impressed by an equity position that is based primarily on outstanding options.

Kazanjian: *How do you put your portfolio together and how diversified do you get?*

Goode: We start on a sector basis by making sure that we're well diversified compared to the S&P 500. We begin by assuming that we'll sector-weight the portfolio in line with the S&P, and then choose to underweight or overweight certain sectors, based on our analysis. We're an all-cap manager, so we'll buy small-, mid-, and large-cap stocks. I happen to believe small- and mid-caps will dramatically outperform over the next five years. We currently have about 80 core positions in the Fundamental Value Fund, which has assets of some $3.8 billion.

Kazanjian: *Why do you believe small- and mid-cap stocks will do better in the future?*

Goode: If you take a look at the historical relationship of these asset classes, you're at the lowest point you've been in 30 years for small- and mid-cap versus large stocks. I think you've gotten to such extreme levels that it's likely you'll see some catching up. The S&P 500 doubled its PE ratio between 1995 and early 2000. The top 10 names—including Oracle, Cisco, and Sun Microsystems—quadrupled their PE ratios. Those big names are now losing PE altitude. The S&P 500 may only be a 5 to 7 percent performer over the next five years. The "not so nifty 450" may do 10 to 12 percent. Many small- and mid-cap companies may generate returns averaging 12 to 15 percent. It's not important whether these are the numbers that actually occur. Instead, they indicate the relative performance from various segments of the market that we think we'll see in the next few years. The best 10-year holding periods since 1925 produced annualized returns of 18 to 19 percent, compared to about 11 percent on average over the past 76 years. I think we'll be in a market that provides returns in the 10 percent range, plus or minus, in the next five years. The market will broaden out because in a 10 percent market, by definition, more stocks can hit this return figure than in one appreciating over 20 percent.

Kazanjian: *How do you define small- and mid-cap?*

Goode: Small-cap would be up to $2 billion; mid-cap would be $2 billion to $10 billion.

Kazanjian: *What percentage of your portfolio is in small- and mid-cap stocks?*

Goode: I lump them all together. I own mostly mid-caps, which now account for about 25 percent of assets. That's a significant weighting for someone who's running an all-cap portfolio.

Kazanjian: *How many stocks do you typically own?*

Goode: About 100, but there are 80 core positions.

Kazanjian: *Will you load up on your favorite positions, or do you stay diversified?*

Goode: I generally won't get above a 2 percent position when I buy a stock. If the stock quadruples and goes to an 8 percent position, I'm happy with that. We'd all like to think we know which stocks are going to be the big winners. I'd say most of the times I have had that feeling it doesn't happen. That's why I'm diversified.

Kazanjian: *How much patience do you have when it comes to holding on to your stocks?*

Goode: We have found that if we buy a stock, nobody rings a bell and says, "John Goode has just bought the stock; now we can mark it up." We are usually willing to hold a stock for six to nine months unless we get information that says we've made a mistake. For best results, we have found you need to be in a stock for 18 to 36 months because it takes a while for low expectations to become moderate expectations, and then for moderate expectations to transition to high expectations. We've got a turnover figure of 41 percent, which implies our average holding period is 2½ years. We've held on to some stocks for 5 to 10 years.

Kazanjian: *What are some of the reasons you'll sell?*

Goode: If a stock completely goes crazy on the upside and goes way beyond what we think it's worth, we'll sell. Also, if we see a lot of insider selling in the stock, we will try to understand what these investors might be anticipating. If you buy a stock and you get information that suggests your analysis was incorrect, it's better to get out and not let the stock drift lower on you. Again, keep the downside limited.

Kazanjian: *What is the primary reason stocks you thought were rubber balls turned into broken eggs?*

Goode: Sometimes businesses have a life cycle. For example, Waste Management was one of the great growth stocks of the middle 1980s. The problem is Waste Management was basically a roll-up. It was buying companies and once it got large, there was nobody else to buy. Many technology companies become broken eggs. Technological change occurs with great rapidity. Companies that once were industry leaders can find themselves faced with new competitive products that erode their market positions.

Kazanjian: *Is this a good time to be a value investor?*

Goode: We're heading into a period when value will continue to do well. A market providing 10 percent–type returns, in combination with broader stock participation, is an environment that means being a value manager probably will be rewarded more than was the experience between 1995 and 2000. In addition, we see a dramatic increase in merger-and-acquisition activity in the next few years. By definition, that's more likely to be concentrated in value rather than in growth stocks. Styles come and go. Clearly growth dominated between 1995 and 2000. If you go back to 1990, though, and fast-forward to the present time, value has slightly outperformed growth. I expect that to continue.

In his spare time, Goode takes to the golf course whenever he can. He's also a writer, having penned eight histories of the annual Big Game between Stanford and the University of California, Berkeley. It's a football rivalry that dates back to 1892.

Goode's tenure at Smith Barney Fundamental Value only goes back to 1990, but during that time he's won a "big game" of his own. He's managed to post positive returns each year, which has kept his shareholders cheering from the bleachers. In addition to Fundamental Value, his organization manages four other mutual funds for Smith Barney and Citigroup Asset Management, as well as several thousand individual accounts. ■

WILLIAM MILLER

LEGG MASON

Bill Miller is arguably the most intriguing and controversial value manager in the business today. This Baltimore-based investment pro has gained fame for beating the S&P 500 each and every year since 1991 as skipper of the Legg Mason Value Trust. That even eclipses Peter Lynch's legendary record. Miller also manages the newer and much smaller Legg Mason Opportunity Trust.

Miller's approach has been criticized by some, who claim he's not really a value manager. After all, the 51-year-old owns such stocks as AOL Time Warner, Dell Computer, and Amazon.com, which are normally found in growth portfolios. These names sit next to more traditional value stocks such as Waste Management and Fannie Mae. How do such companies qualify as value stocks? According to Miller, it's because they were selling at a discount to business value when he bought them. He believes simple benchmarks such as price-to-earnings ratios are insufficient when it comes to valuing complex business entities.

A former philosophy student and longtime market observer, Miller joined Legg Mason as director of research in 1981. He co-managed Value Trust from its inception in 1982 and has run it solo since 1990. Miller still studies the great philosophers and finds that many of their teachings apply to his work as an investor.

I previously interviewed Miller for my book *Wizards of Wall Street*. Given the vast changes in the markets since that book was published, I thought it would be interesting to get an update.

Kazanjian: *You started off as a philosophy student, but one of your former professors says he used to find you in the library reading* The Wall Street Journal *instead of the world's greatest philosophers.*

Miller: I was always interested in things financial. When I was 9 or 10 years old, I was watching my father read the financial pages of the newspaper, which had a different visual aspect from the sports pages. I asked him what *that* was. He said those were stocks and stocks' prices. I then asked what that meant. He pointed to one name and said, "If you look here, you'll see it says +¼. If you owned one share of that company, you would have 25 cents more today than you had yesterday." I said, "What do you have to do to get that 25 cents?" He said, "Nothing. It does it by itself." It was that conversation that got me interested in the markets. I thought, Wow! You can make money without doing any work. That's the business I want to be in.

I probably had come in from mowing the grass for 25 cents for two hours, so stocks sounded like a pretty good deal. It was much later that I realized only the market rate of return took no work. Getting an excess rate of return was a different matter. Then, as an undergraduate in college, I majored in economics and European intellectual history.

Kazanjian: *How did you wind up studying for a Ph.D. in philosophy?*

Miller: The decision to go to graduate school was driven by the lack of finding anything else that was terribly interesting. Economics, both 30 years ago and today, is highly stylized and basically a mathematical exercise. When I looked at other alternatives, law school seemed to be a huge waste of time, since you spent three years trying to figure out where to put commas in documents. Business school would have been more interesting, but I had an Army obligation. While I was in the Army, a friend was at the Harvard Business School, and I was stationed for a short time near Boston. I visited him and saw he was spending two years studying cases that seemed to be very commonsensical. At the end of the day, I had to determine what I found most interesting. I thought philosophy was intellectually interesting, so I studied that.

Kazanjian: *I understand that your father actually discouraged you from getting into the investment field despite your early interest in stocks.*

Miller: It was the worst advice I ever received. When I got out of the Army in 1975, the market had just finished its worst period since the Great Depression. It wasn't the kind of field people recommended as a profession that was full of opportunity.

Kazanjian: *You left the Ph.D. program before getting your degree. What happened after that?*

Miller: In 1977, I went to work in Pennsylvania for a company called J.E. Baker. As assistant to the CEO, I was a jack of all trades, doing whatever he asked. Initially, it was a lot of number crunching on acquisitions. He was looking for somebody who had a conceptual grounding in economics.

Kazanjian: *When did you join Legg Mason?*

Miller: In 1981, as director of research.

Kazanjian: *How did you make that transition?*

Miller: It was fairly seamless in that my wife was a broker at Legg Mason. She had joined the firm in 1975 to help put me through graduate school, and I knew Legg Mason's principals. It was, and still is, a fairly small firm based in Baltimore. They talked to me about joining the research effort, which didn't interest me much. Then they talked about diversifying into money management. I found that much more appealing. By that time I was treasurer at J.E. Baker and enjoyed overseeing the company's investment portfolios. Chip Mason, Legg Mason's CEO, planned to start a fund that would reflect the firm's research ideas. I joined in October of 1981, and we started Value Trust in March or April of 1982. My predecessor as director of research, Ernie Kiehne, and I co-managed the fund. He was the senior manager. Our initial portfolio consisted mostly of stocks Ernie had followed for a long time.

Kazanjian: *Had you ever invested in the stock market at that point?*

Miller: Yes. When I was in graduate school, some friends sent me money, saying, "You always talk about the stock market, and you think you can invest in it. Here's some of our money. See what you can do with it." We formed a little investment partnership, and I invested for them in the early and mid-1970s, before joining Legg Mason.

Kazanjian: *When you joined the firm in 1981, what was your investment philosophy?*

Miller: The same as it is now: value. However, it's much more sophisticated now than it was then.

Kazanjian: *Where did that value orientation come from?*

Miller: From my reading. I've read everything I could about investing for as far back as I can remember. I've always thought the right way to do something is to determine who's best at it and see what he or she does. It seemed fairly clear to me that Ben Graham was the intellectual leader of the security analysis field. Then, reading about Warren Buffett and seeing how he had survived and prospered during the difficult period from the late 1960s to the early 1970s was a real eye-opener. It also always made intuitive sense to me to try to buy things at the best possible price in relation to underlying value. I remember talking to [fellow value manager] Bob Torray over 10 years ago. He believed that if you explained value investing to people, either they got it or they didn't. You couldn't convince somebody it was a good way to invest if they didn't instantaneously see that. Most people, for whatever reason, seem more psychologically attuned to buying companies that are growing, have great prospects, or for whatever reason have something people can get excited about. Valuation tends to be a much less important factor for most people than it is for me.

Kazanjian: *I want to dig deeper into your investment approach in a moment, but given the kinds of companies you own, one might wonder whether you still follow the rules of Graham and Buffett.*

Miller: We are absolutely valuation purists. But we are not valuation simpletons. Many people have taken what Graham said in interviews or wrote in *The Intelligent Investor* and extracted only the simplest possible rules from them. But, if you actually get into Graham's *Security Analysis* or some of the interviews he gave late in life, you see there's much more to it. I was going through some of Graham's later interviews and saw one where he was asked before a congressional committee whether stock prices were too high and what stock prices depended on. His comment was that they depended on earnings and, most importantly, on future prospects and to a minor extent on current asset values. Most people believe that if you talked to Graham, he would be most focused on current asset values and least on future prospects. But that's not what he said.

As to Buffett, if you read his work closely, you find that our methodologies are virtually identical. Buffett says he tries to buy businesses at the cheapest price relative to future cash flows. He doesn't precisely calculate the cash flows. As he says, he would rather be vaguely right than precisely wrong. We do a more extensive and detailed analysis, but it's the same approach.

Kazanjian: *Are you saying people have misinterpreted Graham's teaching?*

Miller: No, I don't think they have misinterpreted it. They just take too narrow a view. Graham believed in low PE ratios and low price-to-book-value. All of that is correct. It's just not the full story. It would be like asking Michael Jordan how much money he makes. If he said he made $200,000 a year, that would be true. But he also makes a whole lot more than that. That's the same thing with Graham. It's true that he was a low-PE guy, but he was a lot more than that.

Kazanjian: *How do you define value investing today?*

Miller: I take it right out of the textbooks. If you go to any finance or investment textbook and look up value or valuation, it will say the value of any investment is the present value of the future free cash flows of that investment. I can't find any textbook that defines value differently. They all get it from John Burr Williams, whose Ph.D. dissertation in the 1930s later became the book *The Theory of Investment Value*. He called it the "rule of present worth." The only way you can compare two distinct investments, such as aluminum and computer companies, is to look at them on a comparable basis. The only reasonable comparison is between the returns you expect to earn from them. That's what I'm trying to do. Investing, as Buffett said, is putting money out today with the expectation of getting more back tomorrow. The question is how you do that. We believe the best way to determine the most reasonable expectation of what we're going to get back from an investment is to think about how our view of future cash flows differs from that of the market.

Kazanjian: *Where do you find your ideas initially?*

Miller: They come from all different sources. Many come from the new-low list. We look at anything that looks cheap statistically and do a lot of computer screening. That's a starting point for many value investors, but some of my peers put a lot more weight on the statistics coming out of computer screens than we do. We just use them to get a universe of names to investigate more deeply. We get ideas from spectacular blowups in the market—Waste Management or McKesson/HBOC in 1999 are good examples—or from companies that are perceived to have lost out in some competitive battle, such as Toys 'Я' Us. Also, people who know our style are always serving up investment ideas. Ninety-nine percent of them aren't interesting, but occasionally we find one that's worth doing some work on.

Kazanjian: *Stocks on the new-low list are obviously companies no one wants right now. They have problems. What makes you decide it's okay to buy? Are you hoping for a turnaround?*

Miller: We do a lot of turnarounds, but we tell our analysts to avoid the word *hope* in their research and instead use *believe* or *expect*. Normally, companies that are perceived right out of the box as terrific companies with strong competitive advantages will not make it into our portfolio because they never hit one of our valuation metrics and therefore don't come to our attention. As a result, we've missed many great companies that it turns out were undervalued—Microsoft and Charles Schwab being prime examples. They are stocks that always looked expensive, so we never took an opportunity to analyze them in depth. If you think about it, the only way you can earn an excess return by owning a particular company is if the market hasn't valued it properly. If the market has it properly valued, you will earn the market rate of return or the rate of return of the underlying company, whichever is lower. The market has to be systematically wrong about the prospects of a particular business for you to earn an excess return over any extended period of time. When growth investors do really well, they do so because the companies grew faster and longer than the market believed. To most value investors, a company is undervalued because the market has overly discounted some negative event or is too pessimistic about something that's weighing on the stock price.

Kazanjian: *How do you know that it's just an overreaction and not something more serious?*

Miller: You analyze the business. You have to get into actually figuring out what the company does and what its competitive advantage is. Most important, you must understand the long-term economic model of the business. How much capital does it require to operate? What returns are normal in that industry? Where is the company positioned in the industry? How can its management execute in a way to deliver the business model?

Kazanjian: *Let's talk about some of the holdings in your portfolio. You own a lot of names that you would not normally find in a value fund, such as AOL Time Warner, Dell Computer, and Amazon. com. Tell me how those stocks justifiably fit into a value portfolio and how you came to find them originally.*

Miller: The important thing to understand is that when we say we are value investors, both of those words are important to us: *value* and *investing*. First, we believe that many people who call themselves value investors often don't do very sophisticated valuation work. Second, and more important, they don't invest. They trade. They buy stocks and flip them out if they go up 50 or 100 percent or trade up to some historical valuation metric. What captures people's attention when they look at our portfolio are names such as Dell, AOL Time Warner, United Healthcare, and more recently, Amazon.com—stocks that are being bought mostly by growth investors. We bought these companies when they were really cheap. We've made 30 to 40 times our money in both Dell and AOL. Most investors rarely hold companies long enough to make 30 to 40 times their money. They're lucky if they make 50, 100, or 200 percent. You get those returns only if you actually invest in companies as opposed to trading them and trying to guess when the stock is going to pull back. We don't spend time trying to guess stock price action. We spend our time trying to value businesses.

When we analyzed Dell, for example, in February 1996, that was a period when everybody thought we were going to have a recession. Investors had sold tech stocks down to levels that looked to us to offer an opportunity. Most value people at the time were buying paper, steel, and aluminum, which also were in the dumps. When we did all the valuation work on those companies, we concluded that they were not terribly attractive or mispriced by the market. Their business fundamentals were poor and were likely to remain so. On the other hand, when we looked at Dell, trading at the time around $1–2 on a split-adjusted basis, we saw a company that had a superior business model and excellent competitive advantages and was growing at 25 to 30 percent a year, earning 30 percent on invested capital, and trading at five times earnings. Why would we ever buy a paper company at five times what they hope to earn if paper prices rise when instead we can buy a terrific company at five times today's earnings? When we got further into the detail of the business, it looked to us like the market had systematically misunderstood the potential of the company. Historically, PC companies traded between 6 and 12 times earnings. Even when value investors were buying PC companies, they would buy at 5 to 6 times and sell at 12 times earnings because that was the peak multiple these companies historically had attained. When we analyzed Dell, we concluded it was worth at least 25 times earnings as a business. If you were to buy the whole company, you would pay up to 25 times earnings, whereas the market had peaked valuation out historically at around 12 times. So we thought it was worth about 5 times what the market thought it was worth. It's highly unusual to find companies that appear to be so mispriced, and we loaded up on it. As it turned out, we were right. We actually underestimated the ability of management to execute what turned out to be a superior business model.

Fortunately, because what we do is dynamic valuation, our models are updated every quarter or more often as we get more fundamental data. We're always trying to figure out the underlying business value and the intrinsic value of the company. Earlier in 1999, Dell reached a level where we though it was moderately overpriced, so we sold a fairly significant portion of it.

Kazanjian: *Was it a similar story with AOL?*

Miller: AOL was much more controversial when we bought it in the fall of 1996. People thought AOL was going bankrupt, and the stock had lost three-quarters of its value from May to November. Our analysis was that the company was worth roughly double what we were paying for it. We do scenario analyses of the companies, since we don't have any idea of what the future is actually going to look like. We try to map out the possible futures, assign probability weightings to them, and figure out which one appears to be most likely. Then we determine the value under that scenario. Under one scenario, we figured AOL could be worth multiples of the central value we had calculated.

Kazanjian: *That was when AOL was having significant capacity problems and people couldn't log on. Scenario one must have been that everybody would switch from AOL to other carriers, which is what a lot of Wall Street was thinking.*

Miller: That was certainly a scenario, but when AOL was being sued by the state attorneys general and there were stories in the news every day about how people couldn't log on, we found it fascinating that it wasn't losing subscribers. The value proposition was very powerful. Ordinarily, if you buy a product or service that you pay for up front and then can't use, you ask for your money back and switch to somebody else. But AOL's customer base continued to grow. That told us there was a very different value proposition going on there. It's like when Coca-Cola changed the Coke formula. People wanted old Coke back. They didn't want the new Coke. Here, people didn't want CompuServe or the Microsoft Network. They wanted AOL. When we analyzed traffic patterns, we found that 80 percent of the customers of the Microsoft Network used it just as a portal to the Internet, whereas 80 percent of AOL's customers stayed on the proprietary service and did not pass through to the Internet. This again supported the view that there was tremendous value in the service. We knew people wouldn't stay with the company forever if they couldn't log on. So we analyzed how long it would take AOL to solve this problem. There were two different issues. One was technological. Could they deploy enough technology over the requisite time horizon to solve the problem? We believed the answer was yes. Second, could they finance it, since it required a lot of up-front capital and they didn't have a lot of money? Would it put too much strain on their financial condition? Our answer, after analyzing the situation, was that adequate financing would be available. We made a big bet on AOL, and fortunately we turned out to be right.

Kazanjian: *Since you bought both Dell and AOL, they're up 20 to 40 times your original cost. Without these two stocks, your fund would clearly not be where it is today.*

Miller: There's no question that without our two largest holdings [Dell and AOL were Miller's top holdings in the late 1990s] going up the most, we would not have done as well. Back when I was director of research, we used to put together a Thanksgiving list—12 stock picks for the forthcoming year. It had a really good record of beating the market. In fact, *The Wall Street Journal* began to pick it up in the early 1980s. They published our Thanksgiving list on Thanksgiving Day. A reporter called me once and said, "I went back and analyzed all your lists. They did beat the market, but there are 12 stocks on each list." I said, "Yeah, I know, one for every month." He said, "If you throw out last year's two best performers, you wouldn't have beaten the market. The year before that, the only reason you beat it was because you had a big takeover." I replied, "If the assumption is we don't own the things that enable us to beat the market, then it follows that we won't beat the market. But we do own them." It's like AOL and Dell. We do own them. Part of the process that has enabled us to beat the market is selecting and then holding these businesses. The other thing people misunderstand about our success is that we've owned Dell and AOL only since 1996. But we've outperformed every year since 1991, long before we owned Dell and AOL. We've also outperformed the S&P 500 over the entire history of the fund.

Kazanjian: *In 2000, Value Trust was down 7.1 percent, even though you still beat the S&P 500. What's interesting is that many value funds did well that year. What happened?*

Miller: First of all, we have a big fund. Counting all the different share classes and assets that shadow the fund, it's a $20 billion-plus portfolio. Unlike many value portfolios, it's also highly focused. The average value fund owns about 100 names and turns the portfolio over between 80 and 90 percent a year. We own 35 names and we turn the portfolio over every 5 to 10 years. Part of the reason we did so well relative to other value funds in the late 1990s was that we correctly identified in 1995–96 that the best values in the market were in technology. By 2000, the market had repriced technology to a level that fully reflected the value. We began selling those tech stocks in the first quarter of 2000. But because we have a large amount of assets, it took us most of the year to get the portfolio to where it currently is, which is underweight in technology. Even though we were behind the market in the first quarter of 2000, we beat the market in the second half of the year, and therefore pulled ahead of it. By contrast, most value people hadn't changed their portfolios in years. They underperformed the market for a long time, many since 1994. They were up in 2000, but had really dreadful absolute and relative results for years, whereas we were able to beat the market handily throughout the 1990s.

Kazanjian: *It sounds like the stocks that helped to fuel your performance during the period when value was out of favor dragged you down in 2000 because you couldn't sell them fast enough before they got clobbered.*

Miller: Yes. We sold tons of stocks that had done really well for us. We still have some AOL, but we sold a mountain of it in 2000. We sold all of our Nokia and most of our Nextel and Dell. You just can't sell millions of shares in a short period of time.

Kazanjian: *You are back in Dell now. What made you return?*

Miller: We sold almost all of our Dell in the first quarter of 2000. By the fourth quarter, Dell had retreated all the way back to levels we thought were attractive, so we bought a lot, and it's worked out well.

Kazanjian: *You've been buying some controversial tech and telecom names.*

Miller: In the first quarter of 2001, we bought a ton of Amazon.com and Nextel.

Kazanjian: *Let's talk about Amazon. That's obviously a name few consider to be a value stock. Take me through how you valued that company and why you consider it to be a bargain.*

Miller: First of all, let me clarify a term here. I don't believe there's such a thing as a "value stock" or a "growth stock." I don't think *value* and *growth* describe companies. They describe styles of investing. It's bizarre when people categorize companies as value or growth. From a pure financial theory standpoint, growth is an input to the calculation of value. It's part of the exercise of figuring out what the intrinsic value of something is. In addition, if you decide that the world falls into growth and value categories on the basis of price-to-book-value, companies such as General Motors that write off a large portion of their book value as they did in the early 90s suddenly get transformed into growth stocks. If companies such as

JDS Uniphase make idiotic acquisitions at very high valuations by is-
suing stock and then capitalizing it as goodwill, they become value
stocks. AOL is 50 times above what we paid for it, yet it's now in
the value index because its price-to-book-value has magically kicked
it into that category due to the acquisition of Time Warner for
stock.

Value and growth do describe styles of investing. There are growth
investors and there are value investors. For growth investors,
growth is the driving force of their investment process. They are
looking for growth. Growth to them is a marker of what will lead to
good returns. They like growing revenues, growing earnings, perhaps a growing return on capital. For value investors, valuation is
the driving force of the process. Some value investors want growth
and others are more like we are, which is agnostic about whether
something is growing or not. We're trying to buy things at the
largest discount to intrinsic business value.

Kazanjian: *How did you determine Amazon's intrinsic value?*

Miller: Intrinsic business value is the present value of the future free
cash flows that an investment will generate over its lifetime. The way
we valued Amazon is we built a model of the company, projected its
free cash flows, and discounted those back in. Because we don't have
any idea—nor does anyone else—about what the actual cash flows of
Amazon will be, we projected a wide variety of cash flows based on
various scenarios. We believe that if you take Amazon's last-quarter
revenues and losses, guidance for the year, and the consensus of analysts' expectations, you get a value of about $30. If we run a variety
of scenarios, including one where you give it 15 years of revenue
growth, you get a wild valuation in the $100-plus range. We don't
believe Amazon is currently worth $100, but we do believe it's worth
$30. If you go out a year and Amazon hits its numbers, the com-
pany's value will probably rise by 30 percent a year.

Kazanjian: *You're about the only value investor I know saying this
about Amazon. Most of your value peers contend the stock is
grossly overvalued.*

Miller: First, I don't know of any other value investor who has actually tried to value Amazon by analyzing its business model and projecting its cash flow. What they are doing is looking at the history of
Amazon and saying this company is losing a lot of money, is gener-

ating negative cash flow, and yet has an equity market value of $3 billion, and therefore is overpriced. Everybody we've talked to who claims the stock is overpriced either is plugging in the wrong numbers or is assuming things that aren't visible and for which there is no evidence—namely, that Amazon's creditors will cut it off. We're trying to make our projections tie in with what is actually occurring. You'll also note that Moody's has put Amazon on credit watch for an upgrade. They have obviously been able to gain confidence that Amazon is actually making its numbers, which gives us confidence that our models are roughly correct. One last comment: The Internet was obviously a huge bubble and many stocks have collapsed to pennies on the dollar. At the same time, Amazon is going up in a down market. Amazon has beat the market every single year it's been public except for 2000. Why? Maybe something is going on at the company that's different from what the general perception is.

Kazanjian: *Are you the largest shareholder of Amazon's common stock?*

Miller: Jeff Bezos, the founder, is the largest shareholder, but we're the largest institutional shareholder, right behind Jeff.

Kazanjian: *Do you look at Amazon the same way you did AOL when you first bought it in 1996?*

Miller: Amazon is similar to AOL in some ways and dissimilar in others. One similarity is that Amazon has a large and loyal customer base. That ultimately is going to drive Amazon's long-term value. The dissimilarity is that Amazon's total value is multiples of what AOL was selling for in 1996. So AOL's theoretical value and economics in 1996 were better than Amazon's. The market has discounted a bit more improvement in Amazon than it did at the time for AOL. From a timing standpoint it's very similar to AOL in 1996. AOL in 1996 was losing gobs of money. People thought it was going bankrupt and were very skeptical of the business model. That's exactly what's going on with Amazon today. We believe that before the end of 2002, Amazon will turn from cash-negative to cash-positive. That's what enabled AOL to get its first big valuation upgrade, and I expect the same thing will happen with Amazon.

Kazanjian: *You also own Amazon convertibles in the Opportunity Trust, along with bonds in distressed companies, such as Exodus Communications. Why buy debt over equities?*

Miller: It has to do with the relative risk and return. The great thing about financial theory is that it provides a way to value any asset. If we buy a bond, it's an asset. How do we value it? By taking the present value of the future free cash flows. If we take a business such as Exodus, we come up with a value for the company. The value of the business is independent of how it is financed. But how it is financed determines who has access to that value. If a company is worth $1 billion and doesn't have any debt, that $1 billion all accrues to the equity holders. If a company is worth $1 billion and has $1 billion of debt, the equity holders don't have an asset that's worth anything. In the case of Exodus, the debt is trading at 15 cents on the dollar subsequent to its bankruptcy filing and default. The current value of the senior debt is around $300 million. We value the company at about $1 billion, so we believe we'll make several times our money through the bankruptcy reorganization.

Kazanjian: *I want to return to a point you made a minute ago about value investors not even looking at Amazon. Do you think a lot of value investors just unintentionally overlook stocks conventionally viewed as being overpriced when, in fact, they represent good values after all?*

Miller: We've certainly overlooked a lot of great ideas and probably still do. If you think about it, Microsoft was a great value 10 years ago. So was Cisco. These companies went up hundreds of times. Even after its severe correction, Cisco is valued at around $120 billion. It was valued at around $1 billion 10 years ago. There are a lot of companies that turn out to be great values that value investors don't look at because they seem expensive at the time. Another good example is Wal-Mart. In the early 1970s, when the stock market was trading at seven times earnings, Wal-Mart traded at 24 times earnings. Had you bought it then and held on, you would have creamed the market over that entire period because Wal-Mart was significantly undervalued.

One thing we've learned over the years is that simple-minded computer screens—such as screens for low-PE or low-price-to-book or low-price-to-cash-flow stocks—do not tell you much about value. They can leave out many great companies that look expensive but are actually worth a lot more than they're trading for. The problem is it's very difficult for a value investor, ourselves included, to actually figure out how to search for stocks that look statistically expensive yet are actually cheap. Looking expensive isn't the same as being expensive, and looking cheap isn't the same as being cheap.

Kazanjian: *Besides valuation, what are the reasons you would sell a stock?*

Miller: We have a threefold sell discipline. The first one is if the company's fairly priced. Second, we will sell if we find a better bargain. We try to remain fully invested. If we find something that's more undervalued on a tax-adjusted basis than what we already own, we'll sell the least attractive thing in the portfolio.

Kazanjian: *What's the third reason?*

Miller: If the investment case changes. Perhaps the government comes in and says it's going to change the reimbursement rates for nursing homes. Guess what? All your cash flows are going to change. Since the terrorists attacked the World Trade Center, the investment opportunities in defense stocks changed.

Kazanjian: *Do you pay much attention to the market, interest rates, and so on?*

Miller: We pay a lot of attention to them. The justifiable valuation of a market with 7 percent inflation is radically different from the valuation of a market with 2 percent inflation. We pay attention, we just don't forecast it.

Kazanjian: *How patient are you with companies that don't move up in price for months or years?*

Miller: We will own a company as long as we're confident of the business value and in management's ability to execute those values. As long as we trust management and believe it's dealing with us in a fair way, we will hold the stock.

Kazanjian: *Tell me more about the additional analysis you do on companies before buying.*

Miller: We do virtually anything we can to help us add value. We talk to management, suppliers, competitors, and analysts. Because we are long-term owners of these companies and don't blow out of the stock because it misses a quarter or underperforms for X periods of time, our discussions with managements center on long-term issues that short-term investors don't care about as much.

Kazanjian: *What are the characteristics of the most successful companies you've ever owned?*

Miller: They tend to have low valuations and are trading way down from their prior highs because of some problem, perceived or real. They are leaders in their industries, have managements who actually care about shareholder value, and, most important, have a fundamental economic model where they can earn above their cost of capital.

Kazanjian: *Value Trust is the only fund to have outperformed the S&P 500 every year since 1991. There are thousands of stock funds out there. Why do you think you're the only manager who has been able to accomplish this feat?*

Miller: I think there are several reasons. Most important, in my opinion, is that most managers do not really invest long term. Their turnover rate is way too high. They trade stocks too much and are not really thinking about what the long-term rate of return is on the asset they're buying. I'd say most managers fail to really understand and correctly value the assets they're buying. One of the points Warren Buffett so correctly makes is that stocks represent ownership interest in businesses. If you understand the value of the business, over time that will help you understand the value of the stock. I think most money managers are focused too much on the stock and the stock price, and not on the value of the business. Furthermore, people tend to get caught up in style boxes and strategy, instead of considering whether those styles and strategies are effective or not. People tend to be too dogmatic. They confuse their objective with their strategy. The objective for an active money manager is to add value over the benchmark. After all, the client can get the market rate of return tax efficiently at an extremely low cost. The only reason to pay for an active manager is because that manager does better than the index. People have confused the objective, which is to do better than the index, with the strategy—for example, to invest using growth or value. What happens is that people get caught up in trying to continue to do what they used to do in the past, apart from whether it worked or not, because they see their job as buying growth or value, as opposed to beating the market. My view is that my job is to beat the market, and the way I do that is by having a valuation-driven strategy.

It's certainly a strategy that has worked for Miller, even during periods when value has been deeply out of favor. By being more flexible than many of his value peers, and keeping his eye on outperforming the market, he has been able to stand far above the crowd.

Going forward, Miller continues to believe that stocks will shower investors with greater returns than any other major asset class, although he's only expecting average annual returns of around 8 percent. He contends that his forecast is bullish, even though it calls for much more moderate expectations than investors became accustomed to in the recent past. ■

RONALD MUHLENKAMP

MUHLENKAMP & COMPANY

R on Muhlenkamp says that investing is a lot like farming. If you plant the right crop, you'll reap a bountiful harvest. Muhlenkamp should know. He grew up on an Ohio farm and still occasionally drives a tractor through his friends' fields.

Muhlenkamp got into the investment business almost by accident. Upon graduating from the Harvard Business School, he learned that some friends were starting an investment firm on Wall Street. They asked him to tag along. Even though the pay was less than other offers he received, he decided to join them, since it sounded like an exciting opportunity. The firm had a hard time growing assets, and Muhlenkamp decided to leave after 18 months. But he has remained in the investment industry ever since.

As an analyst at an insurance company in the early 1970s, he began to do research on company valuation. Through that, he came up with a formula he still uses today to assess the fair price for a stock. Muhlenkamp's method is a form of Graham and Dodd analysis combined with a few tweaks of his own. His approach calls for buying companies of all sizes, as long as they meet his criteria. But he'll also buy bonds if, as he puts it, the "climate" is right. His goal is to produce a high total return regardless of what instruments he has to use to get it.

The 58-year-old investment pro started his own firm in Wexford, Pennsylvania, in 1978. In addition to managing private accounts, he also runs the Muhlenkamp Fund. Away from the office, Muhlenkamp is a motorcycle enthusiast who enjoys taking to the open road. Given his love of bikes, you'll be as surprised as I was to learn that he never invested in Harley-Davidson—his bike of choice—but that mistake taught him a lesson for the future.

Kazanjian: *You grew up on a farm in western Ohio. Did you learn anything about investing while plowing the fields?*

Muhlenkamp: Oh, yes. Far more than I learned at the Harvard Business School. The first thing I learned is that crops don't grow every month. The second thing I learned is that if you don't plant them, they don't grow at all. You've got to know the overall climate. Farming in Ohio is different from farming in Texas or California. Once you know the climate, you have to understand the seasons. The only difference between farming and investing is that we investors don't have a good calendar. We know that we have cycles that tend to be three to five years, but we don't quite know we're at a top or a bottom until six months later.

Kazanjian: *By not planting crops, I trust you mean not buying stocks in the first place.*

Muhlenkamp: Yes. Some investors think it's safer to leave your money in T-bills and never own stocks. When my cousins plant corn, if they want 30,000 plants to the acre, they plant 33,000. They fully expect that 10 percent of their plants won't come up. It doesn't surprise them if they have to replant 10 or 15 percent of the field. When you plant crops, they don't all come up, so you have to allow for some extra margin. Of course, if you don't plant anything at all—or if you don't invest in stocks—you will never reap the rewards.

Kazanjian: *Sounds like an argument for diversification. By the same token, isn't the overall market environment like "weather" on the farm? In other words, you can plant some great crops, but if the rain comes pouring down, it will destroy your crop, even if it was planted properly.*

Muhlenkamp: There can always be something that hits the fan. But it's still more rewarding to plant a crop, to own stocks, than it is to hold T-bills. Bonds are like cash rent. They're analogous to owning the land. You don't want to take the risk of farming, so you rent it out for cash to someone who is willing to take the risk of farming. Of course, you don't get much return there either.

Kazanjian: *Are there ever times to hold bonds?*

Muhlenkamp: Sure. There are climates for bonds, but they're few and far between. The only time you've wanted to own bonds in the last 75 years was when we were in a depression or when inflation was coming down. When interest rates go from 13 to 6 percent, as they did from 1981 to 1993, you can make good money in bonds. We view returns on an after-tax and after-inflation basis. Adjusted for taxes and inflation, the only time you made money on bonds was in the depression years from 1929 to 1937 and from 1981 to 1993.

Kazanjian: *I take it you have no interest in owning bonds at this time or for the foreseeable future.*

Muhlenkamp: No. Bonds look better than cash, but stocks look better than bonds.

Kazanjian: *Did you have an early interest in the stock market?*

Muhlenkamp: Growing up on the farm, I liked the machinery. I went to MIT and studied engineering. I took some business courses my senior year. On graduation, I concluded I ought to get a master's and went on to the Harvard Business School, where I studied marketing, finance, and labor relations. Coming out, all of the job offers looked the same, except for one. Some of my classmates were setting up an investment firm on Wall Street. I had never owned a stock or bond in my life, but it looked like an interesting field to get into. I joined them for a third less salary than was available elsewhere, but it looked very promising. I worked there a year and a half and became totally fascinated with this business. I've been in it ever since. I'm interested in things I know nothing about. I'm in a field where I don't know very much, but neither does anyone else, so it's not a big handicap.

Kazanjian: *Why didn't you stick around with your friends longer?*

Muhlenkamp: After a year and a half, we only had $3 million under management and I was no higher than number three on the totem pole. By that time I had a wife and four kids to support. I went to work for an insurance company in North Carolina. I had time there to fill in the investment knowledge I didn't gain in school. Incidentally, I learned more that was helpful to me about investing at MIT than at Harvard. MIT taught me that if you really understand the basics, everything else falls into place. I did a lot of work from 1970 to 1974 on valuing companies the way other businesses do. I still value businesses the same way today.

Kazanjian: *Tell me more.*

Muhlenkamp: In 1968, all of the studies proved that 4.5 percent was a normal interest rate and 17 was a normal PE. During 1972–74, we saw interest rates go well above 4.5 percent. They went past 7 percent during that period and rose to over 13 percent by the late 1970s. In 1973–74, we saw PEs go from 17 to 14 to 12 to 9 to 7. All the way down, Wall Street said these stocks were cheap. I said to the analysts, "You keep telling me they're cheap, yet I keep buying them and they keep going down. What's the company worth?" The analysts literally couldn't tell me what a company was worth. I started quizzing some of the number crunchers at various firms to see if they could figure out what was happening. They came back and said things like price-to-book [P/B] versus return on equity [ROE] were useful criteria to look at. The key is what return you can get versus your cost of capital. Digging further, we learned that even though P/B versus ROE is useful, you have to adjust for inflation and interest rates. In early 1974, even Ben Graham adjusted his values. If you believed his numbers in early 1974, you would have bought stocks. If you believed mine, you would have sold stocks. I thought, Who am I to argue with Ben Graham?

But by December 1974, prices fell significantly. At that point, I realized I was on to something. I've used the same method of valuing companies, using the Graham format but adjusting it for inflation and interest rates, for 27 years.

Kazanjian: *You realized you were a value investor pretty early on then.*

Muhlenkamp: Yes. If you look at the people with good long-term records, one way or another they're value investors. I'll pay up for growth. I just won't pay an unlimited amount. I would argue that if inflation is less than 1 percent, interest rates are 4.5 percent, and the return on equity is high enough to sustain a high growth rate, PEs should be 2.5 times the growth rate. The flip side is I've never seen a reasoned argument why PEs should be higher than 2.5 times the growth rate.

Kazanjian: *What was your next career move?*

Muhlenkamp: I went from the insurance company to a firm in Pittsburgh as a money manager in early 1975. The trouble was they had read a few books. They had a good start on the disciplines it takes to be a money manager, but they thought they had finished. I was impressed with their start, but every time I tried to do something beyond what they had read in a book, they had trouble accepting it. Finally, at the end of 1977, I stepped out and decided to do my own thing.

Kazanjian: *Did you immediately start a fund?*

Muhlenkamp: No. Funds are expensive and a pain in the neck to start. It's easier to start with private accounts because it's fairly easy to become a Registered Investment Advisor. I worked out of the house for several years and simply beat the bricks trying to find enough clients who would pay me to manage their money. I started out with a $200,000 minimum. Over a period of years, a number of folks said they liked what I did but didn't have $200,000. I brought out the mutual fund in 1988 to serve smaller accounts.

Kazanjian: *How much do you manage altogether?*

Muhlenkamp: It's now a little over $650 million, $500 million of which is in the fund.

Kazanjian: *Do you have a certain type of stock you specialize in, such as mid-caps or small-caps?*

Muhlenkamp: When you study it, you'll find that size doesn't matter. Profitability matters. Growth in earnings matters. Growth in revenues matters. We don't really see a difference between growth and value. We're looking for good companies. We start with return on shareholder equity. If you have a high return on shareholder equity and you sustain it, chances are you're doing a pretty good job as a company. We then look to buy those companies at reasonable prices. The price we're willing to pay changes as inflation and interest rates change. In the early 1980s, we wanted a PE below half of the ROE. Today we want a PE below the ROE. I don't like rules of thumb, but that's as good as any. We always want a good company.

Bad companies keep finding ways of losing money. The question is simply what you're willing to pay for a level of profitability in the current investment climate.

Kazanjian: *You said that capitalization size doesn't matter, but some academic research shows that, over time, small-caps have done better than large-caps.*

Muhlenkamp: In 1983, the studies proved that small-caps did better than large-caps. But in the late 1980s and through the 1990s, large-caps did better. I'd much rather have a good small company than a bad big one, or a good big company than a bad small one.

Kazanjian: *Since, in your eyes, size doesn't matter, how should investors put their portfolios together?*

Muhlenkamp: They should look for good companies at reasonable prices. As it happens, in our portfolio we have a mix of all capitalization sizes.

Kazanjian: *What about mutual fund investors? Which funds should they buy?*

Muhlenkamp: They should go for funds that are not limited by market cap. This whole thing has become a marketing game. If you look at the people who've done a nice job of earning money over time, they've all owned a mix of stuff. Warren Buffett doesn't care about the size of a company. He owns a mix of very small and very large companies.

Kazanjian: *When you put your portfolio together, do you start off by looking at themes or the overall environment before searching for individual companies?*

Muhlenkamp: No. We start with individual companies. If we find a lot of companies in an area, we look to see if there's a general theme to follow. Is it because profitability has improved from what it used to be and people haven't figured it out yet? Or is it because of a political risk? If you can't figure it out, you do some digging. Every now and then, the climate changes. In the last 50 years, such changes have mainly been driven by inflation and taxes. But there's also a change when the public finally realizes what's going on. The public was slow to realize it when inflation ran up in the late 1960s and early 1970s. For years, the public thought the run-up was temporary. The same thing happened on the way down. In the 1980s, everybody saw that inflation and interest rates were down, but figured they were going back up. We made a lot of money for our clients based on that lag in perception. As an investor, my best opportunity for making money is when there is a difference between perception and reality. Wall Street likes to say it anticipates things like earnings, and it does. But it doesn't do a good job of anticipating the big things, such as changes in inflation.

Kazanjian: *You say you start off with a company. How do you find these companies?*

Muhlenkamp: The usual way is to page through Value Line. I have someone who runs computer screens for me. First, you go through and screen for companies with a good return on equity. You then take that list and look for companies that are fairly priced. You follow that with research and analysis to see if the ROE is sustainable. You want to make sure that it's not just a blip and that it's a business you want to be a part of.

Kazanjian: *It sounds like you begin with a primarily quantitative process.*

Muhlenkamp: For the screening process, yes. When the numbers look good, we typically call the company and talk. We have three favorite questions. First, "Are there analysts on Wall Street who do a good job on your company?" That saves us time. The second question is "What criteria do you use to judge your own performance?" Thirty years ago most people used "payback." Today they probably use return on equity, discounted cash flow, economic value added, or something like that. All are valid. We simply want to talk in their terms. The third question is "At what point do your people start earning a bonus?" I want to know what their standards are. If they tell me that their bonuses kick in at 15 percent ROE or the equivalent, I start to get interested. If they tell me that people get a bonus for a 10 percent ROE, I'm not interested. They're not setting their sights high enough to make a good return. Part of our job is to figure out whether, in fact, they can reach the targets they're shooting for. But we at least want to know what they're shooting for and what they're trying to do.

Kazanjian: *You said, "When the numbers look good." What do you mean by that?*

Muhlenkamp: First, I want an ROE over 14 percent, which is the average. I want an above-average company. In today's environment, I want a PE below the ROE. If the ROE is 30, I want a PE below 30. If the ROE is 16, I want a PE below 16. We will pay up for a good company; we just won't pay an unlimited amount.

Kazanjian: *Do you expect an ROE of 30 to sustain itself?*

Muhlenkamp: That becomes the interesting question. Not too many companies can sustain high ROEs for very long. You can't just buy the numbers without doing a little homework to see what's going on behind the scenes.

Kazanjian: *Do you always try to talk to management?*

Muhlenkamp: It depends. If the name of the company is Ford Motor, I don't need to. The smaller the company, the more you've got to know management.

Kazanjian: *Your first question for management was "Are there any analysts who do a good job covering your company?" Many people are skeptical of Wall Street research. Do you find it's reliable?*

Muhlenkamp: It certainly can be useful, but I never ask an analyst what stock to buy. I want an analyst to tell me what's going on in the industry and what's going on in the company. Their job is to know their companies. My job is to figure out what the values are and what companies I want to own.

Kazanjian: *You're looking to get information about the industry or the company as opposed to a recommendation on whether you should buy the stock.*

Muhlenkamp: Exactly. Just as I use Value Line data but don't necessarily use their conclusions. Each of these things adds value to the analysis, but you don't necessarily use their conclusions.

Kazanjian: *Do you invest in international stocks?*

Muhlenkamp: We can, but lately we see no reason to. Any time you step outside the U.S., you take on currency risk and what we call accounting risk. Accounting rules are different in other countries. It turns out that the times you want to be invested overseas are governed more by currency ratios than relative company ratios. We can invest overseas, but we need a higher probable return because of the risks involved.

Kazanjian: *Is there anything else you look at when evaluating a company?*

Muhlenkamp: What we've talked about is just the start. We look at revenue growth. If you own growth stocks, make sure they're growing. In 1998, we saw the revenues of Coca-Cola, Gillette, and Procter & Gamble come down to 5 percent or less over a period of years. Companies can hold earnings up for a little while, but if you're a well-run business and your revenue isn't growing, it becomes difficult for earnings to grow. When the economy is slowing down or the Fed is tightening, you put increased emphasis on the balance sheet. You want to be sure the company can survive all the turmoil.

Kazanjian: *Do you look at things more closely in a small company than in a large company?*

Muhlenkamp: Sure. Things are simply more sensitive, so you have to better understand what management is trying to do.

Kazanjian: *What are some of the warning signs that would keep you away from a company?*

Muhlenkamp: As you work your way through the income statement, you start with revenues. If revenues slow down and margins begin to deteriorate, you get nervous. Typically we look at a company in four ways. First is marketing, or what sales are doing. Second is profitability, which is primarily cost control. Third is finance, which is basically the balance sheet, which becomes more important as things slow down. Fourth is labor relations. The airlines often are more sensitive to labor relations than revenue growth. It became popular for a time to look at price-to-sales ratios instead of price-to-earnings ratios. Companies that look good on a price-to-sales ratio basis that don't look good on a price-to-earnings basis likely have sizable sales but aren't very profitable. That means they're poorly managed. What happened in the 1980s and 1990s as Wall Street got better at driving companies toward profitability was you had a number of poorly run companies get new management from the outside to make their sales more profitable. When that's going on, a price-to-sales basis can identify poorly managed companies. If you see that and believe the new management is making headway, then you've got something.

Kazanjian: *How many stocks do you normally keep in the portfolio?*

Muhlenkamp: In a private account, the minimum is 20 stocks. In the fund, we own around 50 to 60 stocks. In a private account, we might own one or two stocks from a given industry. In the fund, we might own five.

Kazanjian: *So you tend to be somewhat diversified?*

Muhlenkamp: Yes, but by the same token we see no need to own a piece of everything. The most we'll buy in any stock is 5 percent, and typically the most we'll hold is 10 percent. If it gets to be a 10 percent position, we start scaling back, even if we love it. The most we've put in any one industry is about 30 percent.

Kazanjian: *You talked about seasons and cycles earlier. Do you trade frequently?*

Muhlenkamp: No. Our turnover averages less than 20 percent, which means we typically own things for around five years. The "seasons" tend to be three-to-five–year business cycles.

Kazanjian: *What would make you sell a stock?*

Muhlenkamp: If the company starts to disappoint, it gets sold pretty quickly. If the stock starts to disappoint, but we're quite certain that the company's doing all right, we're a little more patient. If the stock disappoints and we can't figure out why, sometimes we'll sell. You usually can't find out the bad news in time to do you any good. It normally shows up in the price first. The rule is that we sell on relative strength. When relative strength breaks down and we can't figure out why, we sell because transaction costs are low in our business.

Kazanjian: *You're like many of the other value managers I've interviewed, in that if a stock you own is going down in price and everything is okay, you'll buy more. It seems that for the average investor, a falling price is the trigger to sell.*

Muhlenkamp: All the average investor knows about stocks is the price. They buy everything else in life—their cars, their house, their clothes—based on value. They look to buy everything on sale because they have a pretty good idea what fair value is. In fact, they don't get excited about a 10-percent-off sale. They might take a look at 20 percent. At 30 percent, they start to get interested. But most people buy stocks the way teenagers buy clothes. They buy whatever is the current fad. When people get a little older, they shop for price because they have some idea of what that article is worth. In stocks, if you don't have an idea of what the company is worth, and all you know is price, you tend to chase price. Wall Street has come to make a big thing about whether companies miss their earnings estimates by a penny or so. We get concerned when a company misses estimates by 10 percent, either plus or minus. If it comes within a couple of pennies, it means it's managing earnings. I'm not sure I should pay a premium for a company that manages earnings. I want to pay a premium for companies that have earnings, but the fact that they try to negate the seasons and pretend their crops grow as fast in December as they do in June is nonsense. The reason people look at price is because they don't know value.

There are really only two disciplines for investing and they go back to Ben Graham and Gerald Loeb. Ben Graham said you should determine the value of a company, buy it below that price, and sell it above that price. Gerald Loeb said he couldn't determine value, but could spot a change in trend. He would then invest in the momentum of the trend. If people are good at identifying trends, the last thing they should do is listen to me. They should go play the trends and the human psychology that are reflected in the marketplace. I'm not very good at that. Because I have derived some disciplines for valuing companies, I play a value game. In the short term, human psychology dominates in the price of stocks. In the long term, the values of companies dominate.

Kazanjian: *Speaking of valuations, in the past you've compared your valuation strategy to buying Pontiacs and Buicks. What is that all about?*

Muhlenkamp: We say that we want better-than-average companies. We define a Chevy as average, so we want Pontiacs and Buicks. We don't want a Yugo at any price. We want better-than-average companies.

Kazanjian: *So you don't want the best and you don't want the worst.*

Muhlenkamp: I'd like to buy the best, the Cadillacs, but they don't go on sale very often. If I wait to buy Cadillacs on sale, I'm missing a lot of good stuff. If I say I never want a company with a less than 25 percent return on equity—a company above that, I would define as a Cadillac—and I want to get it at a good price, I miss too many opportunities. A lot of people would argue that a company like Cisco is a Rolls-Royce. A Rolls-Royce is a great vehicle, but few people own it because to them it's not worth the price.

Kazanjian: *In fact, you don't own a lot of technology in general. Tech stocks tend to have high ROEs. Why don't you have more?*

Muhlenkamp: Because their prices are too high. At one point we bought a fair amount of Intel at 12 times earnings. Every once in a while you get a chance to buy a Cadillac at a cheap price, but not very often.

Kazanjian: *By the same token, not owning tech cost you some in relative performance in 1998–99. Are those periods when you say to yourself, I should have relaxed my constraints a bit?*

Muhlenkamp: The first thing you do in those times is double-check your assumptions. Obviously something is going on that you're not participating in. Once you double-check all your assumptions, if the numbers hold up, you stick to your discipline and explain to your clients what you're doing. My experience indicates that those are the times to tighten your constraints, not loosen them. Our underperformance of 1998–99 was recouped in 2000–01.

Kazanjian: *What do you think of the day trading phenomenon?*

Muhlenkamp: I think day traders have a life expectancy of about six months. They're competing with the specialists on the floor of the New York Stock Exchange and with the Ph.D. mathematicians sitting at Morgan Stanley with computers at their elbows—all of whom can trade for peanuts or less. I realized when I worked in midtown Manhattan that I was too far from the floor of the stock exchange to compete with the specialists, so I've never tried.

Kazanjian: *What have been your biggest investment mistakes, and what have you learned from them?*

Muhlenkamp: It can be anything from not quite understanding the business, to not quite understanding the people, to not quite understanding that something has changed. Sometimes it's the psychology of the marketplace. I've made mistakes across the board. What you learn is that you've got to keep an open mind. The only difficult thing about making money in investing is in changing your mind. Most of the things that we do require making 55/45 decisions. By the time we're 90 percent certain, it's too late. You get information incrementally.

An old friend of mine is very bearish on one of the stocks I'm big in. He calls me once a week and tells me what terrible things are going to happen to the stock. One of these days he'll probably be right. The problem is he's been wrong long enough that rather than taking the information that he provides, I tend to prejudge it because he's been playing the same tune. What I have to do is keep myself open to his information so that I'm able to change my mind when the time comes. I believe most of us would rather die than change our mind. It's tough. You have to rethink all of your assumptions. We all know that hindsight is 20–20, but looking back you can see that there were various things in the wind. Typically the difficulty comes because you were looking at A, B, and C when D, E, and F became more important.

We always look for what we call a "change in climate." We try to look for changes in the climate that can occur on either a macro basis, such as war or politics, or on a company basis. It might be something as simple as getting a new executive or financial officer, or even seeing a competitor who is doing something better. If you are only looking at a company and not its competition, you can get blindsided. The hardest thing to do is sell your successes. It's fairly easy to change your mind when you've been wrong. It's difficult to change your mind when you've been right.

Kazanjian: *Looking out over the next few years at the overall market, do you think the climate is good for people to be investing in stocks?*

Muhlenkamp: Yes. We don't see inflation being a problem. Large numbers of countries around the world are moving toward free markets. The big picture looks bullish.

Kazanjian: *Away from the office, I hear you like to ride motorcycles.*

Muhlenkamp: Sure. I started when I was 17, and when I've been able to afford a bike, I've had one ever since. I like feeling the machine and being out in the open air. Harley-Davidson calls it a 30-minute vacation. That's a pretty good description.

Kazanjian: *Did you invest in Harley stock?*

Muhlenkamp: No, I didn't. When Harley was bought out, the then management asked for and got sizable tariff protection over a five-year period on big bikes. I figured they didn't think they could compete with the Japanese, so I didn't want to own them. Three and a half years later, they asked the government to remove the tariffs. That was the time to change my mind. Unfortunately, I didn't. What I've learned over the years is that no industry is dead forever. I never bought a share of Wal-Mart because I figured retailing was the world's second oldest profession. What could Sam Walton do that JC Penney or Kmart couldn't copy in six weeks? What I failed to recognize is Walton could do a lot because his competition wasn't interested in changing their ways. Sam rewrote retailing and became the richest man in the country. The difficulty is in discarding your old biases when somebody comes up with a new idea. It's tough to change your mind.

Muhlenkamp maintains that for his investment discipline to really pay off, you have to look out at least three years. Since he stays away from fad stocks, it's not unusual for him to be out of tune with the rest of the market over a three-to-six–month period. But when you go beyond that, he says, value almost always wins. As Muhlenkamp points out, some of his peers forgot that in the late 1990s and changed their ways in early 2000, just in time to get caught up in the fall. ▪

WILLIAM NYGREN

THE OAKMARK FUNDS

There is perhaps no value manager who has gained as much respect and prominence in recent years as Bill Nygren. Nygren started out as an analyst at Harris Associates in 1983 and became the firm's research director in 1990. Later that year, Harris started its first mutual fund—The Oakmark Fund—run by Robert Sanborn. Nygren, an analyst at the time, led the effort to help find ideas for the fund. The Oakmark Fund took off like a rocket, posting chart-topping returns.

In 1996, Nygren made a proposal to the Harris board. He suggested that they start a concentrated fund focusing on only a handful of the firm's best ideas. It might own up to 20 stocks, he reasoned, and would be a more aggressive vehicle than The Oakmark Fund. He offered to run the fund in his spare time, while continuing with his research duties. The Harris board bought the idea, and the Oakmark Select Fund was born. The rest is history.

Oakmark Select enjoyed strong performance from the start, and for the first time, Nygren was brought into the spotlight. Before long, Oakmark Select's performance eclipsed the firm's flagship fund. In fact, following an extended period of underperformance, Harris replaced Sanborn with Nygren, giving him two large funds to run. Asset growth into Oakmark Select was so fast that Harris decided to shut the portfolio's doors in May 2001, for fear that the constant stream of assets would be detrimental to performance. Nygren was suddenly the poster boy for all that's great about value investing. A Morningstar analyst even quipped, "All that's left for Bill Nygren is to walk on water and raise the dead." The fund-rating service even crowned him "Domestic Stock Manager of the Year" for 2001.

Unlike some prominent managers in the past, this 43-year-old manager actually had the numbers to back up his industry praise. Not bad for the son of a middle-class family from Minnesota who spent hours in high school reading investment books at the local library. Clearly, all of that reading more than paid off.

Kazanjian: *I understand you first learned the value of a buck as a kid growing up in St. Paul, Minnesota.*

Nygren: There are many anecdotes from my upbringing where you could say the value philosophy was instilled pretty deeply. One would be regular grocery shopping with my mom. We lived near a shopping center with two grocery stores. They both ran weekly specials. We'd go to both stores and buy what was on sale. I grew up in a middle-class family. I learned that if you were a good shopper, you could stretch your budget. I think because of that, when I became interested in the stock market, the value philosophy made complete sense to me as soon as I started reading about it. Warren Buffett says, "The value approach either makes sense to you instantly or you never get it."

Kazanjian: *That's a sentiment expressed by many value managers I talk to.*

Nygren: There was another experience that shaped my value beliefs. When I was around 10 years old, we went on a family vacation and stopped in Las Vegas. I vividly remember my dad taking my older brother and me into a local drugstore. He took out five nickels to show us what a horrible deal it was to put money into slot machines. As my father's nightmare unfolded, he put the first nickel in and about seven came spewing out. We stood there for half an hour as he tried to prove that gambling was a no-win proposition. My dad was a bright guy and he told me gambling didn't make sense, yet I had just witnessed this machine handing him more and more nickels. It made me want to understand the math of risk taking in all different forms. I learned that in a typical slot machine, if you put 100 nickels in, 80 will come back out. If you bet $100 at the craps table, you get about $99 back.

The neat thing about the stock market was it was one of the only opportunities where you had a positive expected return without assuming you had to do better than the next guy. You put $100 into the stock market, get average returns, and a year later you've got $110. Another thing I learned working at a CPA firm was that if you were a very good CPA, you could make fractionally more money than the guy next to you who was average. What I liked about the stock market was how much leverage it gave you based on your talent. An average investor can be equaled or bested by the S&P 500 and is really not of much value to his client. But a superior investor can add a tremendous amount of value.

Kazanjian: *When did you first get interested in the stock market?*

Nygren: It's hard to pick a date. As a student I was always better with numbers than with verbal skills. I was a baseball fanatic as a kid and loved the statistical side of baseball, especially as it related to the Minnesota Twins. In our local paper the baseball box scores were right next to the one-page business section with stock price quotes. I developed an interest in this page. Then, as a high school student, I went to our local branch of the public library and read any books I could find on investing. I graduated from high school in 1976. Clearly, investing was not the national pastime then that it is now.

Kazanjian: *Did you study finance in college?*

Nygren: Yes. I went to the University of Minnesota for an undergraduate degree in accounting. I picked accounting, believing that it made sense to specialize in the language of investing, which is financial statements. I continue to be puzzled at the small percentage of investment people who have done any serious studying of accounting. Given the financial analysis people perform to come up with PE ratios and growth rates, it seems a more difficult task not knowing what goes into making those financial statements.

Kazanjian: *Did you also get a master's degree?*

Nygren: Yes. I went to the University of Wisconsin, Madison, and got a master's degree in finance with a specialization in investments.

I picked that school because of their applied security analysis program. They had a group of 14 students who managed a real investment portfolio. It was only a few hundred thousand dollars, but the group basically formed a management firm at the beginning of the school year and did everything from defining who the client was and what the client's needs were to asset allocations and stock selection.

Kazanjian: *In high school and college, when you did all of your stock market reading, was all of it focused on value-oriented books?*

Nygren: I wasn't trying to focus on those books, but they made the most sense to me, especially *The Intelligent Investor* by Benjamin Graham. When I read books on technical analysis or hyper-growth stock investing, it just didn't click with me the way value did.

Kazanjian: *What was the first stock you bought?*

Nygren: In my first year of college, I had saved up about $1,200 from my earnings as a bag boy. I went to a local brokerage office and bought 10 shares each of AT&T, Gulf Oil, and Texaco. I chose them by going through the stock tables and looking for a combination of low PEs and high yields. At the time the yield I was getting on those stocks was more than I could earn in a savings account.

By the time I was in grad school, I learned that one of the advantages small investors have over large institutions is flexibility. Rather than focusing on names such as AT&T or Texaco, if I could get into the smaller-cap names the professionals really didn't analyze because they couldn't invest enough money to matter, I would have a competitive edge. The first recommendation I had in the program at school was National Presto. This manufacturer of kitchen appliances had more cash on the balance sheet than the company value as reflected in its stock price.

Kazanjian: *What did you do after college?*

Nygren: I went to Milwaukee to work at Northwestern Mutual Life Company as a generalist stock analyst. I was there just under two years. We had three analysts. Each of us had coverage responsibility for a third of the industries. Mine were retail, food, and utilities.

Kazanjian: *Sounds value-oriented.*

Nygren: I'm not a believer that there's an industry with a value orientation. It's all stock-specific. The lesson I learned there that was really important to me, and to the next step in my career, was how important it is to have an alignment of investment philosophy with the group of people you work with. I would go to our portfolio managers at Northwestern Mutual and suggest a stock that had just fallen from $40 down to $20, trading at maybe six times earnings. They used a combination of technical and fundamental analysis, so it didn't look good to them until it rallied to the high $20s. We never achieved a meeting of the minds as to how they could use me as a value person within their system.

Kazanjian: *So you decided to move on?*

Nygren: Yes. I got a call from Steve Hawk, the finance professor who ran the investments program at Madison. He knew I was concerned about this mismatch of investment approaches. He said I'd get a call from another alumni of our program, Clyde McGregor (now manager of the Oakmark Equity and Income Fund). Clyde told me about a position at Harris Associates, which I had never heard of. Steve said I should take the job. This was in February 1983. Harris wasn't even a $2 billion firm then. I hung up and within a couple of minutes, Clyde called and invited me to visit the partners of Harris. Within minutes of talking with them, I saw a match in our investment thought processes that was exactly what I was missing in my prior job. We talked about stocks, and the overlap in what we were each researching was amazing. Driving back to Milwaukee that night, I knew this was the job I wanted. We came to terms very quickly and I started working at Harris in May 1983.

Kazanjian: *Did you start out as an analyst?*

Nygren: Yes. What I really liked about the research department was it was such an important part of Harris's investment process, and further everybody was a generalist. Almost everyone on Wall Street specializes in an industry. I have never liked that way of investing, especially for a value investor. Any investment idea I wanted to look at was open, though it had to be described in a value context, which is how I thought anyway. Still today our research department is made up of experienced analysts who are committed to value investing and who function as generalists. That group of nine professionals sources all the ideas we use in the Oakmark funds. I think it's the best group of analysts in the business and should get most of the credit for the excellent performance our fund family has achieved.

Kazanjian: *You eventually became the firm's director of research, right?*

Nygren: I became the director of research in 1990. A year later we started The Oakmark Fund, which Robert Sanborn managed. I worked very closely with Robert, especially in the first few years the fund was open. My job was to sort through all of our best ideas and make sure Robert and our other portfolio managers had most of their money invested in the names that I thought were our most promising stocks.

Kazanjian: *That fund was phenomenally successful from the start.*

Nygren: That fund launched in 1991 and it peaked in assets in April 1998 at $9.8 billion. We went from being a business that was entirely separate accounts split between wealthy individuals and institutions to one where the mutual fund business was the dominant piece of our asset base.

Kazanjian: *As I recall, a few key stocks really propelled the fund's performance in the beginning.*

Nygren: There were definitely a few standouts that had big performance impact. One was Liberty Media, which is a stock I worked on. Liberty was a spin-off from Telecommunications, Inc. Bob Levy, now our CEO, was a portfolio manager at the time. He had covered Telecommunications, Inc., at his prior job. So he went to the meeting where they discussed spinning off Liberty. He came back and said, "I've got a really strong hunch that Liberty is something we should get interested in, but I've got too much other stuff. Would you mind taking a look at this, Bill, to see if you can figure out what I haven't been able to quantify?"

Liberty put out a 600-page spin-off document that was the most complex thing I had ever seen. I worked through it and felt that Liberty was extremely cheap. The cable area was out of favor at the time. Liberty owned a hodge-podge of investments in various cable programming and cable systems. Most of them were private, so it was difficult to come up with precise valuations.

Our investment philosophy then, as it is now, was to try to identify companies that sell at less than 60 percent of their intrinsic value. Liberty appeared to be priced at less than 33 percent of its value. We also look for companies where that value grows over time. With cable programming we knew each year there would be more cable subscribers. The percentage of time viewers spent watching cable channels relative to network was growing every year and there was a large gap between what advertisers were paying per eyeball for cable versus the networks, which was slowly closing. Those things combined to give dramatic growing values in cable programming assets. The last thing we look for is economic alignment of a strong management team with the outside shareholders. We need to be able to believe that the management approaches their job with the mindset of an owner rather than that of a professional manager. We like to see them own stock, have options, and have incentives that are based on variables we think drive equity values. Seeing John Malone take zero cash compensation in exchange for a deal where he got a large options package was a strong endorsement of the value from the CEO.

From the time we bought our Liberty stock in 1991 until it was taken over by AT&T in 1998, it appreciated 60-fold. (It was up 20-fold when TCI reacquired it in 1994. It was then spun off again in 1995 and tripled before AT&T acquired it in 1998.) It was by far the biggest gainer I've ever been associated with. It was the ideal situation for a value investor—business value grew so rapidly that even though the stock was increasing in price nearly every day, it always traded at a discount to intrinsic value.

Kazanjian: *When did you get to start your own fund, Oakmark Select?*

Nygren: In November 1996. Our firm was going through a generational transition the year before Select launched. The founding partners were getting toward retirement age. They were interested in cashing out of some of their investment and capturing the value they created. We had another group of partners, including me, who was more concerned about what the next 25 years of working at Harris Associates would be like. To satisfy both groups, we sold the business to Nvest. For the first time in my life, I had enough capital that my annual investment returns had a meaningful change on my net worth. I started to become much more interested in how I was going to invest my personal money.

Working in an investment firm, there are tremendous constraints on how you can invest your own money. My thought was I'd like to have a portfolio of fewer than 20 stocks that were the best of the

100-plus names on our approved list. At the same time, I read some research showing how the average mutual fund investor today was so different from investors of 20 years ago. Twenty years ago, fund investors picked one fund for most of their assets. Now they were creating a portfolio of mutual funds. I concluded that the individual was getting into a position of paying active management fees for a portfolio that was likely to replicate the index. As a result, I thought it made sense for individual investors to use concentrated funds to build their fund portfolios. At the time, there were only two decent-sized funds that owned fewer than 20 names: Clipper Fund [managed by James Gipson, who is featured elsewhere in this book] and Sequoia. I was energized by the challenge of selling this controversial idea to the financial press, to investment advisors, and to individual investors. I was convinced I was on incredibly solid academic footing and could show people that concentrated investing made sense.

Kazanjian: *You hoped to sell them on the idea that they should own several concentrated funds, including yours, I assume.*

Nygren: Exactly. At first, I thought concentrated portfolios were too aggressive for the average investor. But when you combine multiple concentrated funds, stock-specific risk disappears from the portfolio.

Kazanjian: *Do you still recommend that investors build a portfolio of concentrated funds?*

Nygren: Yes. There are three very good uses for concentrated funds. One is for aggressive investors who really believe in a stock picker's ability, understand the risk, and are in it for the long term. The second use is as an index fund enhancement. You might think that an index fund is the antithesis of this concentrated approach. But it can be a nice combination. Investors could use an index fund for a large percentage of their assets, and put the rest in one or two concentrated funds.

Kazanjian: *Do you put all of your own money in Oakmark Select?*

Nygren: The majority of my net worth is in the two funds that I manage: Select and Oakmark. More is in Select because I've been involved in it longer and it suits my personality more.

Kazanjian: *Obviously your theory about concentrating in your best ideas has proved correct. Oakmark Select has been a very successful fund.*

Nygren: It seems ironic that five years ago I was sitting in a board meeting with my partners trying to convince them to start this fund. With so few examples of concentrated funds in the mutual fund industry, we argued about the likelihood of raising enough assets to make the fund profitable. Now we've had to close it down to new investors because it was growing to the point where we'd have to change our approach to keep up with the assets.

Kazanjian: *How big is the fund now?*

Nygren: Around $4 billion.

Kazanjian: *Does even that large amount of money impact your ability to be an effective concentrated investor?*

Nygren: I think up to around $5 billion we'll be fine. We don't want more than 20 names in the fund, and we want the ability to invest in mid-caps. The average mid-cap company has a market capitalization of about $5 billion. You couldn't run the fund the way I want to if it was larger than the midpoint of the mid-cap universe.

Kazanjian: *You also took over the flagship Oakmark Fund from Robert Sanborn in 2000.*

Nygren: That's correct. There's been a perception in the press that Robert was asked to step down from the fund because of performance. That is entirely untrue. The mutual decision for Robert to leave was over noninvestment issues. We felt we needed to name co-managers on all of our funds after one of our managers got sick and ultimately retired. Robert had a hard time with that. That was really the biggest issue that we couldn't come to terms on. I took over the portfolio in March 2000. From April 1998 through March 2000, the fund's assets fell from $9.8 billion to $2 billion, almost entirely from redemptions. Basically the sin we committed was having flattish results in a market where technology stocks drove the indices to large gains.

Kazanjian: *A lot of it came from holding on to perennial-value companies such as Philip Morris, which the roaring growth market ignored.*

Nygren: Exactly. The thing that a lot of people have missed is that if you move away from the indexes and look at the average stock, you'll see it was barely up in 1998 and 1999. The bull market was concentrated in a handful of stocks, notably technology stocks and large-cap growth companies.

Kazanjian: *And you generally don't buy technology.*

Nygren: That's true, but it's not that we dislike technology companies. One of Warren Buffett's best lessons for investors—and Warren is clearly one of my heroes in the business—is to invest within your circle of competence. Warren has always said, "I don't understand technology stocks, and because of that, I view them as outside my circle of competence." I think people have mistakenly taken that to mean if you're a value investor, you shouldn't ever look at technology.

We look at a technology company side by side with a food company, a utility, an oil company, or whatever. We don't have industries that we're predisposed to like or dislike. We apply the same criteria to a technology stock that we would a nontechnology stock. Is there an intrinsic value to this company that we think a cash buyer would be attracted to? Is the stock price less than 60 percent of that number? Is it a business where we're comfortable projecting growth over the next few years? Is it a business being run by somebody who's thinking like a shareholder, not a manager? More often than not, we have found that technology stocks are valued at levels that have not allowed us to use them in the portfolio. We've owned a handful of technology stocks over the past year. But we bought them consistent with the criteria we use for any other company. That means we were usually buying a company whose stock price had declined dramatically because they missed an earnings number.

Kazanjian: *We've touched on it as we've been talking, but lay out for us exactly what you're looking for in a company.*

Nygren: Three things. Academic theory says the only way to get higher returns is to take higher risk. We believe each of these three criteria simultaneously reduces risk and increases expected return. The first is a valuation criterion. We want a stock to sell at less than 60 percent of our estimate of intrinsic value. We try to estimate the price a cash buyer would pay if he or she were buying the business today. Each of those terms has important implications.

Word one is *today*. We're not trying to guess what somebody might pay for this business five years from now. We're trying to estimate what the business is worth today. If it hits 90 percent of that value, we sell.

Next is a *cash buyer*. You look back at the peak of the technology market, and there were lots of acquisition transactions occurring for stocks that were trading at enormous valuations. We don't look at stock swap transactions as being reflective of business values unless we're very comfortable that the acquirer's stock is not significantly overvalued. I equate some of the technology transactions to some of the swaps my daughter was making for Beanie Babies. These girls went out and bought their $5 Beanie Babies. Then they read in a magazine that one of them was worth $200. They took two that they read were worth $100 and swapped them for one that was worth $200. They had an economically fair transaction, but they were really trading $5 Beanie Babies. When we look back on the transactions that were occurring in the high-tech sector and the Internet companies in 1999–2000, it had the same flavor as the Beanie Baby trades.

The other word that's important in there is *estimate*. This isn't a precise business of coming to an exact number of what a business is worth in an acquisition. The reality is that if we're estimating a value at $40, we're saying that somewhere from the mid-thirties to the mid-forties is a reasonable guess of what this company would be acquired at if it were to be acquired today. That lack of precision doesn't negate the investment approach because of the discounts available in the market. We try to buy at less than 60 percent. If we think a company is worth $40, our maximum purchase price is $24. If we're wrong on the analysis and it's only worth $32, that's still a substantial discount to where we were buying the stock.

Kazanjian: *So the discount is number one.*

Nygren: Yes. During the time that we own the stock, the analyst's job is to watch how the fundamentals are unfolding, especially if they're different from what we anticipated when we bought the stock. We don't increase a sell target just because the stock went up. We increase a sell target either because cash flows are coming in stronger than we expected, because there's new evidence of similar businesses being acquired at higher prices than we previously assumed, or because interest rates have come down a lot and that requires an increase in the target. The important thing is that changes in our targets are based on fundamentals, not on stock prices.

The second thing we look for is a business where we are comfortable projecting that the value will grow as time passes. As a ballpark number, I would like to see estimated annual per-share business value growth plus annual dividend yield exceed 10 percent. I get to that number because if you go back over a long period of history, 10 percent is typical of the long-term return on the stock market. If we are getting a 10 percent combination of yield and value growth, then we are only depending on the closing of the value gap to produce our excess return instead of producing our entire return.

This criterion keeps us out of the catalyst-driven approach of investing in structurally disadvantaged companies that you see employed by a lot of our value peers. I'd love to have a catalyst in my companies, but generally the market makes you pay up a lot for that. Since our companies have values that increase with time, I can utilize the advantage of patience.

Kazanjian: *To recap, you want to pay at most 60 percent of intrinsic value and you want a business where you're comfortable projecting the value will grow. What's the third thing you look for?*

Nygren: The third thing is management. We want a management that not only has a history of success, but that also is economically aligned with its shareholder base. We look for things like how much stock they own. Is it a large part of their net worth? What kind of options do they have? What kind of incentives do they have in their annual compensation? Are their incentives tied to growing sales of the company? If so, maybe we should be worried that they'll go out and make acquisitions that will contribute to sales growth, but that will dilute per share value. Or are their incentives tied to measures such as return on capital that better track equity price performance? We're likely to own a stock for three to five years. The management team is likely to face a handful of key decisions during that period. We want to make sure they approach those decisions with the mindset of an owner rather than a professional manager.

Kazanjian: *Is your sell discipline equally strict?*

Nygren: The analyst changes the sell target only to reflect changes in business fundamentals. If a stock exceeds 90 percent of value, it's sold. There are two exceptions to that rule. One is for taxes, because we manage our funds to maximize long-term after-tax returns. If a stock price hits its sell target but doesn't exceed it by a lot in less than a year, quite often we hold the position for a year and a day and go long-term. The second exception is we will sell a stock when we believe it no longer fits one of our three criteria. If the fundamentals aren't unfolding in a way that's growing value or if management isn't behaving in the interest of shareholders, we'll sell regardless of how cheap the stock looks relative to intrinsic value.

Kazanjian: *Is that also the rationale for selling a stock that doesn't go up?*

Nygren: Exactly. A lot of people ask how far we'd let the stock price fall before we'd sell. I have almost infinite patience for a stock that's going down if the business is growing well. In fact, lots of times I'll add to my position. I lose patience quickly when the fundamental story isn't unfolding the way I thought it should.

Kazanjian: *Where do you get most of your investment ideas?*

Nygren: As I said earlier, almost all of our ideas are generated by our internal research analysts. They find these ideas from two basic sources. A small percentage come from stocks that have had favorable news developments that we think the market has underreacted to. The majority of our ideas come from stocks that have fallen substantially because Wall Street is treating short-term problems as if they are secular [going to last for an extended period of time]. Our analysts start by looking at stocks that seem cheap—in other words, stocks that have come down a lot, stocks with low PEs relative to other companies in their industry, and stocks with low price-to-sales ratios. We also seek out companies with new management that we think highly of, and companies that our trusted contacts have suggested.

Kazanjian: *What's the main difference between Oakmark and Oakmark Select?*

Nygren: Oakmark Select has 20 or fewer stocks, and anything mid- or large-cap is fair game. Oakmark has about 50 of what I call larger companies—not necessarily large-cap, but large based on business fundamentals, such as sales, income, or equity. Oakmark is designed to have lower risk than Oakmark Select. One way we accomplish that is by having more holdings. Another is by investing in established businesses.

Nygren told me that when I first called about including him in the book, he wasn't sure that he was worthy, since he hadn't run a fund for very long. Then he realized that he'd been in the business more than 20 years, working behind the scenes for much of that time. I'm sure you'll agree that Nygren's inclusion is well deserved. The question is whether all of his recent success will ultimately spoil his returns. So far, it's business as usual. And given this guy's smarts, I wouldn't be surprised to see his unblemished record continue. ■

KEVIN O'BOYLE

ASTER INVESTMENT MANAGEMENT

K evin O'Boyle is by far the most inexperi-
enced manager you'll meet in this book.
He began his career in the investment industry in 1994, and almost immediately began
managing the Meridian Value Fund, which,
during his short tenure, has consistently
posted numbers at the head of its class. As a result, O'Boyle has rapidly
gained the respect of both his peers and admiring shareholders.

Although O'Boyle is only 37, if he had his way, he would have entered the investment business much sooner. Fresh out of Stanford, he
began his career as an accountant with a big-five firm, but quickly discovered that he'd rather analyze stocks than audit books. Getting in the
door was difficult, so he did what he saw as the next best thing: He
joined a San Francisco real estate advisory firm as an analyst. That was
right before the property market crashed.

O'Boyle returned to school, figuring that with an MBA he'd have a
better shot at doing what he really wanted: being an investment manager. During his first summer back at Stanford, O'Boyle interned at a
performance fund in Santa Barbara, where he analyzed a southern California company called Pacific Physician Services. He thought the business had great potential and the ability to take its model nationwide.
When O'Boyle graduated, he went to work for the company as its busi-

ness development manager. Unfortunately, things weren't as rosy as he imagined, and he was soon looking for something else to do.

His big break came in the summer of 1994, when O'Boyle's former boss at the Santa Barbara fund told him about an opening with Richard Aster. Aster ran the Meridian Growth Fund from his office near San Francisco. The two met and immediately connected, discovering that they shared many investment philosophies. O'Boyle began as Aster's assistant, and a short time later was handed the reins of Meridian Value.

O'Boyle's investment technique is derived from some of Aster's theories that O'Boyle set out to prove. In essence, he looks for troubled companies that have fallen significantly in price as earnings have continued to go down. It sounds like a recipe for disaster. But with experienced cooks in the kitchen, the recipe has worked extremely well.

Kazanjian: *You started your professional life as an accountant.*

O'Boyle: I never aspired or dreamed of becoming an accountant. I went to Stanford University and studied economics. My strengths and interests academically were the liberal arts, but I was pretty analytical. Upon graduating, it seemed prudent to pursue a business career. Accounting was a good place to start.

Kazanjian: *Where did you grow up?*

O'Boyle: In Walnut Creek, California, outside of San Francisco.

Kazanjian: *Did you have any exposure to the stock market growing up?*

O'Boyle: *Not really. My father is a retired civil servant and my mom is a homemaker and part-time travel consultant.*

Kazanjian: *What did you do after Stanford?*

O'Boyle: I was hired by Arthur Young, which is now part of Ernst and Young. It's one of the big-five accounting firms. I did not have much of an accounting background, but one of the partners was a Stanford grad and he wanted to bring in some Stanford people. I was hired as an auditor and took accounting courses at night. I sort of learned on the job.

Kazanjian: *What were you doing?*

O'Boyle: I was part of an engagement team that would go out and check over the client's books. Then we would issue an opinion on the financials. I did that for two years. I didn't like the day-to-day work, but I stuck it out and got my CPA. After a while, I decided the rewards for staying in that profession, even if I made it all the way up to partner, didn't outweigh the costs, at least in terms of enjoying my job and the amount of time and effort involved.

Kazanjian: *There's really not a lot of money in accounting, is there?*

O'Boyle: No. To the extent that there is, it's by becoming a partner. When you become a partner, you're paid for your ability to bring in new clients. There isn't money in being an accountant per se.

Kazanjian: *So what did you do?*

O'Boyle: I went to work for a boutique real estate advisory firm in San Francisco called Piedmont Realty Advisors. I found that job through the Stanford career center. It turned out one of the analysts working there was a high school classmate of mine. I think that's what got me the interview. My initial job was as a financial analyst, essentially modeling cash flows to help underwrite real estate acquisitions. I also performed sensitivity analyses on properties that were already in the portfolios so we could make leasing and operating decisions. It was quantitative in nature.

Kazanjian: *How did you like that job?*

O'Boyle: I found it much more interesting than accounting, especially because the thought process that goes into understanding investments is similar to the one used to understand real estate. But I didn't find real estate itself to be particularly interesting.

Kazanjian: *When did you do this?*

O'Boyle: Late 1988. I was there until the end of 1990.

Kazanjian: *I still don't get a sense that you were really interested in the stock market at that point.*

O'Boyle: I should qualify that. When I left Arthur Young, I wanted to get into the investment management business, preferably on the stock market side. I looked hard and tried to get my foot in the door at a few places within the Bay Area, and didn't have a whole lot of luck. Granted, I really didn't know much about the business or how to go about looking for a job in the business, but I took the position with Piedmont Realty to try to get more experience on the investment analysis side, as opposed to financial reporting and accounting, where I started.

Kazanjian: *What made you interested in the investment business?*

O'Boyle: I started saving some money and was trying to figure out how to put it to work. I began reading investment books and investigating mutual funds. I thought it was something I'd like to do on a full-time basis.

Kazanjian: *I take it that after awhile at Piedmont, you decided that wasn't what you wanted to do either.*

O'Boyle: That's right. In 1990, the real estate market started to crash. That had two implications. One, ironically enough, I was given more responsibility within our firm. Two, it meant that our firm's prospects were deteriorating. I decided to go back to business school. I was accepted at a couple of schools and chose to go back to Stanford. I attended Stanford Business School from fall of 1991 until spring of 1993. When I went back to business school, I wrote in my application that I had two possible objectives. One was to move into stock market investing and the other was to position myself in an operations role within an entrepreneurial business. But I really, really wanted to get into the money management business and invest in stocks.

Kazanjian: *When did you finally get that chance?*

O'Boyle: Each summer of my two years back at Stanford, I went to work for a performance fund in Santa Barbara run by a Stanford alum named Tim Bliss. Bliss considered Phil Fisher [a noted growth investor] to be his mentor. I had read both of Fisher's books. As a result, we hit it off in terms of investment philosophies. The fund was focused on investing in what you'd call micro-cap stocks. After graduation, I looked for some full-time jobs in the money management field, but wound up taking an operational position with Pacific Physician Services, a company located in Redlands, California, that had been my principal investment recommendation during my summer internship. I thought that this firm had a chance to take its business plan from the Southern California market and perhaps expand it nationwide.

Kazanjian: *What kind of company was it?*

O'Boyle: It was a physician practice management company. Essentially it helped organize doctors into medical groups and facilitated their management of HMO patients. The key was that when physicians care for HMO patients, they have to be much more cost-sensitive because they tend to get paid a fixed amount of money to treat the patients. They usually don't have the economic training or tools with which to do that effectively. Pacific Physician Services had been quite successful in organizing the physicians, negotiating good contracts with the HMOs, and enabling both the physicians and the company itself to prosper. Unfortunately, the practice of medicine is heavily influenced by local factors. Therefore, you could not take a model from one geographic location and necessarily replicate it in another. It took me a few months to figure that out. After less than one year I started pursuing other opportunities.

Kazanjian: *Since we're already up to 1994, I take it this time you finally were determined to get into th,e investment business.*

O'Boyle: In the spring of 1994, Tim Bliss told me that Rick Aster, who manages the Meridian Growth Fund, was looking for an analyst to assist him. Aster had also started a value fund, which did not yet have a portfolio manager. I sent Rick a letter and asked if I could come up and talk with him. I then did a lot more research on him, his investment approach, his background, and track record. I pursued this opportunity as aggressively as I could. After three months of pestering, he gave me an opportunity to come aboard.

Kazanjian: *You trained under a growth guy. Was Rick more value-oriented?*

O'Boyle: Rick is a growth stock investor, but he has always been sensitive to valuation. His philosophy is to invest in companies generating strong returns on equity that are market leaders and operate in markets experiencing rapid growth. He believes that if those companies have sustainable competitive advantages and are bought at a reasonable price, you can generate very good returns over time. The Meridian Growth Fund, which he still manages, has been one of the best-performing funds for the past 15 years.

Kazanjian: *You started out as Rick's assistant?*

O'Boyle: I was hired to be a research analyst to help him with management of the Meridian Growth Fund.

Kazanjian: *Was the Meridian Value Fund around then?*

O'Boyle: He started Meridian Value in February 1994. I came aboard in September of 1994. He was looking for a manager for that fund and wasn't really doing much with it.

Kazanjian: *How did you get involved with it?*

O'Boyle: In late 1994, Rick came up with a hypothesis for a strategy to manage the Meridian Value Fund. As a result of his long experience in growth stock investing, he had observed that companies with up to a year's worth of negative earnings growth or earnings decline from the previous year tended to decline dramatically in market value. When the company got its operational results back on track, those stocks tended to do extraordinarily well. As a small-cap growth investor, he observed that when small and midsize companies stumble operationally, they can represent compelling opportunities. He thought that could be the basis for a sound value investment strategy.

Rick sprung the hypothesis on me and asked me to do a research study. We established some simple and conservative rules. I went back and looked at 15 years' worth of data—one of those infamous back-tested studies. If we had done X, Y, and Z, what would have been the result? I assumed that there was no fundamental research applied in achieving these results. It was purely a quantitative exercise. I completed the study early in the spring of 1995 and came to the conclusion that if we had employed Rick's strategy, we would have dramatically outperformed the S&P 500 over the period under examination, which was 1981 to 1994. While doing this study, I became convinced it was a strategy that made sense and could produce good investment returns if applied correctly. Rick told me to give it a go in real life. So, in June 1995, I became the lead manager for the Meridian Value Fund, which had less than $1 million in assets.

Kazanjian: *And you employed this strategy in running it?*

O'Boyle: That's right. Obviously we've had to modify the strategy as we've gained experience with it, but it has worked out pretty well so far.

Kazanjian: *Most of the time Meridian Value is categorized as being either a small- or mid-cap fund. Is that your area of focus?*

O'Boyle: We have no market cap constraints. We have always invested in large-caps and always will. A lot of the best investment opportunities have been in the small-to-mid-cap arena, and it also happens to be the area in which both Rick and I are most comfortable operating.

Kazanjian: *Apparently the theory has proved to be pretty successful in action. Sometimes people back-test a hypothesis, get good results, but then find that theory doesn't work as well in reality.*

O'Boyle: In this case, the essence of the strategy definitely made sense. The study confirmed that it made sense, and the actual practice has confirmed this as well.

Kazanjian: *Let's get into the specifics of the strategy.*

O'Boyle: The strategy is based on two key assumptions. The first is that the stock market tends to be very myopic and extrapolates short-term trends too far into the future. The second is that underlying business values tend not to be as volatile as equity prices or the earnings of a particular business.

Kazanjian: *What do you attribute Wall Street's myopic view to?*

O'Boyle: I could give you all sorts of conjectures, but I really don't know. Markets tend to go up and down independent of whether a business enterprise is changing or not. Because stock markets are more volatile than underlying business value, it presents opportunities to buy at lower valuations. Conversely, it can also result in periods of time when stocks are dramatically overvalued.

Kazanjian: *Do you care about the overall market environment then?*

O'Boyle: Not really. We look at each company on an individual basis. Obviously we have to take the macroeconomic environment into consideration when we evaluate the prospects for a company, but we're not really looking at the overall market. In fact, Meridian Value has a mandate to keep the cash level at less than or equal to 10 percent of the overall fund.

Kazanjian: *Given the backdrop you just talked about, what are you looking for in terms of finding individual companies for the portfolio?*

O'Boyle: First, we're looking for companies where the actual or projected earnings-per-share growth for the next three quarters is negative. A company has either suffered three consecutive quarters where earnings have gone down compared to the prior year or this is projected to occur. We're looking for a company whose stock price has dropped 50 percent or more from its 52-week high.

Kazanjian: *Let me get this straight. You're looking for companies with declining earnings?*

O'Boyle: Yes.

Kazanjian: *That's directly opposite of what everyone else on Wall Street seems to be searching for.*

O'Boyle: That's right. And we want situations where the stock price has gone down 50 percent or more.

Kazanjian: *Plus, you are looking for stocks that have already had three down quarters, or those that you predict will have three down quarters.*

O'Boyle: Either/or. The reason why it's either/or is that when we did this study, we looked at companies that already had three down quarters. But markets are efficient enough, and our fund is now large enough, that if a company comes out and makes a negative pre-announcement, it becomes clear that earnings will be down for quite a while. In such cases, the stock drops dramatically the next day and we start focusing on the opportunity. We can't always wait for three quarters of down earnings to materialize.

Kazanjian: *It seems like companies with declining earnings would be the worst investments you could own. They probably have a lot of trouble, and earnings drive stock prices.*

O'Boyle: We're not looking for troubled companies, although we won't necessarily remove troubled companies from consideration. The thesis here is that most companies eventually stumble from an operational standpoint. That operational stumble can result from company-specific issues, or it can result from industrywide problems that are having an impact on this particular company.

We focus on companies that are market leaders, that have a history of generating good returns on capital, or that own an asset that cannot be easily replicated and is capable of generating good returns on capital in the future. We're looking for companies with cash flows that are strong enough to support the capital structure in place even during times when they've stumbled from an operational stand-point, and/or companies with a strong balance sheet that can access the capital market if necessary. Finally, we're looking for companies that participate in mature markets where changes in industry structure or regulations will provide a growth opportunity.

To get back to your original question, the world is not a tidy and neat place. Companies make mistakes. They stumble and have industry conditions turn negative on them all the time. That can cause a temporary decline in profitability. Our observation is that when companies do have these periods of negative earnings growth, their stocks get hammered. Yet the underlying value of the firm and the long-term business prospects for the firm may still be quite good.

Kazanjian: *Is there a particular reason why these companies run into problems?*

O'Boyle: We have identified a number of issues that they seem to have in common. On the company-specific side, those that make acquisitions often have a lot of trouble digesting the acquisition. Either they pay too much and it results in a dilution to earnings, or they actually have trouble integrating the acquired company into the operation from either a cultural or a logistical standpoint. That can result in much higher operating costs than originally projected.

In the technology field in particular, companies often miss product cycles. When they miss product cycles, they lose market share. Sometimes they expect revenue growth to continue. Then they miss a product cycle, and revenues disappoint, though the cost structure is still high. This results in a dramatic decline in earnings.

Companies will often stretch to meet their growth objectives. They may even outgrow their resources. When they stretch or grow faster than the resources can accommodate, operations and customer service tend to fall. This can eventually result in earnings disappointments.

In some companies, revenues are concentrated among a few customers. If one customer runs into difficulties, that can have an immediate impact on the earnings of the company selling to the customer. Back when Y2K was a big issue, a lot of companies were experiencing implementation problems with their information technology (IT) systems. That resulted in costs being much higher than expected and the inability to get product out the door in a timely manner. These are the kinds of company-specific problems that occur and recur that we find all the time.

On an industry-related basis, there are many companies that run into the problem of too much capacity built out in their particular industry. That results in pricing pressure and margin erosion and causes profitability to decline. In industries where there's a change in government regulations, such changes can have an impact on future earnings. That's a situation where a company's business model may no longer make sense and there will be an adjustment period before it gets back on a growth track.

Finally, there are many companies that participate in industries and markets where growth has been rapid and the market becomes saturated. The company's core business experiences a revenue growth slowdown and they must invest heavily in new products or growth opportunities. That usually results in some sort of earnings decline or transition before they can get back on track, if they ever **do.**

Kazanjian: *You're looking for three quarters of down earnings. Is there magic to that number?*

O'Boyle: When we originally tested the hypothesis, what we noticed was that the first time a company reports an earnings disappointment, it's usually just an acknowledgment that there's a problem. There's normally no such thing as one bad quarter. Not only that, it's usually only after the second earnings disappointment that the stock really collapses. We feel that it takes at least two down quarters before the stock price declines dramatically and the problem that cropped up begins to be addressed. It's in the third quarter that problems are getting fixed.

Kazanjian: *Is one of your criteria for buying a stock that you won't buy it until it's had the third disappointment?*

O'Boyle: When we first started the fund back in 1995, we would actually wait until a company had had at least three down quarters before buying. However, if we did that today, the investment returns wouldn't be as good as they are. There are two reasons for this: One is that markets are fairly efficient. After a couple of down quarters, stocks get hammered and those who see compelling value get in. Second, we're investing in a greater number of large companies now than we did five or six years ago. The markets are more efficient for large companies. We do not necessarily wait for a company to have three down quarters. Before we buy, we want to gain confidence that the business has not been permanently impaired. We hope the business prospects for the company have bottomed out or are showing signs of sustained improvement, so the company can get its operating margins back to historic levels and resume revenue growth. But there's a trade-off. To the extent that we have a lot of confidence that business prospects are going to be solid going forward, the valuation tends not to be as compelling.

Kazanjian: *That's the whole risk/reward ratio. You pay more for less risk.*

O'Boyle: That's right. If we have a firm belief that the company is going to be able to achieve a certain margin and the revenue growth over a five-year period is going to be X percent, we will come up with a valuation based on those assumptions. If the stock's present value looks compelling, we'll start buying, even though we know the company is still experiencing tremendous operating difficulties and it could be a while before things get going again. There are other situations where the valuation isn't that compelling and there are too many uncertainties, so we just wait.

Kazanjian: *How do you find your potential candidates?*

O'Boyle: We have a computer screen that we run on a monthly basis.

Kazanjian: *What are you looking for?*

O'Boyle: Companies that have either had or are projected to have three down quarters and a decline greater than or equal to 50 percent in the price of the stock. Second, we follow the news every day. When good companies report an earnings disappointment, they immediately go on our "monitor" list.

Kazanjian: *So if you're watching CNBC, for example, and you hear about a company that's missed its earnings numbers for the quarter, you may put it down as something to monitor, but wouldn't immediately buy it if it was just the first quarter of disappointment?*

O'Boyle: That's correct.

Kazanjian: *But you might on the second?*

O'Boyle: Possibly, but usually we'll wait even longer.

Kazanjian: *So you've found a company, it's missed two or three quarters, it looks interesting, but it obviously has some type of problem causing earnings to go down. How do you properly analyze whether the trouble is going to fix itself after the third quarter, or whether it's a more terminal problem?*

O'Boyle: The first thing that we try to assess is whether the business model has been impaired permanently or whether it's a temporary situation. For example, a change in government regulations is permanent, so I would be cautious about investing in a company whose whole world has been thrown into turmoil. In most cases, a company I'm interested in is a market leader in a growing market that has proven it can generate strong returns on capital. It has simply had some operational issues crop up, resulting in the earnings decline.

The things I look for to resolve the problem include new management, a new board of directors if the problem is particularly severe, a restructuring of operations, and the development and imminent launch of new products. If there's excess capacity, I'm looking to see that there's consolidation taking place within the industry, so that capacity is being reduced, thus reducing the flow of capital and making it tougher for new competitors.

Kazanjian: *Even though you buy a lot of small companies, it sounds like you're really looking for companies that have been around awhile, as opposed to recent IPOs that are missing earnings estimates because they don't have earnings to begin with.*

O'Boyle: Our first preference is companies with strong operating histories that have proven that the economics of their business work. Having said that, we don't limit ourselves to companies that have made operating profits in the past. There's sort of a trade-off. A lot of the companies that participate in the fastest growing markets tend to have somewhat limited operating histories and may not have completely proven their economic model. But we still think those are investments worth considering.

Kazanjian: *How do you determine whether it's a good stock to buy from a valuation perspective?*

O'Boyle: We try to establish a normalized cash-earnings-per-share target. In other words, if the business model is working, what will the profit margins be for the company? Taking the capital structure into account, what could it potentially achieve in earnings? That's where I start. I look at that price to what I would call normalized cash earnings relative to the company's historic valuation, relative to industry comparables, and sometimes compared to market averages. We also run the numbers through a discounted cash flow model and compare that to the price-to-normalized-cash-earnings per share.

The idea here is we're trying to buy the company at what we consider to be a discount to its business value. There are no fixed valuation parameters that we employ because we consider time risk as well as price risk. Therefore, I'm not going to say we'll only buy a stock at X percent discount to the business value. As I mentioned before, if the company has really gotten back on track, and we have a lot of confidence in that, we're willing to buy at a price that may be a bit more than we would if there were more uncertainty.

Kazanjian: *Do you find that, even though you're looking on a company-by-company basis, you tend to run into the same sectors at the same time, since such problems tend to be common among all companies in a given industry?*

O'Boyle: Absolutely. For example, right now about every telecommunications service provider is on our list. There was a huge amount of capital that went into the industry and a tremendous build out of infrastructures. Now it turns out there's too much supply for the demand that's out there. Having said that, there are lots of individual companies with problems that are not necessarily related to the industry as a whole.

Kazanjian: *When you have a case like that, where the whole industry seems to be in trouble, how do you determine which stocks in the sector to buy?*

O'Boyle: We try to find those companies with the strongest competitive position, the strongest balance sheet, and the best management. Often you're not going to find all three characteristics in the same company. We have to weigh the variables and decide which one, two, or three we'll end up investing in.

Kazanjian: *Do you try to limit the amount of exposure you have in any one sector?*

O'Boyle: We definitely try to maintain a diversified portfolio. It's written in the fund's prospectus that we will not have more than 25 percent of the fund in any one sector.

Kazanjian: *How many stocks do you tend to own?*

O'Boyle: Prior to this year, we limited the fund to 40 holdings, roughly equally weighted. Because our assets have increased so substantially, we've increased the number of holdings to over 60. Our long-term goal is to keep the number of holdings as low as possible, but that will depend on the amount of assets we have under management.

Kazanjian: *How much do you have right now?*

O'Boyle: About $700 million.

Kazanjian: *Have you thought about closing the fund?*

O'Boyle: We have decided not to close the fund for the foreseeable future. We'll let the market tell us how much money we should manage. Since we don't have any market cap constraints, we really don't know what that amount is. I will tell you that we are limiting each initial investment in the micro-cap area to 1 percent of the fund's assets, which is something we didn't used to do.

Kazanjian: *What makes you sell a stock?*

O'Boyle: We'll sell if the business fundamentals either stop improving or start deteriorating. We'll also sell if the investment thesis works out, the business fundamentals remain strong, but the price moves far ahead of what we consider the underlying business value to be. Finally, we'll sell if the business fundamentals fail to materialize as we expect and/or we come to the conclusion that we made a mistake in our analysis.

Kazanjian: *How long are you willing to hold out before coming to that conclusion?*

O'Boyle: The first time a business development takes me dramatically by surprise, I become concerned. I will almost always give management the benefit of the doubt. If it happens a second time, which can be as soon as six months, I revisit the thesis and often may decide I made a mistake and sell the stock.

Kazanjian: *What is your average holding period?*

O'Boyle: On average, we'll hold a stock for 18 months.

Kazanjian: *When you do make a mistake or the company doesn't work out as planned, what's the most common reason?*

O'Boyle: Probably the most common underlying reason is that my assessment of management's capabilities was too optimistic.

Kazanjian: *Do you try to meet with management before you buy the stock?*

O'Boyle: We do not always meet with management in person, but I do try to talk to management one way or another before making an investment.

Kazanjian: *One interesting thing about your fund is that it's been pretty successful in different kinds of markets. It did well when growth stocks shined, and outperformed when value was in the spotlight. Is it your theory that this approach will work in all different market environments?*

O'Boyle: We think the fund should do reasonably well in all different environments. In 1999, when the Nasdaq was up 85 percent and the fund was up 38 percent, our technology holdings did better than the Nasdaq. We have found that no matter how strong the economy, we usually have plenty of investment opportunities to consider.

Kazanjian: *On the other hand, since you're buying companies with some type of earnings problems, how will this strategy work now that we're in a recession?*

O'Boyle: It remains to be seen. What I will say is that we are focused on this trade-off between improving business prospects and compelling valuation. If we buy a stock at a cheap enough price, even when things are difficult and not necessarily getting better, we believe our downside should be reasonably limited. To date, it has been our experience that if we make a mistake, our downside is usually about 30 percent, while our upside potential is often 100 percent or more over a two-to-three–year time horizon.

I ended the interview by asking O'Boyle if he felt he might become a victim of his own success. After all, Meridian Value has grown from $700,000 to more than $700 million in a short time. When you buy small stocks, as O'Boyle often does, it's harder to remain competitive and nimble as your assets grow. O'Boyle admits his job was easier when assets were lower, but he believes the strategy will continue to work going forward. And, if he does have a period of underperformance, he'd view that as a perfect time for investors to get into the fund. In his mind, the best time to get into any investment is when it's out of favor. ■

ROBERT OLSTEIN

OLSTEIN FINANCIAL ALERT FUND

Bob Olstein has been a vocal force in the investment business for more than three decades. After learning his craft as a young analyst, he and a partner launched an investment newsletter in the 1970s that blew the whistle on high-flying go-go stocks poised to come crashing down. They found these companies by tearing apart financial statements for signs that earnings were being sweetened through aggressive accounting.

After selling the publication to his partner, Olstein began managing money the same way—only in reverse. Instead of looking for companies that appeared to be cooking the books, he sought out businesses with solid financials that were underappreciated by Wall Street.

At age 59, Olstein isn't afraid to speak out about the stocks he likes or abhors. His early negativity on Boston Chicken got a lot of ink, as did his more recent warnings about Lucent Technologies. When Bob Olstein talks, investors listen. His comments can quickly drive stock prices up or down, although he insists he doesn't think about this power when making his predictions.

Because he is focused on the numbers, Olstein rarely talks with company management, reasoning that they almost always present a positive view of the business and are rarely honest about what's going wrong. He's also leery of most Wall Street research, maintaining that most analysts are afraid to put out negative reports for fear of losing underwriting business for their firm.

Although his fund is one of the more expensive ones out there, Olstein claims it's highly priced for a reason. Among his satisfied shareholders: hedge fund legend George Soros.

Kazanjian: *You've been making waves on Wall Street for some time.*

Olstein: I've been at this for 34 years. I made my name back in the early 1970s when I co-founded a research service called the *Quality of Earnings Report*. This was the largest grossing research service of its kind. My partner, Thornton O'glove, and I looked behind the numbers in financial statements for companies that weren't telling it like it was. In essence, we adjusted a company's earnings for economic reality rather than generally accepted accounting principles. We broke the problems with Penn Central, Levitz Furniture, and others. We were on the front page of *The Wall Street Journal*. We testified before the House Banking Committee. We were called "the watchdogs of Wall Street." Everybody was reading our research reports.

Kazanjian: *You have also taken issue with the value/growth categorization game.*

Olstein: A lot of young people in the industry came up with this large-cap/small-cap and value/growth stuff. Growth is a component of my definition of value. Thus, I buy growth companies in the portfolio. I just value them properly. I say there are two kinds of funds out there: value funds and overvalued funds. Value funds select companies according to a model of discounted cash flow. It is very important in this business to pay the right price for a company whether it is classified as a value company or a growth company. The long-term performers in our industry are the funds that make the fewest errors, as opposed to those that pick the most winners. You must play defense first, and one of the basic rules of defense is to pay the right price.

Kazanjian: *Sounds logical, although some of those aggressive momentum-oriented funds have done pretty well.*

Olstein: A few of those guys are very good at it. They have what I call this extraterrestrial power of being able to judge the psychology of crowds. They have a good gut feeling. I don't know how you do it, but there are some people who can. The crowd determines the price of a stock at any point in time. Investors are always voting. They have a perception about a company. The price of the company's stock is based on that perception at any point in time. A value guy like me tries to predict when these perceptions are wrong and will eventually change. Other people look at the perception out there and play the stock until they actually notice a change. People who can determine the psychology of crowds are the top performers. But there are very few of them.

Kazanjian: *That's a tough game to play, especially because you've got to know the exact time to get out.*

Olstein: They're making money at the expense of others. They're playing the "greater fool" game [hoping a greater fool will come in and pay an even higher price for the stock]. My definition of value is much looser than probably 98 percent of those on the Street. I like to say I run an eclectic value fund. That means I look at cash flow and can buy any category of stock based on a model of discounted cash flow returns compared to U.S. Treasuries. I'll buy everything from technology to cyclical companies. I'll go into large-caps and small-caps. It makes no difference to me.

Kazanjian: *Were you interested in the stock market as a youngster growing up in the Bronx?*

Olstein: No. I didn't even know the stock market existed. I actually thought I was going to be an actuary when I went to college and got my MBA at Michigan State University.

Kazanjian: *An actuary doesn't seem to fit a guy with your personality. What did you do after graduation?*

Olstein: I went to work for Arthur Andersen in their management consulting division. In those days, to work there you had to go to audit school because auditing was a big part of the job.

Kazanjian: *When did the investing bug hit?*

Olstein: I became very concerned about the Vietnam War. In those days there was an exemption for education. I left Arthur Andersen and taught at Hofstra University part-time while studying for a Ph.D. I had one professor who was interested in the stock market. He made us do an analysis on a company. He told me to do my analysis on

Control Data. This was in 1967. After doing a thorough analysis, I was convinced that Control Data had some temporary problems that were going to clear up. I asked my dad if I could borrow some money to buy some Control Data stock. He laughed because he didn't have any money. I watched from the sidelines as Control Data tripled, and I became enamored with the stock market.

In 1968, when I turned 26, I was no longer eligible to go to war. I quit school and took a job as a securities analyst at a small retail firm. It was a wild bull market and I got involved with analyzing go-go stocks. My life's objective was to make $300 a week. I worked for Chuck Royce [who is featured elsewhere in this book]. Chuck was one of the go-go managers of the day. He sent me out to see a company in Texas that was making night vision equipment.

In those days, I didn't understand that management didn't always tell it like it was. I was enthralled with their technology. Not only were they making night vision equipment, which was being sold to the Army for use in Vietnam, but they also had other exciting products on the horizon. For example, they had gamma rays that you could put on your head to get a good night's sleep in 15 minutes. I wrote a research report on the stock and went around selling it to institutions. The stock doubled overnight. I brought in all kinds of institutional business to this retail firm. All of a sudden, the stock started going down. I couldn't figure it out. I learned that another analyst wrote a negative research report on the company. I called him to see what he was saying. He was an MBA fresh out of Columbia. He told me he had all kinds of studies showing this night vision equipment was heading south because the war was winding down. The stock continued to go down and the company continued to report up earnings. One day I called the management and said, "The rumor is your quarter is going to be down." They replied, "Bob, don't worry about it. The quarter will not be down." I came into work the next day and saw that there were no earnings listed for the company in the earnings report section of *The Wall Street Journal*. I thought it was a misprint that it was left blank. It wasn't. The stock opened down 30 percent. Everybody at the firm wanted to lynch me because we had a big position in the stock. I was gravely disturbed that management didn't tell it like it was. I'd never failed at anything, and here I was losing people's money. I was ready to leave the business.

Kazanjian: *You obviously didn't.*

Olstein: For that I have to credit Thornton O'glove, a young U.C. Berkeley graduate who was working at the firm as an analyst. He said, "Bob, you should have looked at those numbers. There was an early warning alert there. Had you read the numbers, you would have realized the company's earnings were turning down a year ago."

He and I decided to team up and founded the *Quality of Earnings Report*. We sold this research to institutions, warning them of where trouble could develop, but without making any buy or sell recommendations. After doing this for 10 years, I realized the real winners in the investment game are the guys who make the fewest errors, not the guys who pick the most winners.

Kazanjian: *How were you finding these potentially troubled companies?*

Olstein: By reading anything we could, looking for hot spots, scouring financial statements, checking out things that looked too good, watching for promotional management [management good at producing hype, but with little or no substance to back it up], and the like.

Kazanjian: *Were people using your information to short stocks?*

Olstein: They were using it to short, to avoid problems, a little bit of everything.

Kazanjian: *You must have been hated by management at the companies you followed.*

Olstein: Oh, they all hated us. Even the analysts hated us when we said bad things about their stocks. They thought that if they shot the messenger, the bad news would go away.

Kazanjian: *Were you relying strictly on accounting to do your analysis?*

Olstein: Financial reporting. We'd go in and look behind the numbers. We were not doing any fundamental research whatsoever.

Kazanjian: *Management probably wouldn't talk to you anyway.*

Olstein: Why would they? We were looking to uncover stones.

Kazanjian: *You sold your interest in the publication to your partner in 1980. Why did you decide to get out?*

Olstein: Because I wanted to go into money management. Every one of my compatriots was running a fund of his own and I wanted to do the same. I thought there was a need for a securities analyst and money manager who would employ my theory—that you win by avoiding errors. I sold my interest and went into individual account management. In 1994 I was running about $150 million. My average account size was about $500,000. My average client was over 60, and I realized I'd be out of business soon because most of these people would want to start taking their money out to live on. I longed to go back to the public marketplace. I had outperformed the market for 10 years and decided to start a public mutual fund. I converted $70 million of my equity accounts into the Olstein Financial Alert Fund in 1995. We're now approaching $800 million in assets today.

Kazanjian: *George Soros is one of your largest investors. That's quite an endorsement.*

Olstein: Other Wall Street money managers who've known me personally over the past 33 years are also invested. We've never had a down year.

Kazanjian: *Tell me how you spend your day.*

Olstein: There are five of us working on the portfolio. We spend a lot of time reading all kinds of publications, including magazines and annual reports, looking for hot spots. We do all our own research.

Kazanjian: *What are you looking for as you are reading through this material?*

Olstein: For misperceptions—where we think the negativity on a stock is not backed by the numbers. We especially seek out problems that are temporary. A perfect example was in 1998 when the Asian crisis hit. Investors were killing the oil drilling companies. I felt that because leases on these rigs were expiring, and with oil down to $10 a barrel, the stage was being set for the next turnaround. I looked for companies with excess cash flow and rigs that I could buy at 25 percent of salvage value. I was willing to wait out the storm because the pessimism was too great. We wound up doubling and tripling our money two or three years later.

Kazanjian: *It sounds like what you're doing now is almost the opposite of what you were doing with your newsletter. Before, you were looking for companies that were hyping too much or on the verge of going down. Now you're looking for companies where the news is more negative than it should be, and therefore the stocks are poised to go up.*

Olstein: That's a good synopsis. Now we're looking for misperceptions in the other direction, where the accounting is too conservative. But we always measure our downside risk before assessing the upside potential. You've got to have a two-to-three–year time horizon for value investing, as opposed to two or three days. The only three characteristics we look at in our stock selection process are price, price, and price. If you buy a good company and pay too much for it, it's like buying a bad company.

Kazanjian: *When it comes to evaluating companies, what numbers do you pay the most attention to?*

Olstein: We look at what we believe the cash flow could be over the next three to five years. We're saying this is what we think the earnings power is. This is what we think this company can grow at. We can put 100 percent of our fund in U.S. Treasuries. Therefore, we want at least a 50 to 100 percent cash-on-cash return over three-to-five–year U.S. Treasuries on any stock we select for the portfolio. So we're looking at discounted cash flow versus what we should pay for the stock assuming we were to buy 100 percent of the company and take it private.

Kazanjian: *When you make mistakes in the analysis, what's the most common error?*

Olstein: Misestimating cash flows. We are wrong on one out of every three picks. But we're usually not very wrong, meaning we rarely lose 50 percent or more. The key is protecting your downside by sticking with companies that have clean accounting and cash on the balance sheet. That gives them time to weather the storm. Cash is a safety net, so to speak.

Kazanjian: *What's your sell discipline?*

Olstein: We sell at private market value. Our annual turnover is about 150 percent. We have a strict sell discipline. We value a company and it's out at that value.

Kazanjian: What if the stock price goes down?

Olstein: We buy more unless our valuation changes. We want to buy at somewhere between a 20 and 50 percent discount to our estimated private market value. The further away the stock price is from that value, the more of a commitment we'll make to the stock. Conversely, the closer a stock is to the value, the more we'll take off the table.

Kazanjian: *You said one out of three stocks doesn't work. At what point do you decide it's not working and sell?*

Olstein: If I have a stock that's $24 and I read something that suggests I was overly zealous or optimistic in terms of what this company can do, or if I see something phony starting to develop in the financial statements, I'll sell. I might see unbilled receivables starting to jump up or deferred taxes. There are certain things that alert me to trouble.

Kazanjian: *So it's really a judgment call.*

Olstein: Yes. And, once again, a falling stock price alone isn't a reason to sell, nor does it indicate I've made a mistake. In fact, you could probably make a living shorting the stocks I have taken an initial position in. For some reason, the stocks we buy tend to drop around 20 percent from the time we take our initial position to the time we build our final position.

Kazanjian: *Why is that?*

Olstein: I don't know. I wish I could solve this puzzle. I tend to think we misjudge the negative momentum or how long it takes to turn a battleship.

Kazanjian: *How diversified are you?*

Olstein: I own between 90 and 100 stocks in the portfolio at any point in time. Some have a weighting of one-half of 1 percent, while others have a weighting of up to 2½ percent.

Kazanjian: *In your previous life as an analyst, you never talked to management. What about now?*

Olstein: Never. I can't say we won't make a call to management to clear up something of a factual nature, like what is this account or what does this mean. But we don't call and ask where they think the company is going, or what is the direction of earnings. I'd rather spend one night with an annual report than two days with management. I can learn everything I need to know by looking at the numbers. I can learn how conservative they are. I can compare three years of shareholder letters and see if they attacked their problems. I can see if they projected something that didn't work, whether they were too conscious about the price of their stock, if they were conservative in the way they financed their company, and how disclosure-conscious they are. I know everything I need to know about management just by looking at the financial statements. I've never met a manager who told me that there are problems and if they don't solve them soon, their stock's going to tank.

Kazanjian: *What about the level of the overall stock market?*

Olstein: Who cares about that? That's what I call the psychology of the crowd. I don't spend too much time on that because I don't know how to predict that.

Kazanjian: *Does that mean you don't keep much cash on hand?*

Olstein: No. On average we've kept 20 percent of the fund in cash over the last four years. The level of cash is determined by how many stocks I can find to buy. I have a strict sell discipline. Cash is a result of whether I can find enough ideas that meet my criteria.

Kazanjian: *Why not just add more cash to your current ideas rather than holding cash?*

Olstein: Because I have a rule that I want diversification. When you're at the house and own the roulette wheel in Las Vegas, the more spins of the wheel you have, the more you can stack the odds in your favor, and the better your chances of making money. I don't want to risk buying 10 percent of one company and have it turn out to be the one I'm wrong about.

Kazanjian: *Are you concerned about taxes at all?*

Olstein: Taxes are of secondary importance. There are idiots out there who believe you should make tax decisions over investment decisions. Investment decisions take priority. Taxes are what they are. If I'm 30 days away from having a long-term gain, and I think I still have a stock that's not overvalued, I may wait the 30 days. But if I have an overvalued stock, I don't care.

Kazanjian: *What is the biggest investment mistake you've made and what did you learn from it?*

Olstein: Donna Karan. We took a big position in Donna Karan, and in the prospectus, I missed the fact that she collected royalties based on sales for designing the product for the company. In essence, she was taking too big a percentage of the revenues [top line] as opposed to the bottom line [profits].

We lost money on that in 1999. That was a company I misanalyzed.

Kazanjian: *What would you say makes you different from other value managers?*

Olstein: Growth is a component of my concept of value. Also, I don't have preconceived notions about what value is in terms of whether I can buy a tech, nontech, or cyclical stock, or whether it's a growth or value company. I have no artificial boundaries to my definition of value.

Kazanjian: *Yet in one of your annual reports you criticized managers who were justifying AOL as a value stock.*

Olstein: Yes, because there was no way to justify AOL in terms of discounted cash flow. Buying that company at 200 and 300 times its multiple of cash flow would require too many years of excess cash flow to justify the valuation.

Kazanjian: *So you don't put yourself among the ranks of managers like Bill Miller who say they take a more flexible approach to determining value?*

Olstein: No. I'm a very strict disciplinarian, and use the discounted cash flow model. The difference is I don't need to have the cash flow today. I need to have it within three to five years.

Kazanjian: *You were really vocal on Boston Chicken back in the 1980s.*

Olstein: I was vocal on two stocks that I broke in the public marketplace: Boston Chicken and Lucent Technology. Boston Chicken wasn't a chicken company. It was a bank lending money to high-risk lenders. It was lending money to its franchisees and taking the money back in fees. I said in the long run there was no real cash flow being generated in this company and that it was going out of business. I turned out to be right. On Lucent, I went on CNBC in March 1999 and was quoted in *The New York Times* about the same time saying that Lucent was fudging its figures. I contended the company wasn't really growing at 20 percent a year and concluded the stock was highly overvalued.

Kazanjian: *What led you to those conclusions?*

Olstein: I owned Lucent and started to see that year-in and year-out management was taking nonrecurring write-offs and reversing reserves. I sold the stock and went out to say the company wasn't growing like it said it was. The financial statements were bizarre. They weren't prepared in accordance with economic reality. At one time, I was very excited about Lucent. The numbers caused me to change my mind. In terms of Boston Chicken, it was obvious to me that the company was lending money to unprofitable franchisees who, in turn, were sending the money back to Boston Chicken.

Kazanjian: *Do you short stocks in your fund?*

Olstein: We can. We're not short any right now because we are not finding tremendous amounts of overvaluation.

Kazanjian: *Do you think the average investor should be shorting stocks?*

Olstein: No. It's a dangerous game. We short very little. We have never shorted more than 4 percent of the fund.

Kazanjian: *Technology was hot from the late 1990s through March 2000. Were you in tech then?*

Olstein: We owned tech stocks. We made a fortune in Intel. There's nothing wrong with technology. Technology today is like the steels of 20 years ago. It's one of the essential pieces of our economy. The problem is that people make technology out to be more than it is. Technology companies are cyclical-growth companies. It's not Jack and the Beanstalk. They can't grow to the moon and beyond without problems along the way. There's nothing wrong with a technology stock. You just have to value it. Everything is cyclical. Nothing grows forever.

Kazanjian: *You don't believe in buying and holding forever?*

Olstein: Absolutely not. You do that today, and you'll own Lucent, Xerox, and Penn Central. You have to watch these companies. I think one of the biggest jokes out there are index funds. They were a tremendous idea in their time. But look at what the index funds had to do. They were forced to buy Yahoo!, AOL, and Qualcomm at any price. Those stocks ran up 50 percent when it was announced they were going into the index. How can you make money that way? We're killing those index funds now. They can't beat us.

There's no way. I can't say they won't beat us in any single year, but in the long run, they're pilotless ships. They're eventually going to hit an iceberg. I can go on and on about why I believe index funds are a fraud. They can't hold cash and they have to buy overvalued securities. It's true that most managers don't outperform the indexes. But so what? Find one who does.

Kazanjian: *What do you think is the biggest lesson people will learn from the big market downturn we had?*

Olstein: If you don't understand how to read a financial statement or you don't understand what you're doing, you're best off finding a professional who does. I was in my dentist's office last week. He was complaining about how Cisco could go down so much. I asked him for his tools. He couldn't figure out what I was talking about. I said, "I have the same chance of fixing my teeth as you do of outperforming me in the stock market." He laughed. If you don't understand what you're doing, leave it to a professional.

The markets are different today than they were 32 years ago when I started. In those days, stocks moved up a quarter for sound reasons. Today, there's too much information out there and people are misusing it. You can't buy and hold. There's no such thing. You must analyze. Stocks aren't lottery tickets. There are real companies behind those numbers.

Kazanjian: *During the boom, we saw a lot of people take their money out of mutual funds and start buying individual stocks on their own. Do you think people will move way from individual stocks and go back to professional management?*

Olstein: There will always be investors who want to play the game. Sophisticated people will go with the pros. If you want to have some fun, that's one thing. If you're going to try to compete with me, that's another. I work on this 16 hours a day.

Kazanjian: *Your comments about a stock have long been able to move the markets. What's it like having that kind of power?*

Olstein: I don't try to move markets. I've become a wealthy man in this industry. I work my butt off. I come from a lower-middle-class background in the Bronx and I honestly believe that I have to give something back to the industry. My comments are really meant to help. I love my shareholders. I respect them. I still work for them. I think the public needs professionals who warn them about investment misconceptions. There are a lot of avaricious people in my industry who only think about themselves. When I speak in public, I believe what I say and I believe part of my responsibility is to give something back through education. I only talk in public about what I believe. I do not talk to move markets.

Kazanjian: *Your fund is predominantly sold by financial professionals.*

Olstein: We'll never offer it in the no-load market. We're a high-cost fund because we pay brokers 1 percent and we take a 1 percent management fee. The reason we pay them 1 percent is because my money is in here and I don't want people trading my fund. We are not allowed to own any stock at Olstein & Associates other than the fund. I want people understanding what I'm doing and what I'm setting out to do. I want to have a financial advisor between us and the shareholder.

Kazanjian: *If you were structuring a portfolio of funds for a friend, what would you tell them to buy?*

Olstein: I'd tell them to buy funds run by managers with a discipline. Discipline, not performance, is the first thing to look for. You want a manager with the courage to stick with his discipline even when it's not working.

Kazanjian: *What about the whole idea of owning a mix of small-caps, mid-caps, and large-caps?*

Olstein: To me, that's a joke. I don't think there's any correlation whatsoever between performance and the size of a company.

Kazanjian: *You would rather go with a manager who could buy anything?*

Olstein: There's no reason to limit yourself to buying anything other than stocks that meet your value and cash flow criteria. Eventually that is the final arbiter.

Kazanjian: *How can the average person reading this book make an educated determination of future cash flow and do some of the analysis you're doing?*

Olstein: They need to learn to trust their common sense. They also must either understand how to read financial statements or have the extraterrestrial ability to call markets. Basically this is a game in which you have to look at the accumulation of wealth over time. People pay too much attention to the day-to-day twists and turns. In the National Football League, the score goes back to zero–zero after every game. In the stock market, it's the one who accumulates the most wealth over long periods who wins. If you go back to zero, you're out of the game.

Olstein speaks with powerful enthusiasm for his job, and exudes incredible confidence in his approach. He doesn't have much patience for amateur investors, which is one of the reasons he makes his fund available almost exclusively through professionals. He even publicly took Barbra Streisand to task in 2000 after reading that she had begun managing money for herself and several entertainment bigwigs. He quipped to shareholders that if she was going to be quoted in financial publications on how to run a portfolio, he might as well moonlight by giving Babs some singing lessons. (Fortunately, it appears that Babs is out of the investment business, while Olstein has abandoned plans to enter the music industry.) ■

ROBERT PERKINS

PERKINS, WOLF, McDONNELL & CO.

B ob Perkins has been investing for most of his life. He first got hooked after using caddying money to buy stock in an Illinois utility company. The shares doubled in a few years. He's been putting money to work in the market ever since. After college and a stint in the Navy, Perkins landed in a bank investment department, before joining a firm that was later acquired by Kemper. It's there that he learned how to be a true value investor. Kemper also gave him a chance to run his own fund.

After 12 years, Perkins decided to leave Kemper for a simpler life. He enjoyed managing money, but didn't like all of the marketing involved in selling a fund. He started a brokerage firm in his Chicago apartment and planned to run a small portfolio for a few friends in the investment business and other select clients. That portfolio eventually became a mutual fund. But because of his disdain for marketing, the fund's assets only grew from $3.5 million in 1980 to $35 million in 1997, and, impressively, most of that came from investment gains.

That year, Berger Funds bought Perkins' fund and renamed it Berger Small-Cap Value. With Berger's marketing muscle, assets quickly swelled to about $2.8 billion, and Perkins decided to close it to new investors. He also co-manages another fund, Berger Mid-Cap Value, with his brother, Tom. That fund remains open.

177

Perkins, now 61, has followed small-cap stocks exclusively for a long time, primarily because he feels that you can add more value as a manager in this area of the market, as opposed to the larger names that everyone seems to follow. He gets many of his ideas by looking at the new-low list in the newspaper, and says the key to success is limiting the size and number of your mistakes.

Kazanjian: *Have you always been someone who has gone against the grain in life as well as investing?*

Perkins: No, I don't think so. I was brought up in a basic, middle-class family and did all the "right things." I grew up on the south side of Chicago and, except for five years of service in the Navy, I've been here ever since.

Kazanjian: *What was your first investment?*

Perkins: My first experience with investing was back when I was cad-dying. I must have been 12 years old. I made $200 during the sum-mer. My dad took $100 of it and bought me five shares of Northern Illinois Gas, which was the local utility. He worked for Marshall Fields and had just gotten involved in the stock market. It was prob-ably the first time he had any extra money. The five shares of North-ern Illinois Gas doubled over the next three or four years. My $100 became $200. That fascinated me. I did absolutely nothing to earn that $100. My folks taught me early on to always live below your means, and when you're making out a budget, the first thing to fig-ure out is how much you're going to save. Even when I was in the service not making much money, I still sent money home for my dad to invest for me. The money compounded very nicely. I'm a rather competitive person. I like the idea of being able to measure how well I'm doing every day by just looking at stock prices.

Kazanjian: *Your brother, Tom, is also in the business.*

Perkins: Yes.

Kazanjian: *Did you have similar experiences growing up?*

Perkins: Yes. He is five years younger than I am. We both worked for 12 years at what is now Kemper Financial Services. I started there in 1968 and left in 1980. He started in 1972 and left in 1984. Back then Kemper was run by John Hawkinson. He ran the firm like a dictator, but everything we know about this business we learned from him. He was very much from the Graham and Dodd school. As a matter of fact, he made his first money back in the Depression buying defaulted railroad bonds.

Kazanjian: *Did you study investing in college?*

Perkins: I went to Miami University and got a degree in general business. I may have had a couple of courses in investing, but it was a very general education.

Kazanjian: *When you got out of school, did you go right to work for Kemper?*

Perkins: No. I went into the Navy for five years. I got out of school in 1962 and out of the service in 1967. I went to work first at a local bank in Chicago. Back then, and I guess this is still true, it was hard to get in this business without a master's degree. I did not have a master's degree and still do not. I thought I had the world by the tail when I got out of the service because I had my military obligation out of the way and I was five years more mature than the average kid coming out of college. But it was really a lucky break that I got my first job in the business.

Kazanjian: *What were you doing?*

Perkins: I was in the bank's investment department. I was a big experiment for them because I did not have a master's degree and they never hired anybody without one. After being at the bank for about 1½ years, I took a job down the street with Supervised Investors, which was bought out by Kemper in 1974. Back then Kemper had five funds. I managed their growth fund, which they still have, and their small-cap equity fund. I ran the small-cap fund from its inception in 1970. I left there in 1980.

Kazanjian: *Those funds don't sound like value funds.*

Perkins: No. The predecessor firm to Supervised Investors was a firm called TV Electronics. As the name implies, they had one fund and it was invested totally in TV electronic stocks. This was back in the boom years for TV electronics. The fund had a great record. When the fad wore off on TV electronic stocks, the fund went right into the toilet.

Kazanjian: *Sounds like the Internet funds of today.*

Perkins: It was the same sort of thing. That's when John Hawkinson got involved. The flagship fund was TV Electronics and they changed the name to Technology Fund. It was the firm's largest fund, even though the performance was quite awful. Then they started the Growth Fund. We obviously bought tech stocks, but I like to think we bought them more on fundamentals and numbers than on verbiage.

Kazanjian: *So even though it was a growth fund, you were still paying attention to value.*

Perkins: Yes, very much so.

Kazanjian: *Today it seems that everybody tries to strongly differentiate between growth and value, along with small-cap, mid-cap, and such. Was that the case back then?*

Perkins: I think it's a more recent phenomenon. Most funds would cover the whole gamut insofar as the size of stocks in the portfolio was concerned. When we started what is now called a small-cap equity fund, we called it the Summit Fund. There was no value or growth in the name. The asset numbers were so much smaller. Technology Fund was one of the largest tech funds. I think it had only $500 million in assets. The Growth Fund, which became the firm's flagship fund, had all of $300 million when I left. The Summit Fund had less than $100 million, yet we were the largest firm in Chicago.

Kazanjian: *Why did you leave Kemper in 1980?*

Perkins: For two reasons. Number one, there are four brothers in the family. The next oldest brother, who was two years older than I, had a stroke at 42. I decided, in all my wisdom, that if it could happen to him, it could happen to me. At that time I was single. I put together enough money so that I didn't really have to worry about a paycheck the next week. Number two, by this time, the firm had been bought by Kemper. They wanted to get me more involved in the marketing of the fund, which I hated.

For those reasons I decided to go out and set up a little brokerage firm, manage some money for the family, and recapture my own commissions. We set up a firm and ran it out of my apartment. We barely paid the rent, but we never really actively went out and solicited accounts. We started our own small-cap fund in 1985.

Kazanjian: *Who is "we"?*

Perkins: Perkins, Wolf, McDonnell & Co. We called ourselves McPerWolf at first because we didn't want to put our names on the firm. If we ended up embarrassing ourselves, we didn't want anyone to know who owned it. Perkins was me, Wolf was my ex–brother-in-law, and McDonnell was Tom McDonnell, with whom I'd worked at Supervised Investors.

At that time, Supervised Investors was 50 percent owned by Kansas City Southern Railroad. Tom, who is five years younger than I am, went to work for the railroad. Back then, the railroad decided it wanted to become a conglomerate. It needed someone to analyze the companies it was going to buy. Tom started coming up to Chicago every Monday morning to be trained by John Hawkinson on how to analyze companies that the railroad might want to buy. In 1970, the railroad put together a software program to keep track of the rail-road cars. At the same time, Supervised Investors was having trouble keeping track of its mutual fund accounts. The company decided to set up a little firm to do the clearing for Supervised Investors. Tom set it up with Kansas City Southern's money. It became known as DST. Kemper was DST's biggest customer for many years. DST never really took off until money market funds gained popularity. DST has now become an $8 billion company and the leading mutual-fund transaction clearinghouse. Tom still runs it.

Kazanjian: *Is he the one who urged you to start a mutual fund?*

Perkins: Exactly. He and I shared a cubicle back when he came up every Monday morning to Chicago. We kept in touch both business-wise and personally. He talked me into starting the fund in 1985. We really wanted to keep it as a private placement. We had 35 people I knew from my days at Kemper who put in $100,000 each. It was a $3.5 million fund. I looked at it as a professional investment club. I would be communicating and exchanging ideas with these 35 people who were money managers at other investment firms. They, in turn, could provide me with a wealth of information. Tom thought we could put together a wonderful track record and take the fund down to some regional brokerage house that would do an underwriting for $100 million. Well, 1987 came along and blew that idea. We opened the fund to the public a week before the Crash of 1987, which says a lot about our timing.

Kazanjian: *You're speaking about what was known as the Omni Investment Fund?*

Perkins: Yes. We never marketed it because I was stupid enough to think that a good product would sell itself. For the next 12 years, I'll bet you we went from the 35 original investors to 150 investors. The fund grew from $3.5 million to $35 million, almost all of which was from capital gains.

Kazanjian: *Was the fund too small for your track record to get noticed and picked up by the major rating services?*

Perkins: That was part of it. More important, we never made an attempt to get our message out. When you're a $15 to $20 million fund, who cares? The institutions don't want any part of you because you don't have enough credibility. The public hasn't heard of you. It took us 12 years to figure all this out. That's the reason we hooked up with Berger.

Keep in mind that Kansas City Southern bought Janus Funds back in 1984. I remember being at lunch with the fellow who ran the railroad and my boss, John Hawkinson, many years ago. They were trying to figure out how to get rid of Janus. They thought it was a terrible investment and they couldn't get along with Tom Bailey. I think they paid about $20 million for the company. The first couple of years they wanted out. Now look at what they have. Tom McDonnell was always the liaison between Janus and the railroad because he spoke Bailey's language better than the railroad people. Then, DST bought Berger in 1994.

Kazanjian: *DST bought Berger, but DST was part of Kansas City Southern, meaning the railroad also owned Berger?*

Perkins: Right. Berger then purchased the fund from us in February 1997. We were hired to continue to sub-advise it. With Berger's marketing efforts and our top-decile track record, we now manage more than $3.8 billion.

Kazanjian: *Your assets have grown so much, in fact, that you closed the fund to new investors in 2000.*

Perkins: Right. One thing I didn't want to do was destroy the character and philosophy of the fund by having it reach the size where we had to either buy larger companies or buy more companies. We've always run it with a relatively small amount of holdings. Right now we're up to around 65.

Kazanjian: *Some people might say that $3.8 billion is still too large for a small-cap fund.*

Perkins: Yes, they could. The fund is actually only $2.8 billion, but we manage another $1 billion for two or three insurance companies. The way I'd answer that is that we really haven't changed the character of the fund. The number of holdings has gone from 45 back when we had $35 million in the fund to 65. The average market cap went from $400 million to something short of $1 billion. Most people think of small-cap as under $1.5 billion. I don't feel we've changed the character or the philosophy of the fund.

Kazanjian: *You also started a mid-cap fund.*

Perkins: Yes, about three years ago. When my brother, Tom, left Kemper, he went to work for Alliance Capital. He was there for 12 years and managed their west coast operation. He got tired of having to be in the office at 5:00 A.M. to do the 8:00 A.M. New York call. He came over to manage the mid-cap fund with me. He and I talked three times a week before. Now we talk three times a day. It's been a good fit.

Kazanjian: *Where does he work from?*

Perkins: San Francisco. He's been out there for almost 10 years.

Kazanjian: *Do you two have the same investment philosophy?*

Perkins: Yes. We were both indoctrinated by Hawkinson.

Kazanjian: *Do you two share ideas with each other?*

Perkins: Yes. We also have a staff of four research analysts. Up until 1995, it was just me. I still keep in touch with many of our 35 initial investors. Most of those who are still alive own shares in the fund.

Kazanjian: *Why do you like to focus on small-cap companies?*

Perkins: For the typical investor, there's more value added in the small-cap area. Everyone knows what General Motors does. There are 8,000 people who follow GM and have an opinion on GM. In the small-cap area, you can be a bit more creative. You can come up with ideas that are truly your own. More original thinking, you might say. In addition, the market in general is very inefficient in the short term and particularly inefficient in the small-cap area. To the extent that you're trying to take advantage of these short-term inefficiencies in the market, there's more opportunity in small-caps.

Kazanjian: *How do you initially find your investment ideas?*

Perkins: We're very much bottom-up investors. We make virtually no attempt to call the general market, interest rates, the economy, etc. We put our primary focus on trying to minimize downside risk. I have always felt that if I make 10 investment decisions, three or four will be wrong. But if I don't lose too much money when I'm wrong, everything will work out just fine. By putting the emphasis on downside risk, I like to think I will minimize the impact of my mistakes. After I've satisfied myself that there is not much risk in XYZ, I start to look at the potential reward.

Kazanjian: *How do you determine whether that risk has been reduced?*

Perkins: We look for ideas in either industries or stocks that are out of favor. They may be out of favor because general economic conditions are working against them, or the problems may be company-specific. We love to look at the new-low list in the newspaper for ideas. After we've found either an industry or a particular company that is selling near its low or has come off its high by a significant amount, we do the number crunching. That's the easiest part. Much of it revolves around balance sheet analysis to make sure a company has the financial strength to get through this period of short-term problems.

Kazanjian: *As you probably know, there is a theory of investing out there that says buy stocks that are going up and hitting new highs.*

Perkins: The momentum game.

Kazanjian: *Exactly. You're doing the opposite. The new-low list can be a dangerous place because these are companies experiencing some type of trouble. How do you know when it's safe to buy a stock hitting a new 52-week low? After all, it could stay on the list for a while if things are really bad.*

Perkins: Once a company reaches a point where its intrinsic value is far higher than the current price, I feel good. If you can buy something at 30 cents on the dollar, you'll usually make out well over a period of time. Your timing might be bad, though. We try to minimize the timing problem by only putting around 1 percent of the fund's assets into any new idea. Ideally we want all the holdings in the fund to be around 2 percent. If we put in 1 percent or less, and the stock continues to go down even though nothing has fundamentally changed, it gives us the wherewithal to average down. If the turnaround starts to develop as we thought it would, it allows us to comfortably add to the position.

Kazanjian: *You said the number crunching part is easy. Take me through the process.*

Perkins: The crunching mostly revolves around the various ratios on the balance sheet. To put it in real simple form, we like to find companies that do not have a lot of debt. Ideally we'd like companies to have zero debt. Certain industries by their nature must have debt. A relatively small amount of debt is acceptable. We want stocks that are very liquid. The easiest way to measure liquidity is with cash on the books. We also like stocks selling at a discount to book value, or at least for not much of a premium to book value, with relatively clean accounting.

Kazanjian: *Why don't you like debt?*

Perkins: Debt is a cost that goes on no matter how well you're doing this week, this month, or this quarter earningswise. Debt can really crimp the style of a company. If earnings are down due to company-specific or industry problems, there isn't a lot of room for error when you have a large amount of debt. If you have no debt, and you're not burning cash, you can go on for a long time.

Kazanjian: *So how are you valuing these companies?*

Perkins: Book value is important, but of equal importance, and where you get your reward, is by trying to ascertain what the company will make when its problem is corrected. In other words, determine the earning power of the company. That's largely based on the company returning to historic profitability levels, sales coming back to historic growth rates, that sort of thing. We try to establish this earnings power looking out no more than two years. After that, it gets real qualitative in nature. We estimate what the market will pay for those earnings. That's where you get your upside reward.

Kazanjian: *Do you look at similar companies to determine that?*

Perkins: Earnings power is largely based on the profitability of the company on a given sales level and is largely dependent on what the company has done in the past along with what the industry is doing.

Kazanjian: *Can you give me an example of a stock you bought that illustrates this process in motion?*

Perkins: The most money I ever made in this business on a relative basis was back in the mid-1970s. Back then, the public became infatuated with real estate investment trusts [REITs]. Wall Street has always had the ability to sell to the public whatever it wants. In other words, they create a lot of paper that the public will buy. We experienced that in the late 1990s and early 2000 with Internet phenomena. In any case, back then there were 80 to 100 REITs created. The early ones were legitimate. They owned a portfolio of property that was occupied and getting good rents. As the public craved more, Wall Street created more and more REITs. These newer REITs were going out and either building property or buying property that was vacant. Then the mortgage REITs came along.

To make a long story short, the boom was busted and a lot of the REITs went to zero because of the overloaded debt and the properties that were not economical. In the process some very good REITs that actually owned good property and were getting nice economic returns got painted with the same brush as the bad ones. I can remember buying these good REITs at 20 to 25 cents on the dollar. Once everything was sorted out, I ended up doubling and tripling my money in sleepy old real estate.

That's where I learned a lesson. If you buy something right and have patience, the returns can be quite large. Bringing all that up to the present, once again a lot of REITs were created. All of this new money overpaid for real estate. After both the junky and quality stocks ultimately tumbled, you could buy quality REITs yielding around 10 percent if you selected carefully. Conceivably you could make an additional 30 percent in capital appreciation. Most important, the downside risk was minimal. That is a good example of buying something that is artificially depressed because of short-term concerns that don't really apply to the specific situation you're looking at.

Kazanjian: *With all the REITs out there, how did you separate the winners from the losers?*

Perkins: By going back to the balance sheet. The ones that went to zero had a mountain of debt and did not own property that was giving an economic return. Most important, they didn't have a means to service the debt.

Kazanjian: *So when you look at a fallen sector, you're trying to find those companies that have the best-looking balance sheet.*

Perkins: Precisely. It's the balance sheet that gives you the financial strength to weather the storm, whatever the storm is.

Kazanjian: *Have any of the fallen Internet stocks made your radar screen?*

Perkins: No. We are opposed to paying much more than 20 times earnings for something. If you pay 20 or 30 times earnings, almost by necessity you have to forecast earnings out a lot further than two years. We don't like to get involved in that. On the other hand, we're not opposed to buying yesterday's technology favorites that have come down in some cases 60, 70, or 80 percent in price after stumbling and not delivering what the market thought they would deliver.

This goes back to the inefficiencies of the market, both up and down. Over the last four years, at any given time, we've been able to find stocks down 60 to 80 percent off their highs. That's when the balance sheet analysis comes in. We like companies with no debt and a lot of cash. We've been able to buy good technology companies at two to four times cash with no debt. Yes, they've had a stumble, which has caused them to come down, but the basic product line is not going to be technologically obsolete at some time next week or next year.

Kazanjian: *What analysis are you doing that those selling these stocks aren't?*

Perkins: We try to establish what the company will make when the problem is corrected. For example, many people forget the semiconductor industry is cyclical. We look at what these companies could make when the cycle is good again. We've been able to find stocks trading at 8 to 10 times earnings that used to sell for 30 or 40 times earnings. The secular growth might not be as robust as it was when the stocks were at their highs, but secular growth of 30 or 40 percent is fiction. In all the years I've been in the business, virtually nothing grows at 30 or 40 percent for very long. Maybe the secular growth rate is 20 or 25 percent. Once the problem is corrected, the Street could legitimately pay 20 or 25 times earnings for that growth. Keep in mind we're buying it at 8 or 10 times that earnings number. Most important, if we're wrong and the earnings do not turn as quickly as we'd like, the balance sheet protects us on the downside.

Kazanjian: *You talked a lot about earnings. Does that mean you only look at companies that have had earnings at some point?*

Perkins: Yes. That's one of the reasons we'd never buy an Internet stock. They've never made money, so there's no way of telling what they could make when times are good. For instance, how could anyone theorize what a company such as Amazon.com could make three to five years from now when they've never made any money?

Kazanjian: *When you're buying these stocks, are most Wall Street analysts typically rating them as sells?*

Perkins: Either they're recommending sells or they give up coverage. If we're right, especially in the fallen growth area, that's when we buy. We sell when everybody on the Street loves them. One of our many faults, and we have as many as the next person, is we establish sell targets and price objectives. When a stock reaches that price objective, we sell. As an example, I might buy something at 8 to 12 times earnings power that I theorize could sell at 20 times that number. In that case, I'll sell when the price reaches 20 times earnings. The Street and momentum guys will buy it from me on the theory that it can sell at 40 times.

Kazanjian: *What else makes you sell a stock?*

Perkins: When we're wrong. And, let's face it, we're not clairvoyant.

Kazanjian: *When do you determine you're wrong?*

Perkins: When the basic reason for why we bought the stock in the first place isn't coming to pass. I'll give you an example of something that worked for us. We made a lot of money in energy stocks over the past two to three years. We started buying energy stocks when oil reached $12 or $14 a barrel. We determined that the supply of oil had been reduced to the point where almost by necessity prices would have to go up. Oil subsequently went down to $10 a barrel. We had paper losses of 20 to 30 percent in some of those original investments. But we stood by our basic analysis and ended up making four to five times on our money in some cases. We never believed that oil would reach $30 a barrel. But we thought buying stock in companies when oil was at $14, $12, or $10 would eventually be rewarding.

Kazanjian: *How about one where you were wrong.*

Perkins: We bought two or three staffing companies with clean balance sheets when they were 70 to 80 percent off their highs. The reason they were down was because earnings estimates had been reduced. Wall Street figured these companies made a bunch of money helping corporate America get staffed up for the Y2K problem, which was now over. We took it one step further and felt the Internet business would replace Y2K as an opportunity for these staffing companies. We were right for a short period of time when everyone was gearing up to be on the Internet. When that came to a screeching halt, the bottom fell out. We probably lost more money on a percentage basis in that group than any group that I can remember. We didn't lose 70 to 80 percent, but I'd say we lost 25 to 30 percent. That had never happened to me before.

Kazanjian: *Is there a threshold where you refuse to hold on to a stock that has gone down by a certain percentage?*

Perkins: There's no set formula, but whenever something underperforms by 10 to 15 percent relative to its group or the market, it necessitates an automatic review of what's going on. You may find nothing other than a reason to add to it.

Kazanjian: *How long do you typically hold on to a stock?*

Perkins: Our turnover is 50 to 60 percent, so by definition we have a two-year holding period.

Kazanjian: *Over the past several years, small-cap stocks have underperformed large-caps, although they've recently come back to life.*

Perkins: You can make numbers say anything you want. The research firm Ibbotson Associates, which has done as much number work as I'm aware of, shows that, going back to 1927, small-caps have outperformed.

Kazanjian: *Over long stretches. I'm talking about more recently.*

Perkins: Yes, over the last few years, you're 100 percent right.

Kazanjian: *What is your thought going forward over the next 5 to 10 years?*

Perkins: The market has a tendency to run in cycles. Obviously small-caps were out of favor for four or five years and have been in favor now for a year and a half. Once again, a biased opinion, but I think we have another good two or three years to run before the cycle starts turning against us. I put more of my emphasis on the long term. I'm a believer that small-caps outperform large-caps over long periods. It goes back to those inefficiencies I talked about. Plus, it's easier to grow something that's small rather than something that's big.

Kazanjian: *You say you're trying to reduce risk, but isn't it true that small-cap stocks are a lot riskier than bigger stocks?*

Perkins: In the very short term, yes, because they're more volatile. I don't think in the long term there's any difference in risk.

Kazanjian: *For an investor who is 100 percent in the stock market, what percentage would you recommend putting in small-caps?*

Perkins: I'd say 100 percent. The one caveat would be, even though I'm biased toward value, that no one should have all their money in one style or with one person.

Kazanjian: *How do you invest your own money?*

Perkins: I'd say 95 percent of the time it is in value stocks.

Kazanjian: *Do you keep all your money in small-caps?*

Perkins: Yes.

Kazanjian: *Why does value make so much sense to you?*

Perkins: Number one, if I'm right in my analysis, I will always be minimizing my downside risk and I will also be minimizing volatility. Second, if the market doesn't want to pay what I think it should for the company, then corporate America will pay it instead. Over the last few years, we've probably had over 10 percent of our portfolio bought out. That to me is a function of corporate America seeing the same values we see. Also, when you're buying value, you're usually buying stocks that pay a dividend. There's nothing better than making a 3 to 5 percent dividend return while waiting for someone to recognize the value that you've recognized.

Kazanjian: *Are you open to owning any kind of stock?*

Perkins: There are certain industries that I will never buy. I've never owned a gold stock. I've never owned a rubber stock or a steel stock. I don't like to buy things that aren't able to create something of economic value.

Kazanjian: *Are you competitive with your brother, Tom?*

Perkins: Yes. Up until I was 18 or 19, I could beat him at anything. When he was 25 and I was 30, I could still beat him at most anything because I was the final arbitor. After age 30, I couldn't beat him in any sport. He always was a better athlete.

Kazanjian: *Who's the better investment manager?*

Perkins: I don't know. You can make numbers say anything you want. Currently he is. I can't figure it out. But we go back and forth.

Kazanjian: *What's the best investment lesson you've learned over the years?*

Perkins: Minimize your risks. I managed a profit-sharing plan at Kemper. The 10 years I managed it, the plan compounded at around 22 percent annually. In 1972, it was down 30 to 35 percent. We had some older people who were planning to cash out that year. When it came time for them to retire, they found they were worth 30 percent less than they thought. Some of them were legitimately unhappy. That's when I learned about the importance of minimizing downside risk.

If you decide to buy small-cap stocks on your own, Perkins recommends owning at least 10 different companies from various industries. If you don't have at least $200,000 to invest, he surmises, the trading commissions can kill you. As a result, he says it's usually better for individual investors to get their small-cap exposure through a well-run fund. Perkins also cautions against overtrading your account, because when you trade too much, more often than not the only person who gets rich is your broker. ■

CHARLES ROYCE

ROYCE & ASSOCIATES

Chuck Royce is a legend among small-cap managers. He's been successfully navigating this part of the market longer than just about anyone in the business. He started off as a researcher in the 1960s and worked as both an analyst and broker for several years. In 1966, he began managing Pennsylvania Mutual, which remains his flagship fund. He started his own firm, Royce & Associates, in 1972, and now has a stable of eight funds and various private accounts, all of which invest exclusively in small stocks.

Royce didn't begin as a value investor. In fact, he was one of the go-go managers of the late 1960s and early 1970s. But after suffering through the 1973–74 bear market, Royce changed his ways. A $1 investment in Pennsylvania Mutual at the beginning of 1974 was only worth 46 cents by the end of the year. That prompted Royce to put a higher emphasis on risk reduction.

The 60-year-old manager and his associates now run some of the most conservative small-cap portfolios you'll find. He looks for three primary characteristics in each company he invests in: a strong balance sheet, evidence of financial success, and promising prospects for the future. Since small companies can be fragile, he wants growing businesses that produce free cash flow and can survive potential difficulties in either the stock market or the overall economy.

Despite his valuation parameters and disdain for risk, Royce does invest in technology stocks. But he says he tends to buy "chicken" tech stocks, those that everyone else is ignoring. The bow-tied manager is also interested in IPOs, but only 6 to 18 months after they begin trading, at which time they are more likely to have fallen in price.

Kazanjian: *Have you always been interested in small-cap stocks?*

Royce: Sort of. Going way back to the 1960s, when I started in this business, small-cap aggressive investing was not a formal category. I don't even remember the term *small-cap* being used until the late 1970s or 1980s. It was just accepted that an aggressive investor bought these kinds of securities.

Kazanjian: *Where did you grow up?*

Royce: In Bethesda, Maryland, near Washington, D.C. I went to college in New England and came to New York City to get a master's degree. I've stayed here ever since.

Kazanjian: *Did you have an early interest in the stock market?*

Royce: I did. It's one of those classic little tales, and I didn't make it up. I bought 10 shares of Syntex, the original birth control company, when I was in high school in the 1950s. I somehow tripped into it by reading Value Line.

Kazanjian: *Obviously you began studying and researching the market at an early age. Did Syntex work out?*

Royce: It did, although I don't recall what I did with the stock.

Kazanjian: *But that experience sparked your interest?*

Royce: Yes. In college I also placed stock bets with other people in the fraternity. We were playing around with a small amount of money, maybe a couple of hundred bucks.

Kazanjian: *Did you study business in college?*

Royce: In graduate school I majored in finance.

Kazanjian: *What did you do after college?*

Royce: I went to work on Wall Street and stayed there.

Kazanjian: *What was your first job?*

Royce: My first job was with Chase Manhattan Bank. I gradually worked my way into the research department. I left Chase and worked for a series of regional brokerage firms as an analyst, broker, and every other thing in between.

Kazanjian: *How did you come to start your own firm?*

Royce: A college buddy of mine was a client. I encouraged him to buy the management company of a defunct brokerage firm that had a mutual fund. The fund had hardly any assets, if it had any at all. The fund had had five or six good years and a couple of horrible ones. When my friend bought the company, I took over the fund.

Kazanjian: *Was that Pennsylvania Mutual, which has become your flagship fund?*

Royce: It was. This happened in 1966, and I took over the firm itself in late 1972.

Kazanjian: *Interesting timing.*

Royce: Yes. The fund promptly lost 40 percent in the first year of my ownership.

Kazanjian: *We started off discussing how no one really talked about small-caps back then. Why have you always migrated toward those companies?*

Royce: It was just sort of the way of the world back in the late 1960s. I was director of research of a small firm that was oriented toward those securities. That's what retail customers wanted. The backbone of small-cap stocks has historically been the individual investor. They bought the things they were familiar with, that were popular in their hometowns, that they were affiliated with, or that they thought they had inside information about.

Kazanjian: *But why did you decide to stick with small-caps, rather than expand into large-caps as well?*

Royce: I'd love to give you a fancy reason, but it's just what I've done. It's a fabulous area because there are 8,000 companies to look at almost all the time. You never run out of things to do.

Kazanjian: *How do you define a small-cap stock?*

Royce: Currently it's a stock with a market capitalization of under $2 billion.

Kazanjian: *So the screening process for you begins by weeding out companies with market caps above $2 billion?*

Royce: Yes, that's our starting point. We make a few exceptions, but everything's in that general area. We actively track our median and weighted market cap size. The median is usually $1 billion or less, and the weighted might be a touch higher.

Kazanjian: *You also have funds specializing in even smaller stocks, called micro-caps. What is the difference between a small-cap and a micro-cap?*

Royce: Only what we say it is. There is no clear definition. We're currently defining micro-caps as stocks under $400 million in market capitalization, but that's a recent change. We've historically put the limit at $300 million. The median market cap of our portfolios is between $200 and $250 million.

Kazanjian: *What is the primary difference between small-caps and micro-caps in terms of the companies themselves?*

Royce: Very little, but as an aggregate I would say the very small stocks—the micro-caps—are followed less closely. They're also less liquid, more fragile, etc., but you would expect that.

Kazanjian: *That makes them sound pretty unattractive. Why are these interesting stocks to own?*

Royce: The more risky something is, the more likely it is to make you money if you invest intelligently. This is a more volatile area of the market, but because of that, you're going to make more money, even adjusting for the risk.

Kazanjian: *I know that risk reduction is very important to you.*

Royce: Personally it is, but I wouldn't say it's true of the universe we cover. I think you can be intentional about risk reduction without sacrificing reward. It's easy to say, hard to do.

Kazanjian: *So how do you do that?*

Royce: We do it a whole bunch of ways. We start at the most obvious level: We're careful about stock selection. We're also careful about the balance sheets and the cash flows of the companies we're buying. We have a deep fundamental bias. Much more important, we think about the significant parts of risk beyond the balance sheets.

This relates to corporate strategy, sustainability, how it fits into the marketplace, the kinds of stocks the company has outstanding, the governing principles of the firm, the overall management style, etc. We think about those things in an effort to do well on both the downside and the upside. You can't do both at once, but you can usually get it mostly right. Usually if we do well with the downside, we don't do so well on the upside.

Kazanjian: *You also have a fund that looks for small-cap stocks paying dividends.*

Royce: Right. That approach really takes risk reduction to the extreme.

Kazanjian: *Do many small firms pay dividends?*

Royce: Sure, about 2,000 of them do.

Kazanjian: *You often hear that smaller start-up companies don't pay dividends. Are these dividend-paying small-caps older companies that have been around a long time?*

Royce: Definitely. These are mature small companies, if that's not an oxymoron. They are advanced small companies that have excess cash and pay dividends for all the reasons companies should pay dividends: Their shareholders want them. There might be a family with a large ownership position that wants it. There may be other special circumstances. In any case, the dividend tends to reduce risk. It also tends to be an indicator that a company is successful. But I can find exceptions for everything I just said. Finding a company with a dividend is in general a positive selection process. It's a way of picking up high-quality small-cap companies.

Kazanjian: *Aren't the majority of stocks out there considered small-caps?*

Royce: Absolutely.

Kazanjian: *How many stocks are in your universe?*

Royce: Let's say there are around 12,000 companies in the U.S. domestic market. About 8,000 are small-caps, but they collectively represent only 8 or 9 percent of the market's total capitalization.

Kazanjian: *Why are most of these companies underfollowed?*

Royce: It's a small category to begin with, in terms of investing. As I mentioned, the universe is only about 9 percent of the country's whole market cap. Brokerage firms are not in the business of recommending small stocks. Securities firms are in the business of doing underwritings. As a result, there is no natural place where these things can get recommended.

Kazanjian: *How do you find your ideas?*

Royce: The old-fashioned way. From my brother-in-law, my stockbroker, the taxicab driver. It could be anything. We run computer screens and have a serious in-house research effort, but we are absolutely nondiscriminatory about where the ideas come from. Where we get highly selective is in what we do with the idea. We have a very rigorous way of looking at a company. We go right to its heart and soul, which is return on assets, and try to understand this. Is it permanent? Is it sustainable? What's going on that will impact the returns of the sector? If you can capture a high-returning company, even if it has cyclical growth or sporadic growth, you're capturing a much better engine than a company with low returns.

Kazanjian: *Give me an example of that.*

Royce: Let's say there are two companies both selling at 10 times earnings. One has return on capital of 25 percent, one has a return on capital of 7 percent. This happens all the time. The company with the higher return is going to be a better investment. If it doesn't have capital opportunities inside its own firm, it's going to generate excess cash. The excess cash will operate as a positive pressure point on the company and on the stock. Over time that excess cash will build up, will be spent creatively, and will be used to retire stock. The company without excess cash is flat in the water. So we're looking for companies with higher returns that tend to generate excess cash.

Kazanjian: *That means that a start-up company with no earnings or prospects of earnings . . .*

Royce: . . . is going to be a minor part of our investment profile. If we do invest in them, we've got to be convinced that the picture will improve down the line.

Kazanjian: *What else do you look at?*

Royce: Frankly, 70 percent of it is looking at returns on capital and understanding the future sustainability of returns on capital. If you get that right, you've really got it right.

Kazanjian: *How do you gauge the sustainability of these returns?*

Royce: You think out loud with the company, other people, and competitors. We go through a Socratic question-and-answer process of trying to understand the company. We keep probing about sustainability.

Kazanjian: *Is a visit with management part of the process?*

Royce: Sure, but I'm not convinced that you get a lot out of that. There's nothing wrong with understanding management and having a social dialogue, but you want to get to the truth. It's important to have a management discussion to understand some of these style issues. However, at the end of the day, it will not answer the question of whether the returns are sustainable.

Kazanjian: *What is the remaining 30 percent of the evaluation process?*

Royce: Asking around, talking to competitors, and the like.

Kazanjian: *What kinds of questions do you ask?*

Royce: We want to know how they regard the company.

Kazanjian: *One of the things people generally say is that small-cap companies tend to be more open and accessible. Is that true?*

Royce: I think that's a valid comment. They're so anxious for a conversation with people. By and large, anybody can call a small company and get a conversation going. You're going to get stuck with the PR person at a large company.

Kazanjian: *But often these smaller companies are so excited about their prospects, management may say a lot of great things without having much substance to back up their enthusiasm. We saw this with the Internet stocks in the late 1990s. Every CEO came out to talk about the multibillion-dollar market they were conquering that never really existed. What's the average individual investor to do?*

Royce: The average investor can read a balance sheet. The average investor has to be instilled with some level of common sense. The qualified average investor can ask the same questions I ask. They are simple questions: Where have you been and where are you going? What does your balance sheet look like? How did you get to this balance sheet? How do you generate these returns? How should we think about your company out three years or five years? Get those answers right—and believe me, anybody can do it—and think about them in the context of the other realities in the marketplace and you'll come out fine.

Kazanjian: *Is there a difference in how you would analyze a large company versus a small company?*

Royce: Not really. I think some general observations are true, such as very small companies tend to be more fragile.

Kazanjian: *What about from a valuation perspective? How much will you pay for a stock?*

Royce: That's a great issue and there are no right answers. Valuation is one part of the risk management. It is certainly an important part, but I don't think it's the only part. At the end of the day, we want to generate an absolute return for our investors. The price you pay does have something to do with that return. But I don't wake up in the morning saying, "The whole world should sell at nine times earnings, and if it doesn't, I won't buy it." I need to understand the qualitative dimensions of the company before I'm ready to talk about valuation. If I can get a deep confidence in the qualitative part of the company, I will address the valuation questions after that. I don't have a simple formula.

Kazanjian: *Could you give us an example of how you might look at a company and determine whether it was valued appropriately?*

Royce: Treat the company as a dynamic enterprise. Look at the historic cash flows, consider future cash flows, make assumptions about the sustainability of and confidence you have in those cash flows, and then value the company as you would a piece of real estate. I want to get a minimum return on my investment, as if I'm making a decision about the leverage of that real estate or the company independently. We come up with a cap rate, by taking operating earnings growing at X divided by our piece of the action. We then unwind the debt and cash, making adjustments for it in the value of the company. We take the shares, the price of the shares, plus the debt minus the cash to get our unleveraged enterprise value. We then use operating income out a couple of years from now as the standard for that comparison.

Kazanjian: *If the companies are underfollowed and undiscovered, what drives prices up?*

Royce: Life. I can give you 20 reasons why the price might go up, but I never know exactly what will happen to a given stock. That's why I buy lots of stocks. It's like firewood. You must have lots of trees in the forest for one to get struck by lightning. You can't just have two trees and expect lightning to find your tree.

Kazanjian: *Once a big institution does discover a small-cap stock, do you tend to see a pretty big move, since these stocks are relatively illiquid?*

Royce: Sure, but these securities are more liquid than you think. It's not unusual for stocks in the small-cap category to trade 50,000 to 100,000 shares a day.

Kazanjian: *Have you seen more interest in the small-cap area over the years?*

Royce: The larger small-caps receive more interest from Wall Street, but it's still a tiny piece of the total pie.

Kazanjian: *What generally causes you to sell a stock?*

Royce: The two extremes are great success—a company being taken over—or total failure. Those both are fine outcomes. Total failure gets it over with and you move on. Most companies, however, are kind of stuck in the middle. They're neither sharp buys nor sharp sells. It's the management of your slow-moving merchandise that is the trickiest part of this game.

Kazanjian: *What do you do with this slow-moving merchandise, especially if the stock keeps treading water?*

Royce: That's the single worst phenomenon. Going up or going down is fine. We can deal with success and disappointment. It's dealing with frustration that's the hard part. And we've got plenty of stocks like that. Unfortunately, there's no magic. It has to be looked at on a case-by-case basis.

Kazanjian: *For how long are you willing to be patient?*

Royce: We are patient, but we really spend time looking at other things. We'll come back and review lagging positions from time to time and at some point make a decision. We make decisions frequently—at least several times a year—after we've made the original buy decision. It's that mass of middle stocks that are not performing well or poorly that gives you the biggest headaches.

Kazanjian: *When the price of a stock goes down, do you have a threshold for how long you're willing to hold on?*

Royce: Most of the time we're buying more, but sometimes we simply give up.

Kazanjian: *Don't you think that's pretty hard for most investors? When the price goes down, it seems like their reaction is to sell.*

Royce: I don't think there is an average response. People operate with a range of emotions, including fear and denial.

Kazanjian: *Small-cap investing has become quite categorized. Asset allocation experts tell us we need to keep so much in large-caps, so much in small-caps, and so on.*

Royce: I'd say that's the biggest change in the last 10 or 15 years.

Kazanjian: *Does that approach make sense to you?*

Royce: The asset allocation approach is no more logical than saying you should have, like an ark, two of every animal. Asset allocation gives you one of everything. What you really want is a portfolio of great stocks and great funds, not one of everything.

Kazanjian: *How would you choose a small-cap fund?*

Royce: I'd look at the history of the fund. That will give you some insight into the future. I spend a lot of time thinking about risk and reward, and I would encourage other investors to do the same. It was easy to throw darts in a bull market.

Kazanjian: Risk *is a word a lot of people forgot about.*

Royce: Right. People are more concerned about the other "r" word— *returns.*

Kazanjian: *What's the key to controlling risk in your portfolio?*

Royce: Being sensible. Being aware of what you're doing and what the company is all about. Is it a speculative company? Does it have a good balance sheet? Does it have a track record? I think you want to get in touch with reality. The closer you are to reality, the better you'll be at making judgments about risk.

Kazanjian: *How diversified do you keep your portfolios?*

Royce: Very diversified. Our mainstream funds might have several hundred stocks.

Kazanjian: *How good is Wall Street research when it comes to small-caps?*

Royce: They tend to be investment-banking-oriented. That can be fine or it can be lousy.

Kazanjian: *Do you rely on this research very much?*

Royce: No. We use it as a secondary source.

Kazanjian: *What about company annual reports?*

Royce: I think investors should read the whole thing cover to cover. I'd read the president's letter, the management discussion, and the balance sheet, and I'd compare this year's annual report to last year's. Investors should line up three or four annual reports, and read the letters and cash flow statements. That will give them the gist of what's going on. Does the average investor bother to do that? Probably not. But it's a simple thing that's available to everybody.

Kazanjian: *Do you ever buy IPOs?*

Royce: Every once in a while. I tend to buy IPOs when they're really out of favor, which is either at the beginning of the cycle or at the very end of the cycle.

Kazanjian: *How important is trading execution when it comes to small-cap stocks?*

Royce: It's pretty important. There are such wide spreads, often of 2 to 4 percent. A $10 stock with a quarter point spread is 2½ percent. That means you give away 2½ percent every time you step into the game.

Kazanjian: *Do you recommend placing limit orders for small-cap stocks?*

Royce: I think you should just be careful. Limit orders are fine. Take your time trading these stocks. You don't have to blast in and get the trade done in 10 minutes. It might take you days to build the position you want.

Kazanjian: *How do you feel about indexing?*

Royce: I think there is a place for it.

Kazanjian: *Does it work in the small-cap area?*

Royce: Less so.

Kazanjian: *Why is that?*

Royce: Because there are too many crummy small stocks. Small stock indexes capture this negative selection, whereas you have positive selection in large-cap indexes because to go from a $20 billion to a $100 billion company, you must be doing something right.

Kazanjian: *Do you own technology stocks?*

Royce: Yes.

Kazanjian: *How do you value them?*

Royce: We value them the same way we value any old company, which is by thinking about their future, understanding their task, and trying to make a judgment as to what they're worth.

Kazanjian: *What is your turnover generally?*

Royce: I'd say 30 to 40 percent a year.

Kazanjian: *That's fairly low by small-cap standards. Do you take taxes into consideration at all?*

Royce: Yes, in two ways. We try to realize losses appropriately, and we try to postpone gains as efficiently as possible.

Kazanjian: *You've been investing for quite some time. The recent bear market is probably the first bear market many investors have ever experienced.*

Royce: What investors now know is that markets go up and down. Those new to the market will never forget that. If the man on the street loses 90 percent in a new issue, he'll be more careful next time.

Kazanjian: *You recently wrote that bear markets are not a time to be conservative. What do you mean by that?*

Royce: It's the wrong time to get cautious. It's the right time to increase risk. It's the wrong time to decrease risk. You want to increase risk because there are higher reward possibilities looking out a couple of years. If markets go down, you want to add to your positions, not subtract from them.

Kazanjian: *What's the best way to approach a bear market?*

Royce: The best way, in general, is to dollar cost average. [Dollar cost averaging involves investing regular amounts on a regular basis in stocks, regardless of what's happening with the overall market.] If you throw a dart on one day, you could get it wrong. Start off slowly and then add more to your portfolio every couple of weeks.

Kazanjian: *How do you invest your own money?*

Royce: The same way. I buy mutual funds.

Kazanjian: *Do you own large-cap funds also?*

Royce: A few.

Kazanjian: *What made you become a value investor?*

Royce: Losing a lot of money in the 1973–74 bear market. I lost most of my money by having undue speculative risk in the portfolio, not understanding the importance of balance sheets, not understanding diversification principles, and not understanding integrity principles as they relate to individual companies.

Kazanjian: *What's the biggest mistake that investors make?*

Royce: Not reading annual reports and understanding the risks involved in their investments. They hear a good story and go into it without doing their homework.

Kazanjian: *What's the best investment lesson you've learned over the years?*

Royce: Lower risk doesn't diminish returns. Contrary to what the academics tell you, risk and reward are not virtually correlated, at least not in my experience.

Kazanjian: *Does this mean that as a mutual fund investor you should look for funds with lower risk, not those that try to have occasional home-run years?*

Royce: Honestly, I'd say yes.

Kazanjian: *It's like the tortoise and the hare story.*

Royce: Definitely. Another lesson I've learned is that you don't have to swing at every pitch. This is a game that goes on and on and on. You can stay out of the game for a while and come back in it with a fresh approach. You don't need to be hyperactive to win.

Kazanjian: *When you do make a mistake and finally decide to sell a stock, is there any common reason why it didn't work out?*

Royce: It's usually some creeping problem that wasn't identified on day one. It gradually enters the picture. For instance, it could be leverage that wasn't there on day one but slowly increases over time.

Kazanjian: *Do you pay attention to the overall market environment?*

Royce: Yes. I want to go against the market. I tend to be more conservative as markets go up and more aggressive as markets go down.

Kazanjian: *Do you hold cash?*

Royce: No. I always try to stay fully invested.

Kazanjian: *Are your valuation parameters changing based on the market? In other words, if the market's going up, are you willing to pay more for your stocks?*

Royce: I hope not. You never know if that subconsciously creeps in, but it's something I try to avoid.

Kazanjian: *In your mind, are there varying cycles between small- and large-caps?*

Royce: Definitely. I don't believe they are necessarily predictable, but I know there are cycles. I get hunches about them. I just pay attention to what's working in the marketplace. Trends tend to persist until they stop. I do think this decade will be a decade of small stocks, primarily because the 1990s were not.

Kazanjian: *What's going to bring interest to this sector?*

Royce: I don't think you need a reason. It just happens. You don't need to buy a stock with a reason that it's going to go up. You just need to know that you've done something sensible. Own five stocks and two will go up more than you think, while two won't go up at all.

Kazanjian: *Would you say investors should be more diversified among small-caps than any other market category?*

Royce: Definitely. Twice as much.

Kazanjian: *There's a debate when it comes to mutual funds in terms of how big is too big in terms of asset size for small-cap funds. Where do you weigh in on this?*

Royce: In the value end of things, you can have much more money because you're generally buying against the grain. In the growth world, you're generally buying momentum. I think in a growth fund, you have to run with much smaller assets.

Kazanjian: *Give me some numbers.*

Royce: I'd be careful with a small-cap growth fund with more than $1 billion in assets.

Kazanjian: *But with value, you could go higher?*

Royce: That's been our experience.

Kazanjian: *Is that because there's not as much demand for these stocks?*

Royce: Precisely. We're buying on down ticks, waiting for the stocks to come to us. That gives you an edge in a large portfolio.

Kazanjian: *What do you like most about your investment style?*

Royce: I think it's as close to an evergreen or all-weather approach as one can have. I think it works in a variety of markets, both good and bad. It probably works even better in bad markets. There's no such thing as a natural value investor. People become value investors through experience. They have to go through some sort of suffering, as I have, to get here.

Royce probably keeps more stocks in his portfolios than anyone else I interviewed. This broad diversification is his way of further reducing risk in the volatile small-cap market. When it comes to choosing a money manager, Royce says investors should look for someone who seeks reasonable returns and uses an approach that stresses absolute—not relative—performance. He also feels that managers should communicate openly and be willing to discuss both their successes and their failures with shareholders.

Royce recently sold his company to Legg Mason, the firm fellow Master Bill Miller works for. Royce plans to remain actively involved in the company and will continue to run several portfolios. ∎

KENT SIMONS

NEUBERGER BERMAN

K ent Simons learned a lot about investing from his dad, even though he didn't realize it until some years after he began his career on Wall Street. His dad was a high school economics teacher who taught Simon about the subject both in the classroom and at home. His dad was a rigorous value investor, who wouldn't buy a company unless it paid a big dividend.

Wall Street, however, wasn't Simons' original career goal. After graduating from Princeton, Simons went to work as a foreman in a soap factory. He loathed the job and was rescued from it by being drafted into the Army. Following his discharge, he found a position at Bankers Trust in pension administration, before talking his way into the investment department.

Simons, now 66, got his first break managing money in the late 1960s. He says the period from 1965 to 1973 was so difficult for stock investors that it led him to become a value manager. He'd buy a stock and watch it go lower by the day. His dad kept warning him to stick with cheaper companies, but it took him a few years to catch on.

Simons came to Neuberger Berman in 1973 and has remained there ever since. Although the firm is revered today as a leading value shop, back then the firm was simply known for its ability to pick good stocks. There were no labels. In fact, Simons feels there's too much emphasis today on the difference between value and growth, even though he's personally more comfortable wearing the value label.

In 1981, Simons took over the Neuberger Berman Guardian Fund, which he ran until 1998. During that time, assets grew from $135 million to $8 billion, making it the firm's largest portfolio. He's been managing the Neuberger Focus Fund since 1991. Running that portfolio, which has been the firm's top performer, is now his full-time job.

Simons keeps a concentrated portfolio of about 30 names. By prospectus, his holdings must be spread across no more than six sectors, although his process often leads him to even fewer sectors than that. He looks for companies with an earnings growth rate higher than the S&P 500, but with a PE ratio that's lower than the index. Just as important, he works hard to figure out why a stock is cheap before deciding to buy it.

Kazanjian: *Did you follow the stock market growing up in Detroit?*

Simons: I did. My father was a high school social studies teacher who taught economic history, so we talked about it at home.

Kazanjian: *That sounds like an unusual subject for high school.*

Simons: It was. I went to Princeton after coming out of the Detroit public schools and had no social life for the first two years. I was so far behind my classmates who went to private schools. But my sophomore year, I took an economics class and just walked through it. My father was a good teacher. I didn't know it then, but it turned out he was also a very good investor. He wouldn't hold stocks in street names. He held them in his own name and used to get dividend checks. Before he'd open the dividend checks, he'd say, "If there are any cents in the check, you can have them." So if the check was for $25.30, I would get the 30 cents. At a really young age I developed this keen interest in stocks in general and dividend checks in particular.

Kazanjian: *Did your dad amass an impressive portfolio?*

Simons: He was a school teacher all his life and never made more than $15,000. When he died, he left an estate of $775,000. Late in life I arranged for him to have lunch with Roy Neuberger (the founder of Neuberger Berman) and me. At the end of the lunch, Roy said, "I think we hired the wrong member of the family." Until the day he died, my father never stopped quoting that comment. Later I said to Roy, "That was really a nice thing to say." He replied, "What makes you think I didn't mean it?"

Kazanjian: *Was your dad a value investor?*

Simons: With a vengeance. He wouldn't put money in the market unless stocks yielded more than he could get on his CDs [certificates of deposit]. I'm not quite that rigorous.

Kazanjian: *Besides, it's not easy finding stocks that yield more than CDs these days.*

Simons: That's for sure. These days if you followed that strategy, you'd kind of be out of the picture.

Kazanjian: *What did you major in at Princeton?*

Simons: I was in a special program called the Woodrow Wilson School of Public and International Affairs. It was limited to 50 people in a graduating class. Most people in the program ended up either going to law school or working for the U.S. Department of State. I wound up going to work for Procter & Gamble, which I loathed. Then I got drafted, which was sort of a blessing in disguise.

Kazanjian: *What did you do at Procter & Gamble?*

Simons: I was a foreman in a soap factory. My father once said to me, "There are two things everybody should do one time in their life. They should work on a farm and work in a factory." After a year in the factory, I said, "Dad, I think I'll pass on the farm. One is enough." After two years in the Army, I went to work at Bankers Trust in pension administration. That is probably the dullest thing a person can do. Even the exciting stuff was terrible, like garnishing poor pensioners' checks because they hadn't paid their taxes. We were literally right next door to the pension investment part. I tried to figure out how I could get from here to there.

Kazanjian: *How did you get into pension administration in the first place?*

Simons: After I got out of the Army, I went on a number of job interviews. The bank made pension administration sound infinitely more interesting than it turned out to be. After about a month of thinking I ended up in the wrong pew, I got called back into the Army during the Berlin crisis for seven months. When I got out, Bankers Trust wanted me back. I told them I wanted to come back to go into investment research. In retrospect, it was the courage of the uninitiated. I had never even taken an accounting course in college. This was in the fall of 1962, right after the Kennedy steel crisis, when the unemployment rate among junior security analysts was 30 percent. Somehow I talked my way into getting the job and managed to survive.

Kazanjian: *Did you start off as an analyst?*

Simons: Yes. The bank's research director thought that with the discovery of antibiotics, the drug industry was mature. So I got to be the drug analyst because it had been decreed from the top that this was an industry not worth investing in.

Kazanjian: *When did you get your first break managing money?*

Simons: I went from Bankers Trust to Lionel D. Edie, a New York–based investment advisory firm. From there I joined Anchor Corp., a mutual fund company that ultimately was acquired by Capital Research. I managed money there from 1965 until coming to Neuberger in 1973.

Kazanjian: *The period from 1965 to 1973 was a tough one to be managing money.*

Simons: It sure was. That is probably why I became a value manager. The experience was scarring. I remember one time buying Texas Instruments at 40 or 50 times earnings and getting chastised by my father. He asked me what the stock's yield was, and I told him there wasn't one. He said, "Kid, you're gonna be sorry." I went home and told my wife, "I think Dad's getting senile." Six months later, he turned out to be right.

Kazanjian: *Were you given money to manage at Neuberger right away?*

Simons: No. I came here as an institutional salesman. It was a total mismatch of talents and job experience. Back then Neuberger had two growth guys and the rest were value. I watched them work for six or seven years and was always begging for a chance to run money. In 1981 they gave me a couple of pension accounts and in

1981 Roy Neuberger picked me to run the Guardian Fund, which stunned everybody. I didn't think he knew who I was.

Kazanjian: *Was the value style immediately comfortable to you?*

Simons: Yes. When I first got here, Neuberger managed a total of $700 million. Everybody knew everybody. The managing partner told me, "Don't pay any attention to what these guys say they're doing. Just look at what they *are* doing." That's what I started to do. I watched the trade sheets, talked to them, and realized the value style made sense. Although we were definitely a value firm, in those days they didn't have labels like they do now. I don't ever remember hearing Neuberger called the great value shop.

Kazanjian: *Do you think we put too much emphasis on labels today?*

Simons: Yes. People talk about whether value is going to beat growth and get nervous about what Morningstar style box you're in. I can understand it in a way, especially in the mutual fund world. A lot of investors want to diversify their investments. But I believe in staying dedicated to a chosen style. Inevitably you'll have a period where you're out of phase for a quarter or even a year. But if you're doing what you say you're doing, most clients will stay with you.

Kazanjian: *You started work on the Guardian Fund in 1981. How long did you manage that portfolio?*

Simons: I managed it by myself until 1988. Then I took on a partner, Larry Marx. He and I ran it together until 1994. We then brought in a third person, Kevin Risen.

Kazanjian: *Because it was getting larger?*

Simons: Yes. When I took over the fund, it was $135 million. When Larry came in, it was around $550 million. Then it got up to $7 or $8 billion. The three of us ran the Focus Fund, the Guardian Fund, and 47 pension funds. It was about 30 percent of the firm's institutional money. Management decided it was too much and consolidated everything. Larry took the pension accounts and went into the pension group. Kevin and I ran the Guardian and the Focus. Then, three years ago they took me off Guardian and gave me full management of Focus. So I've worked on the fund since 1991 and have run it alone since the summer of 1998.

Kazanjian: *Let's talk about your investment approach. As you begin to put the portfolio together, what do you look at?*

Simons: The first thing is valuation. At most, I want the portfolio to trade at a market multiple, ideally below that. As we speak, the PE on my fund is about 16, which is almost a 30 percent discount to the S&P 500 and a 15 percent discount to the Russell 1000.

Kazanjian: *Do you run a screen for stocks trading at below market multiples?*

Simons: Well, it's not anything as formal as a computer screen. I buy what's out of favor or misunderstood. Most people know what those stocks are. But the market is surprisingly efficient. Many things that are cheap deserve to be cheap. As a result, I'm looking for cases where stocks are cheap because of a temporary condition that I believe will be rectified within three to six months.

Kazanjian: *Will you look at stocks from every sector and industry?*

Simons: I used to. But after being in this business for a long time, I've come to realize that some sectors always make bad investments. For instance, you don't want to waste a lot of time looking at the paper industry. At best, paper stocks are trades. International Paper can go up 60 or 70 percent in six months, but that only happens about once every 10 years. I don't want to own commodity companies because virtually every one is in a slow-growing industry or business. They're not good long-term investments. And while many value funds own energy, aluminum, steel, and/or chemical stocks, I really don't.

Kazanjian: *According to your prospectus, you invest in no more than six sectors at all times.*

Simons: Well, that's sort of how it works. The prospectus says that 90 percent of the fund's assets have to be in no more than six S&P sectors. After all, it's the Focus Fund and it's supposed to be concentrated. At the moment, I'm invested in three sectors. It's not because I have a view that these three sectors will do well in the current economic environment. I go where the valuations are. I've found that when a sector goes out of favor, it tends to get cheap from top to bottom. If you find three or four stocks in the same industry that are really cheap, the whole industry is probably cheap. At the moment, those sectors happen to be retail, technology, and finance. We own a total of 34 stocks from these sectors at this time.

Kazanjian: *This approach goes somewhat against the academic argument that you should be diversified across both stocks and sectors.*

Simons: That argument was popular when the S&P was beating everybody. Even then I thought it was specious because if you actually looked at why the S&P was beating everybody, you saw that it was because the top 40 names accounted for 50 percent of the assets. And most of these stocks were in the same industries. The S&P 500 was really a high multiple momentum growth fund. The more something went up, the bigger a percentage of the S&P it became.

Kazanjian: *So you start by identifying an attractively valued company, and then check to see if there are any others in the same industry that are equally appealing?*

Simons: Right, and there usually are. You always find that unique company that is punished for reasons specific to it. It's much more common, however, that the whole industry or sector is punished at once.

Kazanjian: *Tell me about the analysis you do on individual companies.*

Simons: The first question I ask is why did this stock just go from $60 to $25. It's almost always the same answer: It missed a quarter. It's surprising how many really good companies get punished for missing a quarter. Or maybe the company hasn't missed a quarter, but investors are worried that it will because of the economy.

Kazanjian: *Has it always been this way?*

Simons: No. This is more a function of the last three to five years. It used to be no big deal to miss one quarter. Now there's real destruction visited upon you.

Kazanjian: *Is it because there are so many momentum players now?*

Simons: I think so. There are also many people running a bunch of money who have no overriding view of why they actually own what they own. If you give them three drinks, it turns out they really bought the stock just because it was going up. This volatility, however, is actually a value manager's godsend. For example, I really believe in the outsourcing of technology. Cisco only builds about 3 percent of what it sells. Everything else is outsourced. Because of the problems with the big technology companies in 2000, many of these outsourcing stocks went from 40 to 50 times earnings to 15 times earnings. They dropped 80 percent in two to three months. Because of the economic environment, not because of something they did, they missed a quarter. But I'm willing to ride through that. When the momentum investors take those stocks down 80 percent, I'm standing there ready to buy. I now have 5 percent of the fund in electronic manufacturing services companies, which I never thought I'd own because they were always too expensive.

Kazanjian: *What else do you look for?*

Simons: Whether there is something structurally wrong with the company. Are these disappointing earnings a function of something the company did, or are they a function of something out of management's control? In other words, is it a macro-event that will probably be rectified? You also look for evidence that the shortfall will only last for one or two quarters, and that it isn't part of a long-term trend.

Kazanjian: *What's next?*

Simons: There is always an execution risk in these companies. Therefore you must place a lot of emphasis on the people running the company. I usually want to meet them. Because you're buying companies that are under pressure and dealing with adversity, you want to make sure they don't have a 30-mile-per-hour wind at their back. A lot of what I do is quantitative, since I look for low valuations, with high returns on equity and strong long-term earnings. But much of my work is also qualitative. What is the management like? Are they running the company, or is the company running them? Do they have a long-term goal in mind? If so, how reasonable is it? I look at how they are going to get to the goal, and whether their approach makes sense.

Kazanjian: *You haven't mentioned book value or intrinsic value.*

Simons: Book value hasn't worked for me, although some people use it successfully. I've found it to be a trap. For example, if you're looking at a bank, the market is usually astute. If you find a bank selling at a low multiple or a discount to book value, it probably means there are a lot of bad loans on the books. If you find an industrial company selling at a real low multiple or discount to book value, it usually means the plants are obsolete. As for intrinsic value, intrinsic value is in the eye of the beholder. When I buy a stock, I usually don't have a specific price target in mind.

Kazanjian: *Clearly, you're not from the diehard Graham and Dodd school of value investing.*

Simons: No. Their approach was great and there was a time when it worked. If I followed that approach now, I'd own about four stocks.

Kazanjian: *Is there anything else that goes into the buy decision?*

Simons: I look at marketability or liquidity. I like to get at least a 2 or 3 percent position in each stock. I think of how hard it would be to buy $60 million worth of it. You don't want to have to mark the stock up 5 percent to get in and another 5 percent to get out. Interestingly enough, I have found that if you go against the grain, which I do, marketability isn't a big deal. And when these stocks get overvalued, it's the easiest time to sell. Everybody wants them then.

Kazanjian: *What makes you sell a stock?*

Simons: Value guys like me get into trouble by buying stocks at below market multiples and the earnings turn out not to be there. When I buy a stock, I don't have a price target in mind, but I do have a series of assumptions. I assume that the company will earn a certain amount and that these earnings will be legitimate. If those assumptions aren't met, I won't own the stock for long. The worst stock I ever owned was the Bank of New England. I bought the stock at $24 at six times earnings and sold it for $6 at six times earnings. The earnings estimate went from $4 to $1 a share when I got out. The bank ultimately filed for bankruptcy. If the fundamentals aren't coming through, and the assumptions aren't being met, I'm probably going to sell. There are also times when you reach a point in a stock where you think all of the good news is priced in. Selling those stocks frequently turns out to be a mistake, since the market is not stupid. It's telling you that the earnings are going to be better than you thought. Still, once the price gets to that point, I'll cut back at the very least. The final reason I'll sell, since I'm 99.8 percent invested, is to raise money for something else that looks even better than what I'm selling.

Simons believes in holding on to his winners as long as possible. Taking a long-term perspective is something his old boss Roy Neuberger—who is now 98—is always trying to teach him. Just the other day, they met in the elevator and Neuberger introduced Simons to a client. "This is one of our best money managers," Neuberger said. Simons was having a bad day. He responded that things could be going better. "What do you mean?" Neuberger snapped. "Your record has been good lately. I just saw a report that the Focus Fund has been in the fifth percentile over the last 10 years." Simons thought it was odd that Neuberger would consider 10 years to be "lately." Then he realized that since Neuberger had been at this for more than 60 years, 10 years wasn't long at all. ■

BRET STANLEY

Bret Stanley's first lesson in investing came when he got "free money" from the bank as a young boy. That free money was actually interest, but it ignited his interest in the concept of savings and the power of compound interest. As he began reading about mutual funds, while helping to manage his college fund, he decided he wanted to become the next Peter Lynch. He's well on his way.

At 36, Stanley is the youngest Master featured in this book. Although he has only been managing money since 1988, he has shown a real talent for uncovering promising stocks.

Stanley began his career as an analyst with a regional broker in Houston and then moved to a local value shop. It was here that he was first introduced to disciplined value investing. The philosophy immediately made sense to him. In 1995, Stanley joined Van Kampen Investments, where he was hired by fellow Master James Gilligan (who is featured elsewhere in this book) to help run the Growth and Income and Equity Income funds.

After meeting the chief equity officer for AIM at a cocktail party, Stanley learned that AIM planned to expand its growth-dominated product line by launching some value-oriented funds. Stanley was tapped to lead that effort. Today he runs the firm's value research effort and is senior portfolio manager of the AIM Basic Value and AIM Large Cap Basic Value funds.

Stanley seeks out companies with at least a 50 percent differential between the current market price and his estimate of intrinsic value. And although he's a big believer in the teachings of Ben Graham, he thinks that too many value investors focus on poor businesses with lousy economics.

Kazanjian: *Are you a lifelong Texan?*

Stanley: Yes. I grew up in Houston and attended the University of Texas.

Kazanjian: *How did your interest in investing develop?*

Stanley: The impetus probably came from my dad. My grandfather was a private investor, and as a result my dad was always interested in the stock market. My father loved to illustrate the power of compound interest, first with tables and later with a calculator. I became fascinated with the concept of compound interest and saving at a young age. He gave me a savings account when I was 6 or 7, and by the time I was 9, I had opened my own savings account. I always liked the idea of getting money from the bank for free.

At 13, I began actively saving and investing for retirement by starting an IRA. My dad showed me that by starting early and putting money in my IRA every year, I'd be able to retire early. I have put the maximum allowed into my IRA every year since. He also encouraged me to participate in the management of my college fund, which was invested primarily in mutual funds. I began to learn about Peter Lynch because the Magellan Fund was one of our investments. I remember reading an article about a day in the life of Lynch and thought it was fascinating. When I went to college, I already knew I wanted to be a money manager, although I didn't really understand all the elements of the business.

Kazanjian: *You also studied abroad in London for a time. Did this feed into your interest in investing?*

Stanley: No question about it. It allowed me to study finance and do an internship at the sell-side firm Sheppards of London. They gave me, as an American student, a ridiculous amount of responsibility. The first week on the job I was visiting companies and writing research reports. I barely knew what I was doing. They had an analyst training program that I participated in. It was an important bridge from academic work to practical analysis. After graduation, I looked for a job at a number of firms. Since I'm from Texas, a lot of my contacts were here. I got an interview at Underwood Neuhaus, a regional brokerage firm that had been around for a long time in Texas. The principals were still at the firm when I joined. I took the job and figured I would probably be there for 30 years like my dad was at Exxon. I started covering electric utilities, which probably wouldn't have been my choice of industries, but you take what you can get. Anything, if you pour your heart into it, becomes interesting. After that, I spent three years on the sell side.

Kazanjian: *Can you explain what it means to be on the "sell side"?*

Stanley: The sell side is any brokerage firm that sells its research to clients. Underwood Neuhaus was a typical broker that also had investment banking operations. I was on the research side. As major Wall Street firms started to compete more with regional firms, there was a lot of turmoil and consolidation. As a result of mergers, I was actually at three different firms in three years.

Kazanjian: *You never left the firm, it just changed hands three times?*

Stanley: Yes and no. One time, I came back from an Edison Electric conference. The firm had been acquired and everybody was wearing blue jeans. I made the joke, "What happened? Did somebody close this place down?" Everybody said, "Yes." I was the only one offered a job at the new firm, but it was a job for less money and in corporate finance. I walked across the street and started at another firm the following day. The irony is that I was hired back a year later to work at the merged firm. My conclusion from the whole experience was there was too much turmoil in the regional brokerage industry. A friend told me I should contact Gulf Investment Management, which was a local value shop. The principal, Tom Macrini, was pretty much doing all the research himself. I spent more than four years with him. That was my first introduction to a truly disciplined value investor.

Kazanjian: *Were you managing money?*

Stanley: Yes, for the first time. I started out as an analyst and was promoted to portfolio manager. By the time I left, I was responsible for about half of the ideas in the portfolio. It was only the two of us selecting stocks for the portfolio. Then in 1995, I joined Van Kampen as a portfolio manager. I was co-manager of the Growth and Income and Equity Income funds. Shortly after I joined, I launched a Graham and Dodd intrinsic value fund. It was more concentrated and more in line with the way I wanted to manage money. That product led me to AIM because they were interested in expanding the product line to include value. I joined AIM in 1998 to head up our value effort and to launch the firm's first true value mutual fund.

Kazanjian: *As I recall, AIM was a growth shop and didn't even introduce its first blend or growth-at-a-reasonable-price fund until the early 1990s.*

Stanley: That's true. The blend products got so large they rightly concluded they needed a more diversified product line. We started Basic Value in 1998 and Large-Cap Basic Value in 1999. Both are traditional value funds.

Kazanjian: *What is the difference between the two?*

Stanley: Basic Value is a multi-cap fund that can invest in both mid- and large-cap stocks. Large-Cap Basic Value is a dedicated large-cap fund. Some of our clients, such as 401(k) plans, require that we have a fund with a dedicated market cap.

Kazanjian: *At what point did you realize you were most comfortable as a value investor?*

Stanley: It never occurred to me that there was anything other than value investing. Buying something for less than it was worth, I naïvely assumed, was what investing was all about. Until I had exposure to a broad set of clients as a sell-side analyst, I didn't understand what momentum investing was or what it meant to be a growth investor.

Kazanjian: *Was it difficult joining a growth shop such as AIM as a value investor?*

Stanley: I was very cautious about that. I wanted to make sure AIM was committed to a value effort and that it wasn't simply a defensive move on the part of the firm. I spent a great deal of time talking to them and getting my own confidence up about their level of commitment. The first contact was a few years prior to the time I joined.

There's no doubt AIM has a high level of commitment to the value effort, but being the first value investor at a well-known growth shop made me cautious.

Kazanjian: *Tell me about your strategy. How do you put your portfolio together?*

Stanley: The strategy is completely bottom-up, driven one stock at a time. The cornerstone of our approach is Ben Graham's concept of intrinsic value. We think he had it exactly right: Price is independent of value and value is independent of the market. We know intrinsic value is based on the present value of future cash flows. We subscribe to Graham's philosophy, but apply it differently. Instead of trying to adjust PE multiples for all the things Graham suggested, we explicitly make those adjustments in a discounted cash flow approach. We calculate intrinsic value for every company that we own or would like to own at a price, and we maintain a database of these calculations. This gives us the ability to rank stocks based on appreciation potential. We want to invest when we have at least a 50 percent upside potential between price and intrinsic value during our two-to-three–year expected holding period.

We then go one step further. We don't just want to invest in the companies with the greatest upside. We want to invest in the best valuation opportunities—good businesses with a high return on capital that don't require a lot of capital to grow. We want companies with shareholder-friendly management and attractive long-term outlooks. We think far too many value investors focus on poor businesses with below-average economics. We are literally looking at stocks one at a time, trying to find good companies at great prices.

Kazanjian: *Do you pay attention to the overall market and the various indexes?*

Stanley: We're cognizant of that only because our performance is compared to those benchmarks. We have the Russell 1000 Value index as our primary benchmark. The S&P 500 index is our secondary benchmark. But we look for opportunities on an absolute basis. We buy a stock with the idea that we're buying the entire business. We're not trying to find companies that are going to go up in the next six months or are large components of an index. We're truly adopting a long-term horizon. We think about whether it's a business we want to be involved in, and whether there's a big gap between perception and reality that's causing a disconnect between price and value. By concentrating on good businesses, time is on our side because as a company's intrinsic value grows, the discount between price and value grows.

Kazanjian: *Where do you find these companies?*

Stanley: There are many sources. The vast majority of our ideas come from an intrinsic value database we maintain. This is a list of companies, 75 percent of which represent good businesses that most people are familiar with. The other 25 percent are a collection of great businesses I've come across over my years of analyzing companies. For instance, there's a business I'm looking at now that I first became aware of five years ago but never had an opportunity to buy. I put it in the database because I understood the business. I knew it was one I'd like to buy at a price and I liked the management team. Secondarily, we have a variety of computer screens and models, although absolutely nothing is bought off a quantitative model. They simply provide a shopping list and sometimes allow us to catch ideas that are not in the intrinsic value database for one reason or another.

Kazanjian: *Do you put that intrinsic value database together yourself?*

Stanley: I do. I have a team that helps calculate the intrinsic values. These calculations are the product of our fundamental research process. We maintain this information and upload it into a software program for portfolio monitoring and construction.

Kazanjian: *Is the information in this database something we can purchase on the open market?*

Stanley: No. It's based on a proprietary valuation model we use. Every valuation is done by hand and is based on our fundamental research. We value every single company one at a time, put those values into the database, upload it into a software program, and compare it to the market price every day. We are always looking for opportunities where we can achieve at least 50 percent upside to intrinsic value.

Kazanjian: *How do you calculate intrinsic value?*

Stanley: The value of any business is determined by the cash generated by the business. Simplistically, it's the sum of all future cash inflows and outflows, discounted for the value of money over time.
We subscribe to a very classic definition of business value. It's right
out of any business school textbook. But the application may be a
little different. We make a detailed, line-by-line forecast of a company's earnings, cash flows, and balance sheet for the next three
years. For the following seven years, the same financials are forecast
based on a set of important growth drivers.

This is an analytical framework I developed early in my career. It's
what we call a value driver model. This is similar to a DuPont model,
where you make certain assumptions about sustainable growth and
return on capital. But unlike with the DuPont approach, our growth
drivers are the product of economic financial statements that we create, rather than published GAAP [generally accepted accounting
principles] financials. The important thing to understand about the
estimates is that we're making a 10-year cash flow forecast and discounting it back to the present. We use the same discount rate for all
companies. It's derived once a year, and doesn't change that much
year to year. Nothing that we do is relative to the stock market.

Kazanjian: *What question are you trying to answer?*

Stanley: Ultimately we want to know the fair value of the business,
but first we need to understand how much capital was required to
deliver historical growth. We restate 10 years worth of data, adjusting income for all charges, goodwill amortization, and other such
distortions. But the important restatements are on the balance sheet.
We're of the belief that Wall Street spends all too much time focusing on the income statement and earnings, and very little time analyzing how much capital is required to deliver those earnings. We
spend a great deal of time understanding what we call the "economics of the business" or how much capital is required to deliver those
earnings. It's a simple question, but to get the answer, you must add
back all historical charges, restate all pooling transactions to purchase transactions, and treat all operating leases as debt, among
other things. It's a fairly painstaking analysis.

Kazanjian: *So this gives you an idea of how much capital the company put into the business to deliver that growth?*

Stanley: It does. It also gives us a fairly good base on which to estimate what kind of capital is going to be required in the future. Ultimately the value of any business is what the future cash flows are going to be. When we have a good idea of what the cash flows looked like historically, we can make a judgment about what they will look like in the future. These key assumptions drive our long-term forecast. While I said that we subscribe to a fairly traditional definition of intrinsic value, we derive discount rates in a nontraditional manner. We don't use the capital asset pricing model, beta, or any of that. I think a dollar of cash flow from Intel is worth just as much as a dollar of cash flow from Merck. So we use the same discount rate for every company. We want to make judgments about the things we control and understand rather than use the fuzzy logic that stands behind the capital asset pricing model. That's an important difference between how you're taught to calculate intrinsic value in business school and how we apply it.

Kazanjian: *How hard is it for the average person to compute intrinsic value?*

Stanley: The math is very simple. If you come at it from the same framework as I do, even if you choose a different discount rate for comparison, it doesn't matter. You'd make the same mistake across every company and the ranking order would be correct. I think an average individual can definitely sit down and calculate intrinsic value. Would it take him or her a lot of time and be difficult since he or she doesn't have all the resources I have? Probably. But there is no complexity to the calculation. It's the quality of the research and the resulting inputs that matter.

Kazanjian: *Go through an example or two to illustrate this process.*

Stanley: Back in 1998, United Healthcare missed its third-quarter earnings because of one division, which represented about 15 percent of profits. The company's Medicare division was having trouble. The stock declined by 45 percent and estimates declined by 9 percent. Based on my value of the cash flows for the 85 percent of the business that was not impacted—forgetting about the Medicare business—I figured we could more than double our money on the stock. I had followed United Healthcare for years and had met with the company on several occasions. I understood there had been a lot of consolidation in the industry, both within the HMO industry as well as in the indemnity industry. I had evidence a positive pricing cycle had begun, and the company suggested it could fix the Medicare division in one quarter. Conventional wisdom indicated it would take two or three, but from my standpoint, it didn't really matter. The company could have shut down the Medicare division and I would still have believed I would double our money. It turned out the company did turn it around in one quarter, but Wall Street's short-term focus created an opportunity for us. United Healthcare is a good business. It's a business that has an above-average return on capital. I made it a top-five holding below $20 a share and it is still a significant position today.

Kazanjian: *How did you calculate the intrinsic value for United Healthcare?*

Stanley: The same way I always do. I estimated what the earnings and cash flow would be three years out. I used my value driver model for the following seven years. I then took the present value of those cash flows and subtracted out the debt and divided by the number of shares.

Kazanjian: *Is it just a guess as to what the earnings will be going out a few years?*

Stanley: No, not at all. It's based on fundamental analysis. Warren Buffett once said that if you don't have a good idea of what the cash flows will look like over the next 10 years, you shouldn't invest.

With United Healthcare, the primary question was the trends in pricing for the company's products along with the trends in medical costs. I talked to management, competitors, Wall Street analysts, and every resource at my disposal. You must make an intelligent decision about what the future earnings look like. It's important to understand that the way we typically make money is not by having a more accurate future forecast. We make money by spotting when consensus expectations have mispriced the market. In other words, even the analysts who downgraded the stock didn't have dramatically different outlooks from mine for the cash flows of the business. They were just focused on different things and weren't paying attention to what was being discounted by the stock price. They were so disappointed that the company didn't make its quarterly earnings, they didn't realize the stock price was discounting zero percent growth when it seemed likely that the company would deliver at least 15 percent growth. United Healthcare has actually done better than that. It's not always about having a more accurate forecast. It's usually about understanding what is reflected in current stock prices.

Kazanjian: *Do you talk to management?*

Stanley: I personally meet with over 100 companies a year. A tremendous number of companies always comes through the shop to tell their stories. I also try to find out who their toughest competitors are, and I talk with them, too. That's a good way to get a lead on a company that's gaining market share. You have to do those things to be a good fundamental analyst.

Kazanjian: *Do you sell a stock once it reaches intrinsic value?*

Stanley: I'll sell if the stock becomes overvalued relative to intrinsic value, or when I feel like the risk/reward ratio has become unfavorable. Don't forget that intrinsic value is usually growing, so I may not sell an entire position just because it's fully valued. If it becomes overvalued, though, I'll sell the stock based on price alone.

Kazanjian: *Over the past few years, you've had a fairly decent weighting in healthcare management stocks.*

Stanley: That's not because I think healthcare management stocks are the best businesses in the world. I would have loved the opportunity to buy any drug company for half its intrinsic value. But those were the opportunities that were available. HMOs had performed poorly for years and were clearly out of favor. Most investors concluded they were terrible businesses run by bad managers. There was a real disconnect between perception and reality in the marketplace. It's true that I've had a substantial position in healthcare services, but that's really because investors became infatuated with other areas of healthcare and the market.

Kazanjian: *How diversified do you try to keep your portfolio?*

Stanley: I think the right number is 40 to 60 stocks. I have averaged approximately 50. That's enough to get leverage out of our good ideas, but still build a diversified portfolio.

Kazanjian: *How much money do you manage altogether?*

Stanley: I have $4 billion under management. About $3 billion of that is in the Basic Value Fund.

Kazanjian: *We talked about price targets. Do you have any other sell strategies?*

Stanley: I'll sell a stock if it becomes significantly overvalued, or if there's some type of permanent deterioration of the business. I'm not talking about a one-cent-per-share shortfall in the quarter. If the competitive structure of the industry is changed—maybe the company has done an acquisition or maybe a variety of other long-run fundamental issues change the earnings outlook, cash flows, and therefore the business value—I'll sell on that basis alone. The most common reason I sell is because I find something else that's more attractive. I may sell a stock that has modest upside to buy another one that has significant upside, especially if I consider the businesses to be of equal quality.

Kazanjian: *Not every stock goes up. How much patience do you have?*

Stanley: A fair amount on both sides. When I buy a stock, I establish a number of benchmarks that I expect to happen. These are fundamental things that are unique to every investment. As long as those benchmarks are realized [that is, cash flows come in as expected, yet the stock price is going nowhere], that's fine. I'll just keep buying more. I'm a firm believer that in the long run, prices will reflect value. Many times all the appreciation potential comes in the second and third years. There are other instances where a stock declines and the fundamentals are not unfolding as expected. In those cases I try to approach it with a fresh look. Perhaps I'll have another analyst who has never worked on the idea examine it. I'll redo the entire due diligence process. I'm always trying to determine if there's anything I have missed or if I've miscalculated the value.

Kazanjian: *We talked about a stock that worked. Tell me about a stock that didn't work and what you learned from that.*

Stanley: Mattel is a stock that I bought in the mid-$20s after it reported disappointing earnings for the second time. I bought the stock believing that it had substantial upside. It is a great business, but investors were concerned about the Learning Company acquisition. I talked with management and had previously analyzed the toy industry because of an investment in Hasbro several years prior. I was accurate in the value of the core business, but was terribly wrong on a variety of other points.

First, Mattel management was not what we thought they were. The Learning Company transaction created the opportunity to buy the stock, but the acquisition was more dilutive to shareholder value than I originally anticipated. It was one of the worst uses of capital that I can think of and it was devastating to shareholders. The stock collapsed from the low $20s down to $10. At that juncture, I had to decide whether to sell it, buy more, or do nothing. Initially, I concluded there was sufficient upside to hang on to the stock, but I didn't increase our position because of management. After the board hired Bob Eckert as CEO, I increased our position in Mattel because I was convinced that the value would be realized and poor capital allocation was a thing of the past. We have a modest profit from our investment in Mattel because we increased our position near the all-time low for the stock, but our original expectations will never be realized. The original investment thesis was that the business was durable enough to withstand some management and value destruction. The franchise has survived, but the value destruction was greater than anticipated.

Kazanjian: *Do you buy any technology stocks?*

Stanley: Yes. The root of what I'm doing is taking advantage of over-reactions to negative news. I can't think of any sector where there's more overreaction than technology. I have consistently made substantial amounts of money by deploying this value strategy in technology. One example of this was during the Asian crisis in 1998, when everyone was panicked over the economic slowdown and sold semiconductor companies down to ridiculous levels. The top of my intrinsic value database was literally populated with semiconductor companies. Most of those investments went up tenfold.

Kazanjian: *Given what happened in 2000 and 2001, are technology stocks showing up again on your screens, or were they so highly priced to begin with that they're still not trading at a discount to intrinsic value?*

Stanley: Most of the declines in technology have been in the highest-priced segments of the market. I would view the decline as simply creating more appropriate valuations. Any time a sector declines as much as technology, there are isolated opportunities that surface. I have certainly found some of those, but would not broadly say there is a great opportunity today in technology.

Kazanjian: *What do you make of what's happened with the market over the past couple of years?*

Stanley: I think it's a classic instance of a bubble—a virtuous cycle that became a vicious cycle. There were very sexy elements to the mania, with everyone believing the Internet would change the world and the economy and that we'd live in this utopian society as a result. Within professional money management, it became not only acceptable but almost a requirement to own these companies regardless of valuation. That mentality just fed on itself. I think it would have collapsed under its own weight, but it certainly had some help from the Fed raising interest rates.

Kazanjian: *You are the youngest person I've interviewed for this book. Were you even managing money during the crash of 1987?*

Stanley: No. My internship was in 1987, but I wasn't managing money. I was just an analyst.

Kazanjian: *What's interesting is that you had never been through a bear market before, yet you came out of the most recent one unscathed. In fact, your funds were up during this time.*

Stanley: We outperformed because we stuck to our discipline. We even made money in the technology sector during 2000. While it certainly would have been a great advantage to manage money through 1973–74 or 1987, it's wrong for people to assume that I don't know what happened. I've studied market history intensely.

Kazanjian: *We're now seeing stock fund money flow into value in large numbers. Do you think people are merely chasing performance, or are they really coming back to value and starting to pay more attention to what they're buying?*

Stanley: I'm sure with the amount of money that's flowing into value today, some of it is so-called hot money that's chasing performance. I also think this is a fairly typical response to a dislocation in the market. But to me the notion that value investing was ever dead doesn't make sense. It will be here forever. Nothing will ever change the fact that the value of a business is derived from the cash flows the business produces. Even if you spent many years where people didn't believe that, the pure power of that cash flow piling up on the balance sheet would realize that value eventually. I don't know how to answer the question of whether or not people are really coming back to value. I find it hard to believe that they didn't believe this was a valid investment philosophy in the first place.

Kazanjian: *The traditional asset allocation argument is you should put some of your money in both growth and value. What are your thoughts on that?*

Stanley: I think it depends on the individual. If you're an investor who is prone to chase performance or you just cannot stand being in one area of the market that may underperform for extended periods of time, then absolutely you need to diversify. The worst thing that you can do is jump from one hot style to the next.

As an individual, I'm a strong believer in the value approach. I have virtually all of my net worth invested in value. That was true when value was underperforming, it's true now, and it will probably always be true. The difference is I have strong hands. I didn't give up on value in 1998 or 1999 when things appeared the darkest. If you have conviction in a given style, stay with it. If you're with a good manager who has a record of creating value, things will work out fine. If you're not disciplined enough to stay the course, or if short-term volatility is a concern, diversification is the better answer.

Kazanjian: *How do you spend a typical day?*

Stanley: Every morning starts off with going through overnight news on the portfolio and other things that come under the heading of maintenance research. We listen to every management conference call on each of our holdings. I'm constantly reevaluating our intrinsic value calculations and making sure that the fundamentals are unfolding as expected. I spend most of the rest of the day looking for new investments. That due diligence process includes everything from poring over annual reports and Wall Street research reports to getting out of the office and meeting with companies and going to conferences. It's not really all that glamourous, but if you like doing financial analysis, it's exciting. The end result of the due diligence is determining the intrinsic value for whatever company we are working on. I'd say 20 percent of my time is spent on maintenance, and the other 80 percent on generating new ideas.

Kazanjian: *What case would you make to an investor to convince him or her that he or she should follow a more value-oriented approach to investing?*

Stanley: The value-oriented approach is the best approach for wealth creation for a couple of reasons. First of all, you have risk and reward on your side. Rather than trying to buy a stock hoping someone else will buy it from you at an even more inflated price, you have the value of the business underpinning your investment thesis. Therefore, it's a lower-risk approach to creating wealth. It also generates higher after-tax returns because not only are you generating that arbitrage between price and value—in our case, the 50 percent difference between market price and intrinsic value—but you also can compound your money tax-free as intrinsic value grows and over long holding periods.

Kazanjian: *Some academics say value investing is riskier because you're buying troubled companies.*

Stanley: Academia is wrong on its definition of risk. Everything you read in academic research is usually based on defining risk as beta. All of that has really been discredited, even by some of the founders of beta. Nonetheless, it continues to be talked about and taught. Risk has to do with the permanent loss of capital. The probability of a permanent loss of capital is significantly reduced when the price of a stock declines significantly below what it's worth. It doesn't go up as beta would suggest. The notion that risk goes up as stock prices decline is completely backward.

Stanley feels that the biggest mistake most investors make is trading too much and having a short-term time horizon. In his opinion, forecasting where stock prices will be over the next three to six months—or even a year out—is a mindless effort. He further believes that the majority of investors are best off in mutual funds because they don't have the time or interest to develop a credible investment discipline. Stanley puts his money where his mouth is. He says he invests all of his own money in his funds, and doesn't even have an outside brokerage account. ▪

RICHARD WEISS

STRONG CAPITAL MANAGEMENT

Dick Weiss first learned about the stock market from his grandfather. As a young boy, he'd tag along when his grandpa went to see his broker. Weiss remembers staring at the ticker tape in the broker's office. Weiss eventually bought stock in Continental Airlines, because it was headquartered in his grandparents' hometown of El Paso. But it wasn't until an influential college professor rekindled his interest in the market that he decided it might make a good career.

Weiss probably has more affection for growth than any other Master I talked with, perhaps because he started out at Stein Roe & Farnham, which was long recognized as a premier growth shop. Weiss was ultimately handed the reins of the Stein Roe Special Fund at the end of 1991. This fund concentrated on uncovering promising smaller companies. Under his leadership, Stein Roe Special became the top-performing growth fund in the country from 1982 to 1991.

Such solid performance caught the eye of Dick Strong, who invited Weiss to join his firm in 1991. Weiss promptly took over management of the Strong Common Stock and Opportunity funds. Common Stock focuses on small-caps, while Opportunity looks for both small- and mid-caps. Both funds did so well and became so popular that Strong had to limit asset flows into Common Stock to keep it from getting too large. Weiss continues to run both funds today.

While Weiss is clearly interested in growth, he will only buy stocks trading at a discount to his estimate of the company's underlying value. It's a unique take on value that has served him well throughout his career. And while he's a stickler on getting the price he wants when buying a stock, he's a bit more flexible when it comes to selling a holding. Unlike some managers, he'll let his winners run as long as he thinks they are performing in line with his expectations, even if they expand outside of his normal market capitalization range.

Kazanjian: *It's always great talking with fellow USC Trojans who are in the investment business. There aren't many out there, you know, especially in such high-profile positions. Did you study finance there?*

Weiss: I studied marketing and finance at the University of Southern California. I had a finance professor, Dr. Trefftzs, who rekindled my interest in investing. He was a smart guy. I learned a lot from him.

Kazanjian: *How did he rekindle it?*

Weiss: When I was pretty young, my grandpa took me to a broker's office and at my request bought me shares of Continental Airlines. I loved looking at the ticker tape when we visited the broker. So the attraction was there early on. Dr. Trefftzs approached investing not just from financial and quantitative views, but also from a qualitative perspective. That's what I've always liked about investing. It's multidimensional.

Kazanjian: *What happened after USC?*

Weiss: I had a 4.0 grade point average at the school of business. I then had to decide whether or not to get my MBA. A friend and I did an entrepreneurial project where we developed a plan for a travel-related benefits program. I debated starting that company. It probably would have worked out, though we might have been four or five years too early. I applied to the USC and Harvard Business School MBA programs. When I got the application from Harvard, it was so daunting, I put it away for two months. I received a scholarship from USC, which made my decision even more difficult. But Dr. Trefftzs talked me into going to Harvard. So I went straight from USC to the Harvard Business School.

Kazanjian: *Was it the right decision?*

Weiss: Oh, yes. I liked it.

Kazanjian: *Did you know at that point that you wanted to work on Wall Street?*

Weiss: No. There were always elements of it that appealed to me. It's not as financial as people think. It requires understanding business and marketing strategy, which I liked.

Kazanjian: *I get a lot of mail from people asking for advice on how to prepare for becoming an investment manager. What would you recommend?*

Weiss: I think the case study method in business school is a pretty good way to learn investing. They tell you stories, give you some facts and opinions, and make you come up with an answer. But there's never really an answer. You work through it in class and come up with what you think is the obvious answer, although not everyone agrees. Investing is like that. Investing ironically is one of those jobs where you can be precisely measured, yet it's a profession where there is no right answer. I think that's why most investors are pretty average.

Kazanjian: *Did you start at Stein Roe after Harvard?*

Weiss: I was getting offers from different recruiters at Harvard. I really wanted to come back to California, where I grew up, so I was only looking at California companies. Stein Roe was based in Chicago and came to campus. They had a policy of recruiting every year regardless of how bad the market was. I graduated in 1975, so I was being recruited in the fall of 1974, which had the worst stock market since the Depression. I didn't sign up to interview with Stein Roe because I didn't want to live in Chicago. But my roommate thought I would be really good at the job, which was for a research analyst. So later I called them and said, "Sorry I missed you. Could I see you at your New York office?" They said if I could get down there, they'd see me. I was always interested in investing, but it wasn't something I knew I *had* to do. Bill Clinton knew he wanted to be president from the time he was 12. With me, investing was always intellectually interesting, but I never thought of it as a great career. Nevertheless, I met with Stein Roe in New York. They then flew me out to Chicago. Stein Roe had a very hard and extensive interview process. I was interviewed for a whole day by 11 people. When I got on the elevator to go home, I said to myself, If I don't get a job offer from them, I won't get a job offer from anyone.

I tell people now it was only because I was so young and naïve that I was even trying to get that job in the first place. Nobody was trying to get a job in investment management then when they were laying off thousands of people in the worst market in 50 years. I was the only one in the entire business school who went into investment management. Long story short, I got the job.

Kazanjian: *How was it?*

Weiss: I started as a research analyst. Stein Roe could have been a fabulous firm. They were one of the pioneers of in-depth research and going to visit companies. Their structure was quite unique. They had a dual career path. One side was account management and one side was research. There were about an equal number of the firm's senior partners running each of the two sides. That was important to me, too, because at the time the research part intrigued me more than the account management side, which was basically marketing. It was a fabulous place to work. I started under a great guy who gave me a lot of responsibility early on. But the business was different then. It wasn't quite as frenetic. You really could learn an industry.

Kazanjian: *Did you learn how to invest there?*

Weiss: I kind of had that within me. Dr. Trefftzs gave me a framework of what to look for and I already knew what I thought was important in a company.

Kazanjian: *Which was?*

Weiss: Companies that made a high return on investment, had good market share, and had competitive advantages that would sustain their profitability. I started out as a media analyst and as a nonsemiconductor tech component analyst. I was always in the growth areas of the market. What I learned coming in right after 1974 was that valuation did not always accurately reflect the future potential of a company. The Nifty Fifty, while declining in 1974, still dominated the market averages and sported very high PEs. Then you had the rest of the market that was just devastated.

I think the great advantage I had coming in was I could see that value was not related to reputation or what the Street was saying. It was simply inherent within the company. The Nifty Fifty were selling at 22 times earnings back then and maybe growing at 10 percent a year. I was able to buy companies growing at 15 to 20 percent a year for six times earnings. These stocks were available for six times earnings because everything had been devastated in the market. I learned that you don't always have to pay a lot to get a good company with strong growth. You just have to buy these stocks when other people don't want them. That concept has stuck with me.

Kazanjian: *Wasn't Stein Roe primarily a growth shop?*

Weiss: Stein Roe had built its reputation by discovering great companies such as 3M. They liked good companies. They just didn't know what to pay for them. As a result, they always paid too much. The guys that ran the firm didn't have any discipline.

Kazanjian: *Did that bother you?*

Weiss: Yes. I had a pretty good sense of valuation. Starting out on media was a big advantage because I actually liked to watch TV. Most of the people on Wall Street looked down their noses at TV.

Kazanjian: *When did you get your first shot at managing money?*

Weiss: Probably 1980. I was given a small part of a big portfolio. Before that, around 1977, I asked if I could run a paper portfolio. But it was more than a paper portfolio. They set it up so that I had to call up the desk and tell them what I wanted to buy. They then created a paper trade for it. It wasn't like you just make it up at the end of the day. It was actually put into Stein Roe's accounting system. The first year I ran the portfolio, the S&P 500 was up about 5 percent and I was up 20 percent. One day, one of the firm's partners said to me, "That's just a paper portfolio. You're making it up." So I replied, "I'll make you a bet. I won't make another trade from here on out. Even though there may be some things I really don't like that much, I won't do anything and we'll see how well the portfolio does."

Kazanjian: *You sounded pretty confident.*

Weiss: I was. Over the next year, that portfolio was up more than twice as much as the S&P, even though I never made a trade. The year after that, I started getting some real money to manage. The firm kept that paper portfolio going for around seven years with no trading, and it still outperformed the S&P two to one over the period.

Kazanjian: *You also ran a couple of funds at Stein Roe before you left.*

Weiss: In 1979, they gave me a part of a portfolio, which turned out to be the best portfolio at the firm. In 1980, I got a bit more. At the end of 1981, the guy who was running the Stein Roe Special fund left. About a third of the names in the portfolio were names I had brought to his attention. They put me to work on the fund with the director of research, even though I did all the work. From 1982 to the time I left, it was the best growth fund in the country.

Kazanjian: *Was it predominantly a small- and mid-cap fund?*

Weiss: It was mostly small-caps.

Kazanjian: *Were you always naturally comfortable in that space?*

Weiss: Yes. When I started, the Nifty Fifty and the really large-cap stocks were way overvalued relative to the small-caps. The values were all found among the small-caps.

Kazanjian: *When did you move over to Strong?*

Weiss: I started talking to Strong in 1990. Small-cap stocks peaked about 1984 and really didn't do that well from 1985 until 1990. I thought small-caps were going to be a fabulous asset class again. After all, everything goes in cycles. I wanted to start a business running institutional money primarily in small-caps. I talked to Stein Roe about it, and they kept hemming and hawing. Dick Strong called me and we talked for about 11 months before I decided to come to Milwaukee to work here. I started at Strong in 1991.

Kazanjian: *At that time did Strong already have the Common Stock and Opportunity funds, or did you start both of those portfolios?*

Weiss: Opportunity was a pretty big fund. They gave me that to run. Common also existed, but only had about $2.5 million.

Kazanjian: *What's the main difference between the two funds?*

Weiss: It's always been the size of the companies we invest in. Originally Common was really a small-cap fund. Opportunity was a small-/mid-cap fund, meaning we invested in the lower end of the mid-cap range. We closed Common in 1993 because our assets grew so much. Over time, as they got larger and larger, Opportunity clearly became a pure mid-cap fund, while Common is now closer to being a small-/mid-cap combination.

Kazanjian: *What are the assets in those funds?*

Weiss: Altogether we run about $9 billion, including separate accounts.

Kazanjian: *That seems like a lot for the kinds of stocks you buy. Do you have problems managing that much money in the small-/mid-cap space?*

Weiss: Yes. We have to be that much more right. Transaction costs are high. It's very difficult. We also closed our separate accounts in 1993, along with the Common Stock fund. That was the only way we could keep the record going.

Kazanjian: *Is portfolio size as big a problem among mid-caps as it is for small-caps?*

Weiss: The way the markets have evolved, the liquidity among mid-caps is similar to what it was like with small-caps six or seven years ago. There are a lot of large companies that don't have much liquidity.

Kazanjian: *There's an ongoing debate over how big a small- or mid-cap fund should be. When people are considering such funds, all other things being equal, should they look for funds with a small asset base?*

Weiss: Yes. The bigger you are, the harder it is to buy and sell efficiently. If you're dealing with a good manager who's running a big fund, look and see if his performance is consistent with how you think it should be, given where the market is. In other words, if his style is in vogue and he's not doing well, that's a big warning sign. As long as he's performing as you would expect him to given his style and the way it matches up with the market at any given moment, you won't get the home runs like you would have when he had a much smaller asset base, but you'll probably do okay.

Kazanjian: *Let's talk about how you begin the process of putting your portfolio together.*

Weiss: We're really bottom-up investors. We don't do a lot of top-down work, although from our bottom-up work we may develop themes that lead us to similar stocks in the same sector or general area.

Kazanjian: *How do you find your ideas?*

Weiss: One way is through reading. I don't get a lot of ideas from Wall Street. I generate my own ideas and then use the Street to help me monitor them. I also go through the *Value Line Investment Survey* every week. Value Line reviews 1,600 stocks every three months. I get a lot of potential ideas out of that. You can see areas of the market where there's not a lot of activity. That's where stocks tend to be cheap. I'm not looking at Value Line's grades as much as at valuation and cash flow values.

Kazanjian: *You have a unique take on value. Talk about how you go about evaluating these potential ideas to see if there's something you're interested in.*

Weiss: We put a private value on everything. Private value equates to takeover value. In other words, if you could own the company and capture all of the cash flows, what would you pay for it? This process evolved over time because I started as a media analyst. In some areas of media, the only way to really value something is using a cash flow model. Some of the best stocks in history have not made that much money on a PE basis.

It intuitively made sense to me that each company has its own value as a business. One day I was reading *The Wall Street Journal* and I looked through the highs and lows for the year for various stocks in the stock tables. I noticed the spread was huge. It was one of those years in the 1980s when the market wasn't doing much. For most stocks, regardless of industry, the spread from the high price to the low price was 50 to 100 percent. It struck me that in this stable market the underlying value of the business probably hadn't changed at all because nothing was really happening, yet you still had these wild price swings. If you could figure out the company's true value, you would begin to have the ability to play off the emotions of the market. When investors hated a company and took its stock down to half its private value, you could buy it with the confidence that it probably wouldn't go down much more. Conversely, when everybody loved it, you could look at your private value and say, "If it's 80 percent of my private value, that's about what it's worth, so I don't want to buy it." It's a way to take advantage of the way most people operate.

Kazanjian: *How do you determine the private market value?*

Weiss: That's really an art form. I'm a big believer that investing is, in some ways, an artistic endeavor. Everybody perceives the world and the future in slightly different ways. Most people tend to look in the rear view mirror. If you had the ability to see what might be or what could be, and you were more accurate than the rest, you'd have better performance.

The trick with private value is to really understand what you're buying. I think the advantage we have is that most people in the public market are buying next quarter's earnings or a certain earnings-per-share growth rate. If you really were going to buy a company, some of those near-term things would be pretty far down on the list, in terms of what you'd be focused on in the near term. The first thing you'd be focused on is what elements really created and sustained the cash flows of the company—things like whether the company had a key product and whether it was losing or gaining market share. You first have to understand what a buyer would be looking to buy. Sometimes this can give you a much higher price than the market, and sometimes it gives you a lower price. The rough and dirty approach is to put a multiple on the company's cash flows. The key is what multiple and discount rate you use.

Kazanjian: *Private market value is different from book value?*

Weiss: Absolutely. There's really not too much relationship at all.

Kazanjian: *You're looking to determine what another company or outside buyer would pay for the company. What discount from that price are you hoping to pay?*

Weiss: For most of my career, I would have said you wanted to pay 50 to 60 percent of the private market value, because that's where stocks have hit bottom. We have around 12 feet of notebooks containing private values and deals that have happened on the companies we've owned. Anything beyond 50 percent somehow gets arbitraged away. It's just too cheap. Value buyers or other companies and the public market will come in or the board will get disgruntled and replace management to create change. Beyond 50 percent is too big a spread to be sustained for long. But you have to be right on your private market value. If you are, you are very safe buying something at half that price. That said, in the last five years, the market had its own bubble, which also created a rise in private values. As a result, if we now find something selling for 60 to 65 percent of private value, we'll take a shot at it.

Kazanjian: *Why do these companies generally get down to those low levels?*

Weiss: The market is always going from one group to the next. One thing is in vogue this month, and something else is in vogue next month. Sometimes companies have a disappointment and the stock goes down, yet whatever caused the disappointment is no longer impacting results. It could be that the company isn't in a very exciting area, and it's not catching Wall Street's fancy. That's just the way the market works.

Kazanjian: *Once you find a company selling at this discount to private market value, do you automatically buy it or do you do additional research?*

Weiss: When we see a company that looks decent, we do a couple of things. We do a business analysis to see if the company has a business that's consistent with the returns it's generating. Is there something unusual in the numbers? Does it seem to have a competitive advantage that is realistic to what the company says it's doing? If that looks okay, we'll do a rough and dirty private value just to see if there's enough room to even be interested. Any small-cap investor who's serious about it needs to go to see management. So we'll visit the company. If we can't do that on a timely basis, we'll schedule a two-hour phone call or something similar to talk with them. With small-caps, you're really buying management.

Kazanjian: *How do you evaluate management?*

Weiss: I go to talk to them and apply my common sense to their answers. I want to judge their decision-making process and their thought-making process. I look to see if they have a good handle on their business. Is their strategy consistent with what their industry is all about, or at least with what I think it's all about? In a two-hour interview, I might only spend the last 20 minutes on current results. Nobody really knows what's going to happen in a small company. It should be growing, but it's new. Changes occur all the time. What I'm really trying to ascertain is how these managers will adapt and react to changing circumstances. How will they react when their number-one customer goes and does something crazy?

Kazanjian: *Once you take a position, do you remain in close contact with management?*

Weiss: We tend to manage by exception. We spend more time on the stocks that are doing either really well or really poorly than on stocks in the middle.

Kazanjian: *Do you look at debt, growth rate, and things like that?*

Weiss: Yes. That all goes into figuring out what multiple to put on the company's cash flows or what discount rate you use.

Kazanjian: *Are you looking for a certain percentage of growth?*

Weiss: No. I think that's a big mistake. I've heard a lot of people who run portfolios say, "I'll only buy stocks that grow 25 percent a year." They haven't done very well. Stocks that grow 25 percent a year are usually highly priced. We want a growth rate that we think is consistent with what the business is and what the company can realistically achieve. We'll set a value according to that growth rate.

Kazanjian: *Do you generally start off buying a small position and work your way up, or do you try to buy the full chunk you want in the beginning?*

Weiss: We tend to own 70 to 80 stocks in the portfolio. An initial position would be about 1¼ percent. We buy it all as quickly as we can once we decide to take a position.

Kazanjian: *Do you keep the portfolio diversified, insofar as not having too much in any one name?*

Weiss: Yes. I think what makes us unique is that some people tend to apply private market value methodology to one particular segment. We apply it across the board. We have a pretty diversified portfolio. We're bottom-up investors so we never go and say we want X percent in an industry. Nevertheless, somehow it seems to turn out that we cover most industries.

Kazanjian: *Does that include technology?*

Weiss: Yes. Until the past few years we were always overweight in technology. It was only when it got really insane that we became underweight.

Kazanjian: *Is there a certain capitalization range that you limit yourself to because of the fund's tilt toward the smaller stocks?*

Weiss: Obviously, we tend to look more in the smaller areas. However, if we come across something that is bigger, we won't avoid it because the market cap is too high. But we do try to keep the portfolio's median market cap within our set ranges.

Kazanjian: *Which are?*

Weiss: In the Opportunity Fund it would be $6 to $8 billion. For Common Stock it might be $2.5 to $3 billion.

Kazanjian: *What makes you sell a stock?*

Weiss: A few things. When we buy a stock, we figure out our private market value. When it reaches that price, it doesn't necessarily mean that we'll sell, but it causes us to reassess the position. We'll look at such things as how much the private value will rise in the next year. A lot of times something will trade up almost to private value in the current year, but then be at a reasonable discount in the forward year because the company's growing. We have to take that into account.

When we buy a stock, we have key expectations we look for. One thing that triggers a really fast sale is if a company says something that is inconsistent with what we thought it was going to do from a strategic point of view. Say we bought a company that generated a lot of free cash, but had been making several acquisitions. If management previously told us they'd use that cash to pay down debt and they make another large acquisition, we'd probably sell the stock because the company's actions were inconsistent with what they originally said.

Kazanjian: *What about if the stock moves outside of your capitalization range due to its success? Will you sell, or do you hold on to your winners?*

Weiss: We hold them. We put a lot of time and effort into getting to know a company. It's silly to sell because it's executing the way you hoped it would and therefore the stock has gone up.

Kazanjian: *When you make an investment in a stock, how long do you tend to hold on to it?*

Weiss: The average holding length is more than two years. Our turnover is around 70 percent. What tends to happen is we'll buy something and in the first three to four months as we get to know it, we may discover it wasn't exactly what we thought it was. Once it gets beyond that period we tend to hold for a long time.

Kazanjian: *Going through your annual reports, I noticed you occasionally own some foreign stocks. What brings you to those and do you evaluate them differently?*

Weiss: When I got to Strong, I felt that we were moving into a global market. In other words, some industries would be looked at on a global basis and pricing would be normalized across all the different markets. At about the same time, in 1992–93, Dick Strong got interested in Hong Kong because of the opening up of China. For a while we owned quite a few foreign stocks. In fact, I still go to London every 10 months, even though we don't own many foreign stocks now. These trips give me a good sense of how the U.S. looks compared to other places. I've made a lot of money by going to London and playing off the conventional wisdom that I pick up in London on both the U.S. and the rest of the world. The one thing that strikes me when I go to London is that the U.S. market has not been particularly expensive on average compared to many foreign markets. If you look at the S&P, you get a misleading feel for the U.S. market because it's so skewed by overpriced technology stocks. In reality, U.S. companies are cheaper than European companies.

Kazanjian: *What do you think the future looks like for small- and mid-cap stocks?*

Weiss: My thesis is that we're going to be in a market much like the one we were in during the late 1970s. During those years, the market average did not do much, but the average stock was performing well, rising from the 1974 collapse. The Nifty Fifty, which today would be the technology and other momentum stocks, was still so overpriced that they were trading stocks at best. Momentum and tech stocks that reached absurd PEs in 1999 and 2000 will need at least several years for earnings to catch up to stock prices. The average stock is not dirt cheap, but on a relative basis it'll probably do much better.

Kazanjian: *You sound pretty optimistic.*

Weiss: On a relative basis I'm optimistic about the average stock. How that plays out in the market is a little less clear because, as I said, the average stock is not cheap. What you could get is fairly nominal gains in the market resulting in a modest rise for the average stock and flat returns in the momentum stocks.

Kazanjian: *Judging by the composition of your portfolios, you seem to favor growth-oriented businesses more heavily than most value managers in your analysis. Do you agree?*

Weiss: This is a business where most people are well above average in terms of intelligence, but they tend to become average performers because there's safety in crowds. If you're part of the crowd, ultimately you're only going to be average because the market is so efficient. What we've been able to do is take a sound core philosophy of buying good companies when they're not priced like good companies. We take advantage of emotions in the marketplace. Because of our private value work, we try to go where the value is at the moment. If it's in growth stocks, that's where we'll invest. If it's in value stocks, that's where we'll invest. Many people don't have a core philosophy, which I think is the biggest killer because you'll be whipped by the market.

Weiss divides his time between Strong headquarters outside of Milwaukee, his home in Chicago, and his avocado ranch near Santa Barbara, California. As testament to his somewhat eclectic style, he has two certificates on his wall from Lipper Analytical Services, a mutual fund ratings service. One praises Strong Common Stock for being the number-one growth stock fund over a five-year period; the other calls it the number-one–performing mid-cap value fund. Why the discrepancy? The 59-year-old manager says that although he never strays from his discipline, his flexible approach sometimes leads him to pay increasingly high prices for stocks. As a result, at times his portfolio may look a bit more "growthy" than some of his value peers, making it difficult for fund-rating services to keep him in one particular style box. ∎

WALLACE WEITZ

WEITZ FUNDS

There aren't many value managers who are regularly compared to the most famous investor of them all—Warren Buffett. Wally Weitz is one such manager. Weitz and Buffett do have a lot in common. They both hold a rather concentrated portfolio of stocks bought at a significant discount to their private market value. Both play bridge. And both live in Omaha.

As it turns out, Weitz and Buffett are friends, and Weitz has long been a shareholder of Buffett's Berkshire Hathaway. But Weitz is quick to distance himself from the other oracle of Omaha, reasoning he doesn't deserve to be compared to a legend such as Buffett. Certainly some of Weitz's shareholders would disagree. As *The Washington Post* noted, Weitz's funds have actually outperformed Berkshire Hathaway in recent years.

Weitz got his introduction to the market at age 11. His grandparents gave his single-parent, social worker mom some money to invest in stocks. Weitz tagged along when she went to meet with a broker on Wall Street. His mom was bored stiff, but Weitz was fascinated. He started corresponding with the broker and reading about the market. Before long, he made his first investment. After college, he wound up working at the broker's firm as an analyst.

Feeling the itch to start running money, Weitz moved to his wife's hometown of Omaha in 1973 and became a broker. He didn't earn much in the way of commissions, but was good at making money for his clients. Ten years later, he decided it made more sense to manage the accounts on a pooled basis, earning a set fee for his advice, rather than commissions on each trade. That's when he started his own company.

All of the assets he managed were placed into three private partnerships, which were similar to mutual funds. Almost two decades later, his firm now runs five funds and three private partnerships.

In determining a company's value, the 52-year-old Weitz focuses on free cash flow, or the amount of money left for management to use after paying its bills. He's a patient investor who sticks closely to his discipline. And if he can't find enough stocks that meet his criteria, he's not afraid to sit on a pile of cash until some bargains come along.

Kazanjian: *You live close to Omaha's other famous value investor, Warren Buffett. Have you two ever met?*

Weitz: Yes. I know him, I like him, and I've learned a lot from him. One of my finest hours was taking $9 from him in a bridge game a long time ago, thanks to my duplicate bridge teammate's skill, not my own.

Kazanjian: *Do you try to emulate his investment style?*

Weitz: I've learned a lot from watching what he does, going to his annual meetings, reading his annual reports, and such. But our portfolios have little overlap most of the time. From him I've learned the concept of thinking about the business behind a stock and what a realistic, sensible private owner would be willing to pay to own it forever. Value investors are looking for ways to screen out dangerously expensive investments. That private owner mindset is my version of the screen, and it comes from Buffett.

Kazanjian: *You've been investing since you were a kid. Tell me how your interest in stocks first developed.*

Weitz: My grandparents worried about their social worker, single-parent daughter, who lived in New Orleans. When I was 11, they gave her $25,000. This was a lot of money in the 1960s—about five times her annual salary. My grandparents introduced her to the family stockbroker in New York. She and I went to Wall Street and had lunch with him. She was absolutely bored, and I was enthralled. On the way back home I picked up a copy of Louis Engel's *How to Buy Stocks* and got excited about it.

Kazanjian: *What did you learn from the broker?*

Weitz: I corresponded with him, and he would send me things to read. He got me interested in life insurance stocks, which were hot at the time. He sent me a list of 40 or 50 insurance stocks and I bought the one ranked highest on the list. It didn't work out, and it was an early lesson that investing isn't as easy as just doing some arithmetic.

Kazanjian: *Did your mom buy any stock?*

Weitz: Yes. She bought Atchison, Topeka and Santa Fe Railroad, Standard Oil, and a couple of other stocks that he recommended. My first stock was General Telephone. I bought it in 1961, when I was 12, with my grass cutting money.

Kazanjian: *How did it work out?*

Weitz: My wife teases me that even though I can't remember to pick up the laundry on the way home, I do remember paying $26⅜ in September 1961 and selling the stock for $42½ in 1966.

Kazanjian: *Sounds like a pretty good experience.*

Weitz: It was. Nine months after buying it, we had a sharp market collapse in May 1962. The stock went to $19. That was an early experience in market volatility.

Kazanjian: *Did your interest in stocks continue in college?*

Weitz: Yes, although there was one other little chapter in between. I belonged to an investment club when I was in high school. The teacher would bring in stockbrokers and other guests to talk. One guy who came in got me interested in technical analysis. He recommended *Technical Analysis of Stock Trends* by Robert D. Edwards and John F. Magee. This book is the technician's version of Ben Graham's book for fundamental investors. I asked for the book for Christmas, which probably made my mother fear that she was failing as a parent. For several years, I kept as many as 100 charts a day on different stocks, and traded from those charts. That was another wonderful lesson because it didn't work out very well. I was trying to make a mechanical science out of it.

Kazanjian: *That was your first and last experience with technical analysis?*

Weitz: Right. I remember people wrote things in my high school yearbook about expecting me to become a stockbroker. I went off to Carleton College and majored in economics. I tried to talk several of my professors into letting me do independent-study work on the stock market. They thought that was absolutely beneath an academic institution such as Carleton. One of my professors told me the stock market was nothing but astrology.

Kazanjian: *Did you take any finance courses at Carleton?*

Weitz: They didn't teach finance. It's a small liberal arts school. I'm probably better off for having had to sample lots of "impractical" subjects. We did have a fabulous professor who, among other courses, taught a two-semester course in accounting. That was my only formal finance training of any kind. She taught us about the choices that companies have in terms of being aggressive or conservative about the way they account for things. She also showed us how to read the footnotes, to avoid being tricked by all the different kinds of maneuvers that can go on.

Kazanjian: *Were you trading stocks in college?*

Weitz: Yes. But that was in the 1960s, and I didn't have a lot of spare money. When I lost $50 because my trade in Tootsie Roll didn't work, that was a major tragedy. In retrospect it was pretty cheap tuition. It made a big impression on me at the time.

Kazanjian: *What happened after Carleton?*

Weitz: My senior year I got a copy of *The Wall Street Transcript* and wrote to a dozen brokerage firms asking for a summer job. The 13th firm I wrote to was the little firm my mom and I visited when I was a boy. I wrote to the personnel guy and he said I could come meet him when I came to New York at Christmas. I got a summer job there by sheer luck. I showed up the next June. It turned out to be the bottom of the 1970 bear market. I found out later that the firm was just about bankrupt. He looked at me and said, "Oh, I forgot you were coming, but we're only going to pay you minimum wage so you might as well stay." It was supposed to be a summer job, and I planned to go to New York University in the fall for business school. I liked what I was doing that summer, so I arranged to go to

NYU at night instead of full time and stayed at the firm. I ended up dropping out of NYU after one semester because I hated it. But I stayed at the brokerage firm for two and a half years.

Kazanjian: *What did you do at the firm?*

Weitz: At first I was the assistant to the one self-taught analyst who followed the 500 stocks we made over-the-counter markets in. The list changed every month. We certainly didn't cover them closely, but it was a wonderful experience. A trader would come running out of the trading room screaming, "My stock is down five points! What's wrong?" I'd call the president of the company, because I didn't know any better. I don't think I did the traders any good, but it was a terrific experience. I'd go to analyst luncheons and annual meetings and such.

I also helped some guys who were managing accounts for people, trying to find stock ideas for them. One day the president of the firm called me in and said, "You're doing fine and we're not paying you much so there's no problem, but what do you want to do with your life?" That was a cold slap in the face, but it made me stop and think further ahead than next week. I told him I'd like to manage money. He said, "That's great. Go get some money to manage." I had to think about whether to try it as a broker, which is what those guys were really doing. They had discretionary accounts, but they were brokers.

I decided I was willing to try that, but my wife and I didn't want to bring up our kids in New York City. If I was going to try being a stockbroker and finding accounts, we wanted to be in a place we were willing to live in for a while because once I developed a clientele, if I could, we'd need to stay there. We looked in Omaha, where she was from, New Orleans, where I was from, and Minneapolis near Carleton, where we'd gone to school. A little Omaha regional firm, Chiles, Heider & Co., agreed to hire me on the basis of a tiny research salary—so at least I wouldn't totally starve while trying to get some accounts to manage—and a share of any commissions I could generate. I did that for 10 years, from 1973 to 1983.

Kazanjian: *Were you a successful broker?*

Weitz: Well, it depends on how you look at it. I was a very small producer from a commission point of view, but I always approached it as trying to get people to give me accounts on a discretionary basis so that I could really be a money manager. I didn't want to sell them individual ideas one at a time.

Kazanjian: *Did you have an investment discipline at that point?*

Weitz: Yes. I don't think it was so different from what it is today, although I couldn't have explained it at the time. The head of the firm I worked for, Charlie Heider, was close to Buffett and a Berkshire fan. He would take me to the Berkshire annual meetings back when there were six or eight outsiders that went to them. He was a mentor to me in the sense of indoctrinating me about the virtues of free cash flow and the Buffett approach to thinking about a good business, taking a long-term approach, buying at a discount, and so on. It fit with the Graham theoretical stuff I had read. I always thought about assets under management even though that's not the way the brokerage world worked. I wasn't successful in the sense of earning high commissions, but after 10 years I had a small group of clients who were willing to come with me to form the new company.

Kazanjian: *The company you have today?*

Weitz: Exactly. I wanted to pool the accounts for efficiency. I wanted to charge a fee instead of commissions, because it seemed like being paid by the trade was the wrong way to go. I also wanted to be on my own.

Kazanjian: *When did you start the firm?*

Weitz: In 1983. I had $11 million of client assets willing to come with me. I pooled their funds into three private partnerships that, in most respects, were just like mutual funds.

Kazanjian: *What did you call your company?*

Weitz: Wallace R. Weitz and Company. As time went on, we started some mutual funds. Now, 19 years later, there are five public mutual funds and three private partnerships.

Kazanjian: *How much do you manage altogether now?*

Weitz: Around $7.5 billion.

Kazanjian: *It wasn't until the mid-1990s that you really started to get significant assets. What was the catalyst that brought you into the spotlight and caused all of this money to flow into your funds?*

Weitz: I think there were three or four things that happened along the way. In 1993, Morningstar picked up the Weitz Value Fund and gave it five stars. The fund had $50 million at the time. Morningstar also wrote an article called "Five Undiscovered Funds," which included Weitz Value. Several newspapers around the country picked up this article and reran it. Up until then, 80 percent-plus of our investors had been local. The fund's assets went from $50 million to $100 million in six months. Everybody here was stuffing prospectus packages. We did our own fulfillment. We got 20 or 30 calls a day. Four years later, at the end of 1997, assets were up to $800 million.

We had another huge deluge of new investment in early 1998, after the Hickory Fund got some press for its strong performance. We had 1,000 phone calls for information in all of 1997. We had 1,000 a month in the first quarter of 1998, then 1,000 a week in the second quarter. Then we got 1,000 in one day. It was unbelievable. It was almost a "success disaster." Hickory grew from $20 million to $500 million in eight months. We closed the fund in August 1998.

Kazanjian: *Has all that money impacted your ability to be a good manager?*

Weitz: I have $2.8 billion in one fund and $4.1 billion in the other. It sure is different. There are certain ideas that come up that I would have pursued five years ago that I don't today, since I have too much money to buy a big enough position in the stock. The large asset base hasn't hurt performance yet, but I don't know if that's a coincidence or not. I've been comfortable with bigger companies, but the fund has always been characterized as a mid-cap fund. The universe I focus on seems to accommodate our size, but I do wrestle with the question of whether we should close the two funds I manage.

Kazanjian: *Let's move into your investment approach. How did you come to be a value investor?*

Weitz: It's a combination of ingredients that have come together over time. Reading Ben Graham during college was part of it. Being in a value-oriented firm from 1973 to 1983 was a big part of it. Having Warren Buffett so visible helped. My first boss in New York, Artie Dunn, was an intuitive value investor, although nobody called it value investing then.

Kazanjian: *Take me through your process for evaluating stocks.*

Weitz: At the most basic level we're trying to find situations where the odds are seriously stacked in our favor. That means buying companies where you can be fairly certain of the underlying business value. That way you can identify when something is a bargain. It sounds so simplistic. Buffett talks about waiting for a fat pitch in a game where they do not call balls and strikes. You can pass on 100 ideas while you wait for the one you want. It's looking for the easy plays.

It really does start with thinking about the company as a business that you would like to own for a long time. Being statistically cheap or having unused assets that make something appear to be statistically cheap can be helpful, but that isn't enough. We're not looking for the quick hit. My ideal situation is a solid business that has some control over its destiny, that generates what I call discretionary cash flow, meaning the money may be plowed back into the business but doesn't have to be. Ideally the company is growing and at some moderate rate. If anything grows too fast, I get nervous because fast growth is unsustainable most of the time. The company must also have management that I really trust, who treat me like a partner, whose motives and aspirations match up with mine as an investor.

Next, the stock has to be available at a deep enough discount that we have what Ben Graham called the "margin of safety." Often it will go down for a while after I buy it. Many of the really big scores in my portfolios over the years have been good businesses that got cheaper before the stock took off. I'm very price sensitive. If a stock starts moving up right off the bat, I often don't get a very big position in it.

Kazanjian: *How do you put a proper value on the company?*

Weitz: It's absolutely an art, not a science. I don't mean to lapse into Buffettisms, but he has said that if he can't do it in his head, or if being off by a percentage point or two on the discount rate makes a difference, it's not cheap enough. Of course, he can do complex discounted cash flow calculations in his head, so maybe we shouldn't take him too literally.

The idea is to think about how much cash you would be able to pull out of the company over a long period of time, discounted back to the present. I use 15 percent as a discount rate because it's a handy number. I like to think of 15 percent as the rate of return I'd like to get over the long term. Others use the long-term Treasury bond rate. There's nothing magical about it. It's what you do with the valuation that counts.

Kazanjian: *Explain what you mean by the 15 percent discount.*

Weitz: A dollar today is worth $1, but $1 to be received in five years is only worth 50 cents today, assuming you could invest the 50 cents today and earn 15 percent per year. So to calculate the "present value" of a stream of future payments, you look at each payment, work backward to see what today's investment would have to be, and then add up the present values of each of these payments. The arithmetic is easy, but guessing what those earnings payments will be is very hard. I am very cautious about what I'm willing to believe will happen in the future.

Kazanjian: *You're not really looking at intrinsic value or book value?*

Weitz: I like to call it "business value," defined as what a sensible, informed business person would pay if he expected to own the company for a long time and wanted to make a 15 percent return on his investment. Some people would say that's another definition of intrinsic value.

Most of the time, the generally accepted accounting principle [GAAP] version of book value starts with the historical cost of everything—some of which was bought yesterday, and some of which was bought 100 years ago; some of which is growing in value, and some of which is sinking in value; and so on. The number that accountants come up with for book value may have zero meaning for some companies and be very meaningful for others. One of the problems with any investment formula is that one measurement doesn't fit all.

Kazanjian: *How do you start uncovering your ideas?*

Weitz: They come from all over. We tend not to do much mechanical computer screening, partly because the raw numbers you put into the screens are sometimes suspect. I have friends in the business and we exchange ideas. Things sometimes emerge from Wall Street research, although we're really not interested in the Street's recommendations.

A lot of my ideas are recycled from the past. For example, in the summer of 1999 when the Fed started raising interest rates, it was the kind of environment I had been through several times before. I remembered that Wall Street thinks you should automatically sell all of your financial services companies when the Fed begins raising rates. If your time frame is several years instead of a few quarters, you know the Fed isn't going to raise rates forever. What I've noticed in the past is that earnings for vanilla thrifts often don't even go down during those periods. The growth rate may slow down or drop for a few quarters, but it doesn't change the long-term value of the business. The cash flows over the next 10 years are pretty much the same whether the Fed raises rates periodically or not. In the summer of 1999, I started buying these financial stocks as Wall Street sold them. When they rebounded, they made our performance in 2000. It didn't take special insight. It just took being willing to be out of step for a while.

Kazanjian: *In addition to pricing considerations, what other characteristics do you look for in a company?*

Weitz: Ideally, I'd like a company with some kind of control over its own destiny and pricing. Monopolies are good in that sense. For example, I've been fond of cable companies over the years. The local cable company does have competition from satellite, over-the-air broadcasters, and, in some cities, a second cable company. But, for the most part, they really have this multichannel, video delivery system pretty much to themselves. They have pricing power. A lot of people will pay an extra $10 a month to get 10 or 15 new channels with a digital converter. If you can offer customers a cable modem for an extra $30 or $40 a month, many people will buy that because they don't have a realistic alternative for high-speed Internet access. I'm much more interested in that kind of company with its recurring revenues than I am in an equipment maker of cable modems or set top boxes. Equipment makers generally have multiple competitors and, therefore, less control over their own destiny.

The same is true in the cellular telephone world. When we first got started in that area, there were two competitors in every market. Now, in some cases, there's a fourth, fifth, or sixth competitor, but it's still a limited number. You have recurring revenues in both cable and cellular. The company gets a monthly check even if subscribers don't use the service. When they do, the check goes up. I'd much rather own a company that owns the network and supplies the cellular service rather than the handset makers or the Ciscos of the world. So I want companies that have recurring revenue, insulation from competition, and control over their destiny, and that are not particularly capital intensive. That way, when they do generate cash, they have a choice of whether to reinvest or give it back to shareholders.

Kazanjian: *When do you sell? Is the decision based on price considerations?*

Weitz: In theory you're looking at the price compared to the underlying business value. When the price gets too far out of line in either direction, it gives you an opportunity to buy or sell.

Kazanjian: *Do you set price targets?*

Weitz: I could say I try to buy it at half of the business value and sell it at 100 percent of value. I don't have targets in the sense that I buy the stock at $50 and put a sell order in at $75.

Kazanjian: *What if the stock price goes down after you buy it?*

Weitz: I recheck the story. If I still believe that I've got the valuation right and that the company is good, I celebrate and buy more. As I said before, that's the ideal situation. It can cause some indigestion when the price goes down. By the time it drops the 14th time and you recheck and buy it again, you start to doubt yourself.

In the fall of 1990, I went on a 20th-anniversary trip to France with my wife. At the time, financial stocks were weak. There were questions about credit quality, and commercial real estate was in the tank. The Bank of New England went under, and people were starting to worry about the single-family mortgages guaranteed by Fannie Mae and Freddie Mac. I had owned Freddie Mac for a long time. I bought it all the way up to $60, before it went to over $100. That fall, it came back down to the $60s and I started buying again. The week we were in France, it was at $46 on Monday and $42 by Tuesday. So I bought more. By Friday, it was at $31. I gritted my teeth and told our trader to buy some more. I really was starting to doubt myself a bit. My wife still reminds me that I had no appetite for my incredible French meal that night. Adjusted for all splits, my cost basis on the stock today is $2 or $3 a share and the stock is in the $60s. If the price hadn't gone down that much, I never would have been able to get such a big position in the stock. It turned out to be one of the companies that really drove my performance.

If you look at the performance record on Weitz Partners Value, it's about 18 percent annualized for 18 years. There are probably a dozen stocks that accounted for the vast majority of that performance, and almost every one was a good idea that started off badly. We doubled up on cable stocks in 1994 when deregulation hit and the stocks went down. By the end of 1996, there were other fears and the stocks got really cheap. We doubled up again. Then, from 1997 to 1999, the cable portion of the fund bumped up against 30 percent because they rose in value so much. The big names went up five times. The small ones rose about 10 times.

Kazanjian: *It sounds like you're an extremely patient investor.*

Weitz: Very much so. I really think the underlying approach is important. You need to have patience and a willingness to look dumb for a while.

Kazanjian: *How diversified is your portfolio?*

Weitz: I worry a fair amount about specific company risk. I rarely let a stock get much over 5 or 6 percent of a portfolio. There are all sorts of things that you can't avoid with individual companies. I would like to have 8 or 10 totally different, unrelated industries represented so that I would have industry diversification, but that hardly ever happens. I've had as much as 40 to 50 percent of the portfolio in financials of one kind or another. I like to think that within that category there are all kinds of companies that are affected differently by different factors, which provides a level of diversification.

Kazanjian: *For some time, you have kept a very high cash position of 35 to 40 percent. Why so much?*

Weitz: I claim that it's not a market timing call. I'd love to be fully invested, but I can never find enough ideas that I'm really excited about to be fully invested. So, when new money comes in or I sell something that's too expensive, if I can't find something else to buy, I'm happy to own a Treasury bill. Realistically speaking, I've felt that stocks in general have been overvalued for a number of years. Being slow to reinvest new cash has been a function of a sense that tomorrow I was likely to find something better. I guess some could call that market timing.

Kazanjian: *If it really was a lack of ideas, couldn't you put more money into the stocks you already own and/or close the fund so you don't get any more cash?*

Weitz: Yep, I could do either one. One other factor is that the market has become more volatile in recent years. It's really not unusual to have a company's stock drop 20 or 40 percent in a day. When a stock I really like falls for the wrong reason, it's handy to have that cash.

Kazanjian: *But investors send you their money to buy stocks. Do you think you're serving them well by holding all this cash?*

Weitz: I think so. What I tell anybody who will listen is that this is the way I am. All of my own money is invested in these funds and I'm doing it for myself, too. Measure me against other equity investors and if the cash hurts, it's okay to penalize me for it. There are lots of ways to approach it.

Kazanjian: *Given your approach, do you invest in technology stocks?*

Weitz: Hardly ever. For a long time I'd use the "I don't understand it" line. It's true that I'm not very mechanically inclined. I only recently found out that CDs are read from the bottom, which is why you can have pictures on top. I'm not a technology person, but that's not why I don't invest in technology. I really like to look for the easy high-probability investment. Those tend to be the ones where either the value of the business is already there or there are very predictable cash flows that will be coming along, such as in a cable system that's already mature. Technology changes so dramatically every few months that it's really hard to predict whether today's leader will even be in business five years from now.

Kazanjian: *Is there anything else you'd like to add?*

Weitz: There are an infinite number of facts you can learn about a company, but there are usually two or three very important variables that make the company succeed or fail. A lot of Wall Street research gets so bogged down in the minutiae and details that it misses these two or three big things that make or break the investment. Part of what's worked for me over the years is being able to distinguish what matters from what doesn't. That's one of Buffett's great gifts. He focuses on the critical issues involved in analyzing a company. I don't pretend to be able to do it like he does, but it's one of the most important things you can do.

Weitz tells me that being too trusting or tolerant of management has traditionally caused his biggest investment mistakes. Unlike his fellow manager, Richard Lawson, whom I profiled in my book *Wizards of Wall Street*, Weitz is less willing to swing for the fences, and would rather go for the sure single than the possible double or triple. That's why he's been able to keep the volatility of his funds relatively tame.

As we finished the interview, it struck me that Weitz is like his neighbor Warren Buffett in a few other ways. For one, both are modest about their abilities. For another, both live rather low-key lifestyles considering the wealth they have amassed. Finally, both are more comfortable dressed casually (plaid shirts are Weitz's uniform of choice) than in three-piece suits. ■

MARTIN WHITMAN

THIRD AVENUE FUNDS

Marty Whitman goes one step beyond value investing. On Wall Street, he's affectionately known as a vulture investor, a title he wears proudly. Whitman invests in the securities of distressed companies, looking for those he calls "safe and cheap." Whitman started out in research before moving into investment, private money management, and "control investing." He defines control investing as taking a sizable equity stake in a smaller company, thus buying a significant voice in corporate decision making. Whitman began specializing in distressed companies in the early 1970s, after realizing it was an area where the larger investment firms weren't competing. He started out by giving advice to troubled companies, but soon realized he could make more money investing in them instead.

Whitman initially planned to teach economics following a stint in the Navy. But after finishing graduate school, he figured there wasn't much of a future for him in academia. Instead, he went to Wall Street. While Whitman describes what he does as a form of value investing, he pays little attention to traditional indicators of value, such as dividend yields and PE ratios. In fact, he claims Graham and Dodd—the godfathers of value investing—are "all screwed up."

As you might have guessed, Whitman is quite candid and not afraid to call it as he sees it. He presides over the Third Avenue Value Fund, a portfolio comprised mostly of small-cap stocks. Whitman says that's because he often finds bargains among small-caps, not because he concentrates on that market segment.

Whitman frequently starts off buying the debt of troubled companies, hoping to turn it into equity at fire sale prices once a reorganization has taken place. That's how he became a large shareholder in oil services concern Nabors Industries in the 1980s. Today his firm owns large stakes in a handful of companies. Whitman pays no attention to the overall market, feeling it has as much relevance as reading tea leaves. Instead, he concentrates on uncovering new investments one at a time.

Kazanjian: *You've often been described as a vulture investor. Does that title bother you at all?*

Whitman: I would much rather be called a vulture investor than an asset allocator, market strategist, or academic.

Kazanjian: *Why is that?*

Whitman: Because they're clueless. To be a vulture investor, you really have to know something about value.

Kazanjian: *Why are you so critical of academics?*

Whitman: It's not that I don't think highly of them. They're all chartist technicians. They know nothing about analyzing securities or analyzing companies. Their whole thesis is based on the study of prices and the study of markets with no weight placed on understanding companies, understanding information, and understanding long-term investing.

Kazanjian: *You think that looking at individual companies is the key to success?*

Whitman: Yes. No question about it. And having a long-term outlook unless you're involved in risk arbitrage.

Kazanjian: *How do you define a "vulture investor"?*

Whitman: A vulture investor is someone who invests in the credits of distressed companies.

Kazanjian: *Credits meaning both bonds and stocks?*

Whitman: No, not stocks. Nobody in their right mind buys the common stock of a distressed business at any price. We buy the stocks of cheap companies, but the senior paper [high quality debt] of distressed businesses.

Kazanjian: *You've been dealing with distressed companies for some time, but not always as an investment manager.*

Whitman: That's correct.

Kazanjian: *When did this all begin?*

Whitman: In the early 1970s when I decided to work for myself, I wanted to do corporate finance. There were two areas in those days that no respectable investment bank would touch. One was stockholder litigation and the other was bankruptcies. I went into both fields. I first became an advisor to other firms. Then I found out that I could do a lot better as an investor than I could as an advisor.

Kazanjian: *What did you study in college?*

Whitman: Economics.

Kazanjian: *Where did you go to college?*

Whitman: I went to Syracuse and did graduate work at Princeton.

Kazanjian: *What was your first job out of college?*

Whitman: I was a research analyst at Shearson in the brokerage business.

Kazanjian: *Where did that lead you?*

Whitman: I ended up at a private family trust, which invested in both passive and control investments.

Kazanjian: *That was in the late 1950s?*

Whitman: Yes. In 1960, I became a partner of a New York Stock Exchange member firm in Philadelphia. In 1967, I moved back to New York and went with a New York Stock Exchange firm for a few years. I went into business for myself in the early 1970s. In 1984, I did a hostile takeover of a closed-end investment trust, and that got me into the money management business.

Kazanjian: *What led to that takeover?*

Whitman: The stock of Equity Strategies Fund was selling at a discount. After I got control, I made it an open-ended fund and used it as a vehicle to buy out the bank debt of a company now called Nabors Industries. In the late 1980s, Nabors went into Chapter 11. It was a tremendously successful transaction. To solve some tax problems, Equity Strategies was merged with Nabors Industries and all the shareholders of Equity Strategies received Nabors common stock, most of which we still hold. By this time, I had decided that I liked the money management business, so I started a new fund called Third Avenue Value in 1990.

Kazanjian: *What got you interested in takeover investing?*

Whitman: I certainly didn't want to be in the general stock market. It seemed like an easy way to make money. The risk/reward ratio was fantastic.

Kazanjian: *Do you do takeover investing at Third Avenue Value?*

Whitman: No. Third Avenue Value strictly does passive investing [buys stock, but doesn't try to run or get control of the company]. We don't do any takeover investing, with the exception of a few distressed securities. In common stocks, we're strictly passive investors.

Kazanjian: *How much do you manage altogether now?*

Whitman: About $3.5 billion in three funds and privately managed accounts.

Kazanjian: *Let's talk about your investment approach. Some people have described it as growth at dirt cheap prices.*

Whitman: That's the way I'd describe it. Any common stock we buy has to be safe and cheap. In order to be safe and cheap, each issue has four characteristics. One, the company has an extremely strong financial position, starting with the balance sheet. Two, it has reasonably good management from a stockholder point of view. Three, it has to be a business that we understand, which can mean many things, but always means comprehensive documentary disclosure. Those first three characteristics—strong balance sheet, good management, and an understandable business—are what make a security safe. The fourth characteristic is cheap. We try not to pay more than 50 cents on the dollar for each dollar we think the security would be worth if the business were to go private or be taken over.

Kazanjian: *Surely there are trade-offs with this approach.*

Whitman: For sure. In order to get our pricing, the near-term outlooks for the businesses are almost always terrible.

Kazanjian: *Let's talk about each of these points. For example, you want companies with extremely strong financial positions. Specifically, what does that mean to you?*

Whitman: It's a combination of three things. First, a relative absence of liabilities, whether off the balance sheet, on the balance sheet, in the footnotes, or out there in the world.

Kazanjian: *Does that mean it can't have any debt?*

Whitman: It can have some debt, but a relative absence of liabilities. Two, the existence of high-quality assets, meaning cash or assets that might be converted to cash. Three, we want—if we can get it—a lot of free cash flow from operations available to stockholders, which is something far more rare than most people think. A mix of those three things generally constitutes an extremely strong financial position.

Kazanjian: *What about book value or other traditional value measures?*

Whitman: In evaluating whether a company is cheap, we might do book value. But that measure has nothing to do with safe. The PE ratio is another figure that goes to price, but has nothing to do with safe.

Kazanjian: *Next is management. How do you determine whether a company has reasonable management?*

Whitman: It's the toughest thing we do. All managements have both communities of interest and conflicts of interest with their public stockholders. We try not to go into companies where the management either looks incompetent or is overreaching relative to the stockholders as measured by stock option programs, compensation levels, and other transactions as disclosed in the SEC filings. An awful lot of managements are out to rape the public stockholders. We try to avoid those people.

Kazanjian: *How can you tell from talking with management whether you want to do business with them or not?*

Whitman: It's a combination of both a careful review of the documents and interviewing them. We would never appraise a management just by listening to them talk—not when there's a public record that tells you a lot of things about them. That's for amateurs.

Kazanjian: *The third characteristic is a business you can understand.*

Whitman: That means many things, but it always means that there are comprehensive disclosure documents and audited financial statements, which we rely on as objective benchmarks. Financial statements do not tell us the truth. We don't expect them to tell us the truth. We expect them to give us objective benchmarks that we then can use as a tool of analysis.

Kazanjian: *Warren Buffett has said he does not invest in technology because he doesn't understand how the technology works. Is that true with you as well?*

Whitman: No. We invest pretty heavily in technology.

Kazanjian: *So you don't necessarily have to understand how the business operates?*

Whitman: You have to be comfortable. Warren, after all, is a control investor. We're very different. We're doing passive investing and we'll invest in technology as if we were a venture capitalist. You must have more than one investment. We're diversified. You still get huge returns, but you expect to have a pretty high strike-out ratio. That's part of the understanding.

As a control investor, I don't know that I would invest in high tech. We invest in high tech as if we're a first-stage venture capitalist, and only when we get the right pricing.

Kazanjian: *That leads us to number four, which is paying 50 cents on the dollar. How do you determine how much a company is worth so you know whether it's selling for 50 cents on the dollar?*

Whitman: It depends on the company you're analyzing. Let's say we're doing high tech. We want to price that like a first-stage venture capitalist. We figure what the future earnings will be and calculate an internal rate of return. The internal rate of return is the compound annual growth rate. We have never bought the common stock of a financial institution unless it was selling at a substantial discount from adjusted book value.

Kazanjian: *Is this also where you take a look at book value?*

Whitman: Book value is a good benchmark. It's an accounting figure. I would say that once you get away from Wall Street, once you get away from where the inmates are in charge of the insane asylum, book value is every bit as important as earnings. They're both part of the accounting cycle, derived from, modified by, and a function of all other accounting numbers.

Kazanjian: *Speaking of earnings, how important are earnings to you?*

Whitman: It depends on what we're doing. In general, all businesses that are any good are involved in wealth creation. Away from Wall Street, given the choice, most intelligent people would prefer to create wealth by methods other than earnings [for tax reasons]. They'd rather have unrealized depreciation, have realized depreciation, take out proceeds from refinancing, or restructure. Most of our portfolio companies have no choice but to create wealth through earnings, although it's the least desirable method. Obviously earnings are the key variable in analyzing strict going concerns that aren't tax shelters, but earnings tend to be unimportant in analyzing a real estate company, an insurance business, or a company with investment trust characteristics. For companies that are either investment companies or investment companies masquerading as something else, earnings aren't important.

Kazanjian: *What, generally speaking, makes the companies you invest in cheap?*

Whitman: First and foremost, most of the time the near-term outlook is not good and they're not in industries that are popular at the moment. The market believes their prospects are dismal.

Kazanjian: *So why are you interested?*

Whitman: We don't pay attention to the market.

Kazanjian: *How far out are you looking in evaluating the future prospects for these companies?*

Whitman: Right now, we're buying huge portfolios of high tech and financial companies selling at under eight times peak earnings. These are very well capitalized companies where we have a strong belief that the next peak is going to be a lot better than the last one. I think the next peak will occur in three to five years. That's always been my experience. We go on the assumption that these industry wide depressions always are going to be deeper and last longer than we think.

Kazanjian: *Three to five years. That's like an eternity for most of Wall Street, right?*

Whitman: Yes. That's why they keep messing up. We would only have a short-term perspective in risk arbitrage situations, with risk arbitrage being defined as relatively determinant workouts in relatively determinant periods of time, such as in anticipation of an announced merger. Other than that, we would never do anything short-term. It has to be risk arbitrage.

Kazanjian: *Do you find that you're generally in smaller companies as a result of your investment style?*

Whitman: It depends on timing. In recent years it's been almost entirely small companies. I suppose going forward it's going to be very much that way for the simple reason that most of the companies building up strong balance sheets were beneficiaries of the IPO phenomenon. It's like a company went public at $14 and the stock went to $60. Now it's selling at $2 to $5. It's all anti-momentum, yet some of these companies have big balance sheets.

Kazanjian: *Have you been buying any of those blown-up dot.com IPOs?*

Whitman: No. We're looking far outside of that area. Most of those companies are junk.

Kazanjian: *Do you buy IPOs?*

Whitman: We only buy busted IPOs. We wait for the IPO to fall down. That's our style.

Kazanjian: *What percentage of your portfolio is technology now?*

Whitman: Twenty-nine percent.

Kazanjian: *Is that high or normal for you?*

Whitman: It's about normal. We target opportunity, so there is no perfect number.

Kazanjian: *Are the companies you're buying those that were hot and high-flying in the late 1990s when technology was hot?*

Whitman: Precisely.

Kazanjian: *I know you have a long-term outlook. What makes you sell a stock?*

Whitman: We sell because we made a mistake or the issue gets grossly overpriced.

Kazanjian: *You also invest in a lot of foreign companies, especially in Japan. How do you feel about Japan now?*

Whitman: We began investing in Japan in 1997 when the Tokyo market was 20,000. It's now 12,000, yet we have a profit in the companies we're in. A large part of Japanese investments are affiliates of Toyota Motor, including an insurance company, where we're buying in at a 40 to 50 percent discount.

Kazanjian: *Yet not all of your Japanese investments have been good ones. You sued Japan's distressed Long-Term Credit Bank a few years ago for not managing its bad loan portfolio in the interest of shareholders.*

Whitman: I had a sizable stake in that company. The bank planned to forgive 520 billion yen, which is around $3.7 billion, of defaulted loans. They were doing that without any consideration of shareholders. You're talking almost $4 billion of forgiveness. That would bankrupt Citigroup!

Kazanjian: *Do you now consider that investment to be one of your mistakes?*

Whitman: I do. I realized that you can't replicate the American experience in Japan. There is no system to work out nonperforming loans and no consciousness of the problem. If Japan doesn't come up with a way to rescue troubled companies and banks, like a Chapter 11, the country's financial and economic system will collapse and bring the rest of the world down with it.

Kazanjian: *Do you evaluate foreign companies in general any differently than U.S. companies?*

Whitman: Not really. It all goes down to management and the financials.

Kazanjian: *In some cases you take some pretty substantial positions in the companies. What are some companies you own a large portion of?*

Whitman: We own about 30 percent of the common stock of Tejon Ranch, a big California real estate company. We own about 15 percent of Capital Southwest, and 5 to 10 percent of AVX Corp. We also own 45 percent of Innovative Clinical Solutions, 20 percent of C.P. Clare, 10 percent of Stewart Information Services, and 15 percent of FSI International, to name a few.

Kazanjian: *In those cases where you own such a huge percentage—in some cases 20 to 40 percent or more—do you get involved in the companies? Are you an activist shareholder?*

Whitman: We like to be passive, but I had to go on the board of Nabors Industries. I'm also on the board of Stewart Information Services and Tejon Ranch. They are three extremely well managed companies. I wish they'd let me alone to just be passive.

Kazanjian: *Do you find that when you're on the board of these companies, it's harder to be objective as an investment manager?*

Whitman: Not at all.

Kazanjian: *If the company is not doing what you want it to do, do you still feel free to sell your position?*

Whitman: Yep. I work hard for my funds. I'm really not interested in being close with company management.

Kazanjian: *Let's move on to distressed securities and bonds. When would you buy a bond, for example, of a company instead of the stock?*

Whitman: We would not buy the stock if the company did have a strong financial position.

Kazanjian: *What would make you willing to take on the risks of even a bond?*

Whitman: We try not to take risks. We try to buy the most senior securities that would participate in a reorganization. We are presently the largest creditors of USG Corp, with its asbestos liabilities. We're large holders of Safelite Glass Bank debt. Safelite is a good company. We own 50 percent of the outstanding subordinated debentures of Home Products International. We own 7 million of the first mortgages of Pacific Gas and Electric Company [PG&E]. We're one of the largest senior creditors of Armstrong World Industries.

Kazanjian: *You own no common stock in these companies.*

Whitman: Well, we own common stock in USG, which I think was a mistake.

Kazanjian: *What makes these benchers securities "safe" in your mind?*

Whitman: No matter what happens to USG, there's no way the senior notes will ever be subordinated to asbestos claims. Indeed, they're likely to get paid before the asbestos claimants. The PG&E mortgages yield 25½ percent to maturity. We bought Home Products at about a 25 percent yield. I think that's going to be a performing loan. If it isn't, Third Avenue will end up the majority common stock holder. Again, I'm looking for the most senior debt that will participate in a reorganization.

Kazanjian: *Are you burned very often?*

Whitman: Occasionally. It's no different than with common stock. Most of the investments work out, but we unfortunately do make mistakes.

Kazanjian: *How do these companies come to your attention?*

Whitman: I definitely don't read Wall Street research. The ideas come from various sources. On the distress side, I read the *Daily Bankruptcy Reporter*. On the common stock side, we do run computer screens. We also read the newspapers, annual reports, proxy statements, 10Ks, and the like.

Kazanjian: *Are you looking for stocks on the new-low list?*

Whitman: I do that sometimes.

Kazanjian: *But you don't pay attention to Wall Street research or earnings?*

Whitman: No. That's mostly nonsense. It's a waste of time.

Kazanjian: *Do you set price targets on your stocks?*

Whitman: No. Value is a very dynamic thing and it's continually increasing. It's silly to set a price target. That just gets you into tax disadvantages.

Kazanjian: *You don't pay a lot of attention to the overall market, right?*

Whitman: Don't pay any attention to it.

Kazanjian: *But do you find that companies in the same sector all tend to be distressed or cheap at the same time?*

Whitman: I don't know about distressed. They all tend to be cheap at the same time. The reason we get all these great opportunities in high tech at four and five times earnings is that the market fails to distinguish among them.

Kazanjian: *As a result, is your portfolio generally concentrated in certain sectors?*

Whitman: Yes. As I mentioned, around 30 percent is invested in high tech as we speak.

Kazanjian: *What other areas are you heavily invested in?*

Whitman: Financial institutions and real estate.

Kazanjian: *I know you actually have a real estate fund as well. I assume that's mostly invested in real estate investment trusts [REITs].*

Whitman: No. There are some REITs, but we prefer other kinds of real estate.

Kazanjian: *Such as?*

Whitman: Operating companies, such as Tejon Ranch.

Kazanjian: *In your mind, is real estate a good area to be invested in going forward?*

Whitman: It's a great area. Real estate securities are a hell of a lot cheaper than real estate.

Kazanjian: *Your fund did quite well in the early to mid-1990s. In fact, you were Morningstar's domestic fund manager of the year in 1990. Then, along with many other value managers, your performance suffered a bit in the late 1990s when everybody was into high tech and aggressive growth. What did you think about that market environment?*

Whitman: I think what went on up until March 2000 was the greatest speculative excess in the history of man. The inmates were running the asylum. How are you going to compete with that? Obviously we did very well in 2000 and we're doing okay now.

Kazanjian: *What do you think will go down as the biggest lesson from that time period?*

Whitman: Not a thing. This craziness will all recur again. Since I've been in the business, there have always been periods of great speculative excess. As far as I know, it will happen again.

Kazanjian: *We don't learn from our mistakes then?*

Whitman: I don't think so.

Kazanjian: *Maybe we can talk about a couple of stocks—one or two that worked out and one or two that didn't—that demonstrate your approach in terms of how you find and evaluate companies. Let's start with the ones that worked out.*

Whitman: We had a big score with Applied Materials. That was a 10-bagger [increased in value by 1,000 percent].

Kazanjian: *When did you first buy that?*

Whitman: In 1996 or 1997, when the semiconductor equipment business was going into a huge depression. This was the best company in the business and could be bought at 10 times peak earnings with a very strong balance sheet. It worked out like a dream. At the same time, we bought into C.P. Clare, Inc. It's a company in the same industry, with the same story. This company wasn't very well managed. Since we've owned it, the stock has gone from $9 to $3. Management is very important.

Kazanjian: *Is bad management the primary reason when your stocks don't work out?*

Whitman: I'd say so. Even though our stock picking formula is good, we occasionally wind up with stinkers. Appraising managers is the toughest thing we do.

Kazanjian: *If you were to buy 10 stocks, how many of those would work and how many of them would eventually bomb?*

Whitman: Probably seven would work and three would bomb.

Kazanjian: *Those are pretty good odds.*

Whitman: Yeah. But then again, it's really a long-term approach. How much of what we're buying now will work out this year? As far as I know, zippo. In three to five years, seven out of 10 should work. You previously asked me what I thought about academics. They all measure everything by what happens next week. That's silly.

Kazanjian: *In the late 1990s, when your fund wasn't doing as well as some of those formerly high-flying technology funds, you had a lot of outflows. Are you getting inflows again?*

Whitman: Yes.

Kazanjian: *Doesn't that prove that investors always react in the wrong way? They buy high and sell low.*

Whitman: Yeah. I wish we didn't attract as much hot money as we apparently do. But I have no control over that.

Kazanjian: *Is it individual or professional investors who are most guilty of this?*

Whitman: Both. The professionals are probably worse than the individuals. I bet you most individuals take a buy-and-hold approach.

Kazanjian: *Does that mean people are better off managing their own money?*

Whitman: Probably. People should buy what they know.

Kazanjian: *You closed your fund at one point. Do you think you'll do that again?*

Whitman: No.

Kazanjian: *Why not?*

Whitman: There are too many opportunities. I would close it if there weren't investment opportunities available.

Kazanjian: *Do you think that people should put all their money in value stocks and funds?*

Whitman: Yes.

Kazanjian: *You don't believe in having both growth and value?*

Whitman: That is a misnomer. You used the word *growth*. We're a growth fund. We just don't buy generally recognized growth. When people talk about buying into growth funds, they talk about buying into generally recognized growth, and when you buy into what's generally recognized, you have to pay huge premiums. A growth manager is someone who is price unconscious.

Kazanjian: *What do you think of index funds?*

Whitman: Index funds are better than poorly managed mutual funds and much less attractive than well-managed value funds. I think index funds peaked in 1999.

Kazanjian: *Do you think that the excesses of the late 1990s will prove to be healthy in the end?*

Whitman: Yes. It's so funny. I don't think we would have had the economic boom we had were it not for the speculative excesses. We got a terrific allocation of resources in high tech issues. That's the area where the economy expanded and made the U.S. very competitive and rich. We wouldn't have had this expansion if it weren't for those speculative excesses.

Kazanjian: *Did the venture capitalists get carried away?*

Whitman: Sure, and a lot of people and the economy were hurt by that. But, in the end, it served a terrific purpose.

Kazanjian: *Are there any areas or industries you won't invest in at all, or are you open to everything?*

Whitman: I wouldn't invest in tobacco.

Kazanjian: *Why is that? For personal reasons or because you think it's bad business?*

Whitman: Both, but mostly personal reasons.

Kazanjian: *Are there any other areas besides tobacco that you avoid?*

Whitman: I don't do liquor anymore. I wouldn't invest in companies that damage the environment.

Kazanjian: *So you're a socially conscious value investor as well.*

Whitman: Oh, sure. But making money is the primary goal.

At 77, Whitman still comes to the office every day, often in his trademark sweatshirt and sneakers. Although he has no plans to retire, he has gradually been handing over responsibility for some of the other funds at his firm to the younger managers he has trained. But this doesn't mean that Whitman's slowing down. He remains active and says that he'd quit money management in a second only if he could somehow talk his way into becoming a professional tennis player. ∎

DAVID WILLIAMS

U.S. TRUST

Fund companies are forever coming up with gimmicks for new funds. A few years ago, there was even one called the Tombstone Fund that invested in companies involved in the death industry. Fortunately, that one met its own demise after a period of dismal performance.

Dave Williams runs a fund that also sounds a bit gimmicky on the surface. It's called the Excelsior Value and Restructuring Fund. As the quirky name implies, Williams' mandate is to find companies undergoing a change or restructuring that will make them more competitive or profitable. As it turns out, the concept works. In fact, Williams was already investing this way when his employer, U.S. Trust, first approached him with the idea in 1992.

After spending five years flying in the Navy and earning a degree from Harvard Business School, Williams began his investment career at T. Rowe Price in 1974, at the peak of a brutal bear market. He then went out on his own for a couple of years, before becoming the chief investment officer of a New Jersey bank. In 1987, he moved over to U.S. Trust. Initially he managed individual accounts for wealthy clients. Today most of the assets he runs are in the fund.

Williams, 59, tries to find companies that are under a cloud. They've disappointed Wall Street for one reason or another, but are going through some type of restructuring. Because they're out of favor, Williams can buy them at relatively cheap prices. While uncovering such companies isn't hard, separating the junk from the diamonds in the rough is. That's part of the art of what he does.

Kazanjian: *Did you have childhood ambitions of working on Wall Street?*

Williams: Not really, although I always liked stocks. I taught in Athens, Greece, for a year after graduating from Yale. I was in the Navy for five years after that. Then I went to the Harvard Business School.

Kazanjian: *How was the Navy experience?*

Williams: I loved it. What's not to like? There was a great esprit de corps, which you never experience in any civilian job.

Kazanjian: *When you graduated from Harvard in 1974, did you go right to work in the investment business?*

Williams: Yes. I started at T. Rowe Price and was there for four years.

Kazanjian: *That was a pure growth shop back then, wasn't it?*

Williams: I don't think it is anymore, but it was definitely the place to work if you were interested in growth stocks. Back then I didn't know growth from value. I think you learn along the way that you have a natural predilection toward one or the other. I learned early on that I was more cut out for value than growth.

Kazanjian: *Did they teach you how to invest as a growth manager at T. Rowe Price?*

Williams: It's fair to say that. Nothing against T. Rowe Price, because it's a great place, but I don't think any of these firms really teach you anything. You go there and by some process of osmosis you pick up how they do it, why they do it, and how they're thinking, but there's no actual teaching that goes on.

Kazanjian: *How long after you got there did you realize that you were more of a value guy?*

Williams: Even from the very beginning, I just had this natural instinct that wouldn't let me pay up for stocks. This was in 1974 and the world was coming to an end back then. It really was. Inflation was something new and people didn't know how to deal with it. PE ratios were collapsing. Experiencing the meltdown of the market back then made me very risk averse. I think it was as much the times as my temperament that led me to value.

Kazanjian: *How long were you at T. Rowe Price?*

Williams: Four years. Then I worked with a friend for about two years. We started a small investment firm in New York that never really got off the ground. I left and went to a bank in New Jersey called Horizon Trust Company. I was a chief investment officer there until 1987.

Kazanjian: *That's when you joined U.S. Trust?*

Williams: Correct. In the beginning, I managed private accounts that were invested in our mutual funds. In 1990, I began picking stocks for our individual accounts. It became apparent that I was the value guy around here. We started a value mutual fund in 1993. It was one of seven theme funds the firm launched that year, and I was tapped to manage it.

Kazanjian: *What were some of the other theme funds?*

Williams: Among others, we had an energy fund, a demographic fund, a telecommunications fund, and mine, which was a restructuring fund.

Kazanjian: *Did the funds sell very well?*

Williams: Not at all. Investors and consultants couldn't relate to a theme fund. As a result, they phased most of these funds out. They kept the energy fund and mine because we had good performance records. The name of the fund was changed to Excelsior Value and Restructuring. It was called Business and Industrial Restructuring before.

Kazanjian: *It sounds like your marketing department needs help coming up with sexier names.*

Williams: That's true. But for a relatively small firm, compared to the Fidelitys and the T. Rowes of the world, we've done well.

Kazanjian: *Do you still manage private accounts as well as the fund?*

Williams: Oh, yes. As a matter of fact, in the value area, I manage about $3 billion—$2 billion of that is in the fund, and the rest is in individual accounts.

Kazanjian: *Was the whole value and restructuring theme something you walked into because it was a creation of the marketing department, or was that the way you were investing in the first place?*

Williams: It was the way I was investing anyway.

Kazanjian: *What's the rationale behind this?*

Williams: We try to differentiate ourselves a bit from other value styles by having this restructuring theme along with the value approach. Pure and simple, we look for companies where there's a change going on. Of course, we hope it's a change for the better, but it doesn't always work that way. It simply must be a change that will improve the company's outlook. For us to buy it, it must first be cheap. Equally important, we want something going on that will keep investor interest in the company and lead to better earnings in the long run. If the company executes well, the PE will automatically go up.

Kazanjian: *We'll get back to cheap in a minute. In terms of the restructuring, are you looking for significant change to take place in every company you buy?*

Williams: Either present change, or if there's not anything going on in the company per se, then I like to see a good possibility that something will happen in the future. Maybe the company doesn't have the necessary scale or is underperforming a bit. I like to see the potential for the company to be acquired. That strategy worked a few years ago, but it's getting tougher in this market environment.

Kazanjian: *How do you find these companies?*

Williams: First and foremost, I do an awful lot of reading. Without question, that's where I get most of my ideas. I also look through various brokerage materials. I'm searching for cheap stocks, number one, and if I read a story and get a sense that some restructuring is going on, I get even more interested.

Kazanjian: *Do you rely heavily on Wall Street analysts?*

Williams: A lot of my ideas come from Wall Street. We also have 15 analysts here. Ninety percent of the time, I like to hear from top management at the company before I make an investment. The nice thing about working in New York is that you have that opportunity.

Kazanjian: *It's interesting to hear you say that because most of the managers I've interviewed for this book say they don't trust Wall Street.*

Williams: They're absolutely right. Maybe I was naïve when I first came into the business, but I think the credibility of Wall Street has declined immeasurably since I entered this business 27 years ago. You have to somehow corroborate what the analysts are saying with your own instincts. Wall Street research is really a starting point for me. Then, I dig in and do my own analysis.

Kazanjian: *You mentioned cheap a few times. How do you define cheap?*

Williams: To be a value investor, you must have confidence that everyone else is wrong and you're right about the stock being undervalued relative to its future potential. You look over the horizon to either when the company turns its business around, when the cycle turns around, or when the company is bought out.

More to your point, how much is a stock worth? That varies, of course. If the market's down, you like to look for stocks that can double. If the market is up, finding doubles is more difficult. You like to see a big spread between what the stock sells for and what you think it's worth. The benchmarks may be better earnings in the future, the return of a positive business cycle, or a correction in the morass the company has gotten itself into. An easy way is to look at what the assets would sell for to a willing buyer and determine the percentage gain you might get in the best of all worlds if the company is taken over.

Kazanjian: *Is that book value?*

Williams: Not so much book value as the value of the assets to a buyer. It might be two or three times book value. For example, many of the cyclicals recently were selling around book value. Of course, the fundamentals were awful. You can eventually count on the cycle turning, at which point these companies might sell for two times book value.

Kazanjian: *Do you base that on history?*

Williams: Yes. A more common approach is to look at what similar companies have been selling for. For example, cable companies need scale, so we buy the number-four or -five company in the sector. If the consolidation continues at some point, you're almost certain to make 50 to 75 percent on your money if the companies are taken out.

The other way to look at valuation is to search for stocks with low PEs and low price/cash-flow ratios, and then look at what the company's doing, and give it the benefit of the doubt. A great example of this is Duke Energy. Duke is transforming itself from an old regulated utility to a company that has its fingers in all kinds of energy-related businesses. Over the foreseeable future, a bigger and bigger portion of its business will be in unregulated parts of the energy business where it can capture a multiple of 20 or 25 times earnings. When I bought Duke, it sold at 11 or 12 times earnings. All the analysts said it was going to grow at 7 to 9 percent annually. The company was transforming itself, but the analysts for whatever reason weren't giving Duke the benefit of the doubt, in terms of its future growth rate.

Kazanjian: *What first attracted you to Duke?*

Williams: At the time I bought it, I owned a company called Dynergy. Dynergy was buying generation assets, marketing energy, and acting as a middleman between the generation of energy and the marketing of energy. I saw what kind of multiple that stock had. Duke was doing the same thing, yet Wall Street wasn't giving it credit for being successful in turning its business around. I saw that as an opportunity.

Kazanjian: *Do you find that companies in the same industry all tend to undergo restructuring at the same time?*

Williams: Companies restructure when something is wrong and to improve productivity. It's hard to generalize. If business is bad for the industry, chances are that all companies will be doing something—some in a major way, others in a minor way—to get earnings back to a more growth-oriented mode. On the other hand, you can have the number-three or -four player in an industry with good cash flows that has fallen short for whatever reason. The company may announce a restructuring to get back into more of a growth mode than the rest of the industry is in.

Kazanjian: *So just because you find a bank, for example, that's in the process of restructuring, you won't necessarily go looking for other banks?*

Williams: That's correct, although in the case of the utility industry, that whole industry has been restructuring.

Kazanjian: *You look at companies on an individual basis, rather than on a sector basis?*

Williams: Yes, but if I've had a good stock pick and can find another company doing similar things, that's a pretty good low-risk way to make money.

Kazanjian: *Actually, it sounds more like a high-risk strategy, since you're buying companies that clearly have problems.*

Williams: I suppose you're right. I admittedly make a lot of mistakes. Growth managers tend to make mistakes by paying too much. Value guys tend to make mistakes by buying junk. I try to mitigate risk by paying close attention to what management has to say. Often you don't know until after the fact if management is any good or not. They may tell a good story, but it's not until after they have performed well and the stock triples that you know they're doing a good job. You take some risk in assuming what they're saying makes sense and that they're going to execute well.

Kazanjian: *Do you always talk to management before you invest?*

Williams: Ninety percent of the time, yes.

Kazanjian: *In the end, does it come down to intuition?*

Williams: Definitely. We don't know everything that's going on in the business. We don't do in-depth research on all of their customers and the suppliers. It's mostly a big-picture approach. I had a course at business school called "Business Policy." I enjoyed it because it involved seeing what a company's assets were, looking at their market position, examining their financial position, and evaluating whether the company could put it all together. I think investing is just a real-life business policy course. We look at what a company does, its business plan, how it ranks in the industry, and whether it makes sense.

You do the best you can, but you're wrong a lot. I love to buy stocks that are way down, but many times they go down more than you ever expect them to. I've got a closet full of corpses here that didn't work out. So what do you do? You monitor the company very closely and you diversify well. I like to buy stocks that are down and double up on them when they're down even more. However, at some point you get the sense that the company is being successful at what you hoped it would accomplish; that's when you begin to add more money and make it a bigger portion of your portfolio.

Kazanjian: *Why don't we talk about one or two corpses and what went wrong.*

Williams: I'll give you a good one and a bad one. I tend to like big-name companies with new management. I think names are a valuable asset. A couple of examples are Xerox and Kodak. Not long ago, I sold Xerox and lost money. My average cost was $30, and I sold it around $20, give or take. I recently bought it back at $5 and change. The price implication was that the market assumed that this company was going under. Yet, in my mind, the company seemed to be doing all the right stuff to turn its business around. It got rid of the CEO who botched things up. It brought back the old CEO. It outsourced the financing of its copier business, which was causing its balance sheet to deteriorate. It also sold off half of its Fuji Xerox position to reduce debt. In my mind, the company was doing all the right things to get on a good financial footing. Our analyst here said she thought Xerox was going under. But I saw management and thought what they were doing made sense. Lo and behold, the stock was one of my best-performing positions in 2001.

Kazanjian: *It was a mistake before, but worked out the second time around.*

Williams: Right. I don't usually do that. If I make a mistake, I don't like to lose twice. But I thought Xerox was different. Another one that didn't work out so well was Kodak. Kodak had slowing cash flows, was losing market share to the Japanese, and had outdated technology. I thought it could use the Kodak name to advance its technology base and get into some areas that were growing faster than its traditional chemical photography business. Lo and behold, Kodak continued to lose market share. Again, what got me interested in Kodak initially was management. But they never executed, and the stock suffered as a result.

Kazanjian: *Looking through the list of names in your portfolio, I see that you own some stocks that most people would consider growth stocks. Qualcomm and Citigroup are two examples.*

Williams: I think Citigroup can probably go either way, although Qualcomm is obviously a growth stock. Keep in mind that I bought Qualcomm in 1994, when the company was having all kinds of trouble. It wasn't making money. It owned the rights to this great CDMA technology, but didn't know what to do with it. The whole wireless area had not taken off. It wasn't until the fourth quarter of 1999 that the stock exploded. In hindsight I should have wised up and sold all of it then. Instead, I just trimmed my oversized position. The stock went from $50 to $200 before you could blink. My original cost basis is about $10.

Kazanjian: *What you're saying, then, is that when you have these growth stocks in your portfolios, it's because you've held on to them from the time they were value stocks.*

Williams: That's exactly right. The same is true of Nokia. I bought that very early on. Nokia was once a conglomerate with four businesses. Its largest product when I bought it was rubber boots, believe it or not. Now, of course, it's a telecommunications giant.

Kazanjian: *What is your sell discipline?*

Williams: I like to trim my winners. If the fundamentals are good, I'll reduce the position in the portfolio. If the fundamentals are bad, I'll sell. Or if I bought a company for a restructuring and it has been completed, I'll eliminate the position. That's really good advice for anyone. When you buy a stock because you think something is going to happen and it happens, get rid of it. Move on to something bigger and better when the transformation is complete. Once the transformation is behind these companies, the reason for owning them doesn't exist anymore unless it's a very long-term restructuring story. When the fundamentals are disappointing and you don't have confidence in the company, sell it. But it's hard to sell a company if the fundamentals are still pretty good and working in your favor, so what I do then is trim.

Kazanjian: *What if the restructuring has taken place, as you expected, but the fundamentals are still good?*

Williams: That's the dilemma. As often as not, I make the mistake of holding on too long when fundamentals weaken and, as a result, the stock again underperforms. One of the professors at my 25th business school reunion presented a study of this very syndrome. He discussed how stocks typically outperform leading up to the consolidation or restructuring, but underperform thereafter. His conclusion was exactly what I had intuitively believed. The time to get out is when the restructuring is completed and behind you. Once the restructuring is done, such companies tend to underperform for a couple of years, even though the fundamentals may be good. I am forever trying to convince myself that things are different this time. But they usually aren't.

Kazanjian: *Is that what happened with Qualcomm?*

Williams: Exactly. I trimmed that position along the way, but held on to more than I should have.

Kazanjian: *It's like a father who falls overly in love with a certain kid.*

Williams: Yes, in the sense that emotion takes over when more calculated reasoning should prevail. The problem is you tend to get too many names in the portfolio. I try to limit mine to about 65 or so. With many more than that, I find the fund essentially mirrors the S&P 500, which we are being paid to outperform. With so many small positions, you don't have the focus you need to really outsmart the index. That's the risk of not selling judiciously.

Kazanjian: *Are you well diversified among those 65 or so names, in terms of sectors and such?*

Williams: Definitely. I like to use the cash flow to build up small positions in the beginning. I usually put about 1 percent of the portfolio in a new position. If I'm not convinced that all of the bad news is out, I'll buy a smaller position and add to it when the price goes down. I like to buy when prices are down. Of course, I'm no better than anyone else when it comes to picking the exact bottom. It's a tough thing to do. You think a stock is cheap, but then it gets cheaper. One good bit of wisdom is that when we're in a bull market, stocks go higher than they should; conversely, when we're in a bear market, they go lower than the fundamentals warrant.

Kazanjian: *Do you find yourself mostly in large or small stocks?*

Williams: I invest in companies of all sizes. Right now because large-caps have performed so well for so long, I'm investing around the edges a bit. There's more opportunity in some of the small- and mid-cap names. But my fund is big enough now that I really can't own too many small names.

Kazanjian: *You seem to do well in both growth and value markets. Is that because you hold on to some of the value names when they turn into growth stocks?*

Williams: Yes. I've heard other people describe my approach as being a good fund to own for all seasons. Even though I buy cheap stocks, I think I've got enough "growthy" names in the portfolio that I tend to do relatively well when growth stocks are in favor.

Kazanjian: *You own foreign companies as well. Do you evaluate those the same way?*

Williams: I try to keep an open mind. It's more of a bottom-up approach. If I see an interesting idea and it's a foreign stock, I become interested. It's not so much that it's a foreign stock per se, but just the fact that it's a cheap stock that happens to be headquartered overseas.

Kazanjian: *Do foreign companies tend to deal with the same restructuring issues, and is management key for those companies as well?*

Williams: I tend to invest in just the biggest foreign companies. In many cases the management was educated at the same business schools that CEOs in this country have gone to. I think U.S. companies deserve to sell at higher multiples now than foreign companies because the environment in this country is better for business. In Europe, even though policies seem to be improving, nations are still overtaxed, have a socialist mindset, and are very protective of labor—all of the things that reduce productivity and make it difficult to make money. At this point it would take a pretty convincing story for me to invest overseas in a big way. I think the U.S. is still the better place to be, especially because our stocks are cheaper now than they were a year or two ago.

Kazanjian: *What's the biggest lesson that will come out of the bear market that began in 2000?*

Williams: The obvious lesson is don't overpay. That's what went on here and is being corrected now.

Kazanjian: *Will all of the damage be healthy for the market in the long run?*

Williams: It's what markets always do. We used to have 4-year cycles. Now it looks like we may have 8- or 10-year cycles. Maybe the cycles are a bit different, but the market always goes from extremes of fear to extremes of greed. We went through a period of extreme greed and we're going back to extreme fear. Markets tend to go both up and down more than you think they should until regressing to more realistic valuations. That's another one of the lessons. It's very hard to time these things with accuracy.

Kazanjian: *Do you expect the tech sector to come back like it did before?*

Williams: Yes, in the long run because of the growth potential. But don't hold your breath. Stay only with the good technology companies. Like location in real estate, it's quality, quality, quality that counts for long-term results in investing. I have a great deal of confidence long-term in Texas Instruments and Nokia, but I still have no confidence whatsoever in some of the junkier tech names that were so popular in recent years. None of these companies has earnings, and companies must have earnings to support higher stock prices in the long run.

Kazanjian: *You said earlier that you sell when the restructuring isn't working out. Do you have a time limit for that to take place?*

Williams: If a company doesn't perform up to expectations after a year, it's time to evaluate what went wrong with a bias to eliminating the stock from your portfolio. Too many losers "torpedo" performance, and there has to be a discipline to freshen up a stale portfolio. I prefer to put the money into a new company that I have more confidence in, or add to an existing company in the portfolio that is performing better.

Kazanjian: *That sounds logical.*

Williams: If you want to understand what makes my portfolio work, it's the simple arithmetic of what I look for. I like companies that are growing a bit faster than the market and that I can buy for a valuation that's less than the market overall. My companies typically have a higher return on equity than the market. They almost invariably have a better near-term earnings outlook, yet I pay anywhere from a 33 to 50 percent discount to the market.

That being said, you get what you pay for in this business. Yes, my stocks are cheaper. But you have to be careful. They also have a greater risk of not making their numbers because they don't have the earnings visibility shared by many of the better, "growthier" companies. I have more earnings risk, but if I'm correct at picking out the companies that really will produce better earnings growth, I'll get these earnings at a cheap price and profit on the way up. Earnings really do ultimately drive the market, even for the more troubled companies that I invest in.

Williams is also competitive away from the office. He plays golf, hikes, and is an avid runner. That's why it came as a shock in early 2000 when Williams began having muted chest pains while working out. A visit to the doctor revealed he had seven clogged arteries, even though he otherwise felt fine. Williams was forced to undergo a quadruple bypass. Fortunately, he has fully recovered. Could it be that the stress of Wall Street finally caught up with him? Williams doubts it. His doctor told him such diseases are largely hereditary.

In addition, Williams has a new boss, now that discount broker Charles Schwab has taken over U.S. Trust. So far, Williams says the new ownership hasn't caused any major changes, since Schwab has lived up to its promise to leave U.S. Trust alone. ■

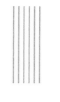

PART TWO

INVESTING LIKE THE MASTERS

WHAT THE MASTERS
HAVE IN COMMON

When I wrote *Wizards of Wall Street,* an earlier collection of interviews with investment managers, I uncovered several traits that the best managers all seem to have in common. Perhaps not surprisingly, the Masters share many of these same characteristics. Other characteristics are unique to their value orientation.

A feel for value in their bones. Most of the Masters are inherently value-conscious people. Many grew up in middle-class families and learned the value of a buck early on. By and large, they look for bargains in life as much as they do in the stock market. As several of them point out, you don't really learn to become a value investor. You must have these inherent beliefs within you in the first place. If you're the kind of person who spends money freely, never buys anything on sale, and doesn't pinch pennies, it will likely be harder for you to truly adopt the value philosophy.

Unbridled passion for their jobs. As with the Wizards of Wall Street, the Masters have a real love for the work they do. Investing is more than a profession. Although these managers also have outside interests, their work clearly takes the front seat.

Allegiance to Graham and Buffett. The Masters almost universally admire and study the two most highly regarded value investors of all time: Benjamin Graham and Warren Buffett. Many true value afficionados have read and reread Graham's *The Intelligent Investor,* and they pay close attention to the actions of Buffett, both personally and through his doings at Berkshire Hathaway.

A taste for their own cooking. The Masters invest their own money according to a value style, usually in their own funds. All other things being equal, it's desirable to invest with a manager whose own money is in the same pot as yours. These managers are bound to be more careful about how they run the portfolio when they have a personal stake in its performance.

Ability to stick to their knitting. Even when the value approach seems to be out of favor, the Masters hold firm to their convictions and stay with their discipline. Granted, it's not always easy to do, especially when it causes your performance to lag the overall market. But they realize that over time, holding to their convictions will lead to solid long-term investment results. (For more on this, see key number 7 in the next chapter.)

THE 10 KEYS
TO SUCCESSFUL VALUE
INVESTING

As you have no doubt gathered from reading these profiles, each Master has a slightly different way of defining value and uncovering promising investment ideas. Nevertheless, I have identified 10 traits that most of the Masters share. They are what I call "the 10 keys to successful value investing."

1. **Stick with the market.** Although there are some exceptions to this rule, the Masters by and large remain invested in the market at all times. Christopher Browne, for one, says that he keeps his portfolios as fully invested as possible to avoid missing those sessions when the market posts favorable returns. "Research shows that 80 to 90 percent of investment returns occur during just 2 to 7 percent of your total holding time," he points out. As a result, sitting on the sidelines is likely to hurt your performance, especially in the long run.

   David Dreman says that he raises cash only when the market is in the middle of a freefall, which happens very rarely. "I've seen too many good money managers get hurt trying to outsmart the market," he says. "They wind up missing the rallies."

   In fact, when the markets fall, Chuck Royce maintains that's the time to be putting more money to work, not taking it out. "If the markets go down, you want to add to your positions. The best way, in general, is to dollar cost average." Dollar cost averaging involves investing regular amounts on an ongoing basis, regardless of what's happening with the overall market. This technique allows you to buy more shares for your money when the market is lower. As a result, by continually investing regardless of the climate, you can use market volatility to your advantage.

2. **Think like an owner of a business.** Warren Buffett has often said that his favorite holding period for a stock is forever. That's because he doesn't view stocks as pieces of paper. When he buys shares in a company, he does so with the attitude that he's becoming a part owner of the entire business. That's the same philosophy followed by the Masters. As a result, they don't make a purchase without doing careful due diligence, and they buy with the idea that they will remain a shareholder for some time to come. "If you view yourself as a long-term partner of the business, you're happy to stay put," according to James Gipson.

Likewise, rather than paying constant attention to the company's stock price, the Masters concentrate on how well the business itself is progressing, which they know will lead to increased returns in the long run. "We're not trying to find companies that are going to go up in the next six months," notes Bret Stanley. "We're truly adopting a long-term horizon. We think about whether it's a business we want to be involved in, and whether there's a big gap between perception and reality that's causing a disconnect between price and value."

3. **Pay attention to price.** Although they have different ways of defining it, all of the Masters are looking to buy stocks at what they consider a bargain price. Often they seek to purchase shares of their targeted companies at a hefty discount to what is called intrinsic value. (Some also refer to this as either business value or market value.) Intrinsic value is often defined as the price a company could fetch on the open market if it were sold entirely to a private investor.

In most cases, the Masters also search for stocks with low PE ratios, especially relative to the overall market. "As we speak, the PE on my fund is about 16, which is almost a 30 percent discount to the S&P 500 and a 15 percent discount to the Russell 1000," says Kent Simons. Others, like Jim Gilligan, are a bit more flexible. "We don't use a strict PE measure," he points out. "We look at the potential relative to the price. For example, we bought AOL right after the accounting problems surfaced in 1996. It was a value stock then, even though it didn't have earnings." Why? Because, in Gilligan's mind, the potential for earnings was there.

In Ron Muhlenkamp's eyes, all successful investors pay attention to price. "If you look at the people with good long-term records, one way or another they're value investors," he maintains. "I'll pay up for growth. I just won't pay an unlimited amount."

In fact, says Dave Williams, overpaying for growth is what caused the huge technology and Internet bubble to burst in 2000. "The obvious lesson [from this event] is don't overpay," he insists. "That's what went on then and is being corrected now."

But not every Master follows a pure cut-and-dry, by-the-numbers approach. Some are more flexible in defining value than others. "We are absolutely valuation purists," says Bill Miller. "But we are not valuation simpletons. One thing we've learned over the years is that simple-minded computer screens—such as screens for low PE or low price-to-book or low price-to-cash-flow stocks—do not tell you much about value. They can leave out many great companies that look expensive but are actually worth a lot more than they're trading for."

4. **Buy what's out of favor.** When you're price conscious, you frequently wind up buying merchandise that's not in great demand at the time of purchase. It makes sense when you think about it. The greater the demand, the higher the price. It follows, then, that the stocks that go on sale are those that the rest of Wall Street is less interested in at the moment. "In 1993, for example, when Hillary and Bill were going to rewrite healthcare in this country, all of the pharmaceutical stocks were trading at low double-digit PEs," notes Christopher Browne. "Johnson & Johnson sold at 12.5 times earnings. If you took out the pharmaceutical business altogether, you were paying a fair price for Tylenol, Band-Aids, Johnson's Baby Oil, and all of the other products. In essence, you got the pharmaceutical business for free." Browne loaded up on the stock and still holds it today.

There are many reasons investors grow disenchanted with stocks. "Investors are always voting," Bob Olstein reasons. "They have a perception about a company. The price of a company's stock is based on that perception at any point in time. A value guy like me tries to predict when these perceptions are wrong and will eventually change."

"The market is always going from one group to the next," says Dick Weiss. "One thing's in vogue this month, and something else is in vogue next month. Sometimes companies have a disappointment and the stock goes down, yet whatever caused the disappointment is no longer impacting results. It could be that the company isn't in a very exciting area and it's not catching Wall Street's fancy. That's just the way the market works."

Other times, as Kevin O'Boyle explains, such negative perceptions are caused by problems the company creates for itself. "A lot of times companies that make acquisitions have a lot of trouble digesting the acquisition," he says. "Either they pay too much and it results in a dilution to earnings, or they actually have trouble integrating the acquired company into the operation, from either a cultural or logistic standpoint."

The trick is to determine if and when the problems will be corrected, at which time investors will once again get interested in the stock. As a result, you must be a forward thinker. "For example, many people forget that the semiconductor industry is cyclical," Bob Perkins offers. "We look at what these companies could make when the cycle is good again. We've been able to find stocks trading at 8 to 10 times earnings that used to sell for 30 or 40 times earnings. Once the problem is corrected, the Street could legitimately pay 20 or 25 times earnings for that growth."

5. **Build your portfolio from the bottom up.** There are two primary approaches to portfolio building: top-down and bottom-up. Top-down investors generally start by looking at the overall economic landscape, market environment, and sector fundamentals. They then make predictions about what companies and industries might benefit from these conditions, before going out and finding individual stocks that fit into these themes. By contrast, bottom-up investors pay little attention to these more macro considerations. Instead, they seek out individual companies one by one. As it turns out, most of the Masters take a bottom-up approach.

"We look at each company on an individual basis," insists Kevin O'Boyle. "Obviously we have to take the macroeconomic environment into consideration when we evaluate the prospects for a company, but we're not really looking at the overall market."

Jean-Marie Eveillard even applies a bottom-up approach to building his global portfolio. "There is never a concern about any countries or sectors being underweighted," he maintains. For instance, when he couldn't find any Japanese securities that met his value criteria in mid-1988, he had no money in that country, even though most analysts were positive on the market's fundamentals at that time.

And although the big picture is always in the background, Ron Muhlenkamp says that sometimes the bottom-up approach leads you to a more general trend that you can latch on to. "If we find a lot of companies in [a given] area [or sector], we look to see if there's a general theme to follow. Is it because profitability has improved from what it used to be and people haven't figured it out yet? Or is it because of a political risk? If you can't figure it out, you do some digging."

6. **Know when to sell.** It is often said that the decision to sell a stock is harder to make than the decision to buy. That's why the Masters have clearly defined criteria for determining when to sell a stock. In fact, most set a sales price target before making the initial purchase. "We will sell a stock when it reaches intrinsic value," says James Gipson, echoing a theme that's common among his fellow value investors. "It can [reach intrinsic value] in two ways. Either the price can go up, or the value can go down."

Because intrinsic value is always changing, a sell target set when a stock is bought is always subject to revision. "Don't forget that intrinsic value is usually growing, so I may not sell an entire position just because it's fully valued," says Bret Stanley. "In other words, there are companies that can be bought for $75 or $80 today where the intrinsic value is $100," Jean-Marie Eveillard explains. "If they continue to create value, next year intrinsic value may be $115, and two years down the line it could go up to $125, etc." Adds Bill Fries, "If the company has done everything it was supposed to do, earnings are higher, and the multiple is still at a reasonable level, then we may end up hanging on to the stock and coming up with a new price target."

In addition to reaching a given price target, there are a few other reasons the Masters might sell out of a position. "The most common reason I sell is because I find something that's more attrac-

tive," notes Bret Stanley. "I may sell a stock that has modest upside to buy another one that has significant upside, especially if I
consider the business to be of equal quality."

And, given that they view buying shares of stock as taking an
ownership position in the company, the Masters also sell when
they no longer want to be part of the business. "When there's a
change in the fundamentals strong enough that the outlook isn't
as promising, we'll sell immediately," David Dreman says. "We
found it pays to sell, not if there's a bad quarter, but if there is a
major fundamental change in the longer-term outlook."

7. **Have patience.** No one ever said that value investing was easy.
Because you are buying what's currently out of favor, it can take
months or even years for the rest of Wall Street to see the potential you have uncovered. In addition, there are times when investors throw valuation out the door and become enamored of
high-flying glamour stocks trading at outrageous prices. This
happened during the late 1990s and into early 2000, a period
when value investors as a group seemed to be completely out of
step. Perhaps Wally Weitz puts it best when he says, "You need
to have patience and a willingness to look dumb for a while" to
be a successful value investor.

The Masters have all made a commitment to stick to their discipline, even during the tough times. "Your readers should realize
that whatever investment style they select, periods of superior
performance generally come in unpredictable lumps," Jim Gipson
says. "This is one of the things that frustrates people who are trying to get rich quick or making long-term judgments about the
deployment of capital based on short-term performance."

By the same token, because they are patient, the Masters don't
automatically sell a stock just because its price goes down. "A lot
of people ask how far we'd let the stock price fall before we'd
sell," Bill Nygren observes. "I have almost infinite patience for a
stock that's going down if the business is growing well. In fact,
lots of times I'll add to my position."

8. **Be wary of Wall Street recommendations.** Research reports and
recommendations by Wall Street analysts have come under significant scrutiny in recent times. Much of this stems from the Inter-

net and technology debacle, in which analysts gave glowing recommendations to companies their firms brought to the public market, but which went bust a short time later. The Masters have always been wary of such research. "Maybe I was naïve when I first came into the business, but I think the credibility of Wall Street has declined immeasurably since I entered this business 27 years ago," Dave Williams observes. "You have to somehow corroborate what [the analysts] are saying with your own instincts."

That doesn't mean the Masters ignore this research altogether. "We look at outside research, but we don't trust anybody," Jean-Marie Eveillard insists. "There is a conflict of interest associated with investment banking and research. Most of the research is done for growth investors who are looking for securities to move into today and out of in six or nine months."

Still, such reports can provide many general insights into a company's overall operating environment, as Ron Muhlenkamp points out. "[The research] certainly can be useful, but I never ask an analyst what stock to buy. I want an analyst to tell me what's going on in the industry and what's going on in the company. Their job is to know their companies. My job is to figure out what the values are and what companies I want to own."

9. **Get to know the company and those who run it.** Similarly, the Masters view research as a crucial component of their jobs. They just like to do most of it themselves. Before buying any stock, they try to get a firm grip on what makes the company tick, which often involves spending quality time with management. "There is always an execution risk in these companies. Therefore you must place a lot of emphasis on the people running the company," says Kent Simons. "Because you're buying companies that are under pressure and dealing with adversity, you want to make sure they don't have a 30-mile-per-hour wind at their back. A lot of what I do is quantitative, since I look for low valuations, with high returns on equity and strong long-term earnings. But much of my work is also qualitative. What is the management like? Are they running the company, or is the company running them? Do they have a long-term goal in mind? If so, how reasonable is it? I look at how they are going to get to the goal, and whether their approach makes sense."

Wally Weitz also pays close attention to management. "I look at whether they have a good handle on their business. Is their strategy consistent with what their industry is all about or at least what I think it's all about? In a two-hour interview, I might only spend the last 10 minutes on current results. Nobody really knows what's going to happen in a small company. It should be growing, but it's new. Changes occur all the time. What I'm really trying to ascertain is how these managers will adapt and react to changing circumstances. How will they react when their number-one customer goes and does something crazy?"

Marty Whitman's due diligence process involves not only talking with management, but also closely examining all publicly available company documents, to see if their story bears out in reality. "We would never appraise a management just by listening to them talk," he insists. "Not when there's a public record that tells you a lot of things about them."

10. **Minimize risk.** If you do your homework carefully and follow all nine of the previous rules, you should have not only a potentially profitable portfolio, but also one with relatively low risk. In fact, most of the Masters maintain that controlling risk is at the forefront of what they do. Jean-Marie Eveillard often says that he pays more attention to how much money he can lose than to how much he can make from investing in a given stock.

Risk reduction is also important to Chuck Royce, although that wasn't always the case. Royce was once known for buying the go-go growth stocks of the late 1960s and early 1970s. But after losing a great deal of money in the 1973–74 bear market, he changed his ways. "I lost most of my money by having undue speculative risk in the portfolio, not understanding the importance of balance sheets, not understanding diversification principles, and not understanding integrity principles as they relate to individual companies," he admits. "Lower risk doesn't diminish returns. Contrary to what the academics tell you, risk and reward are not virtually correlated, at least not in my experience."

How do you lower risk? "[By] being aware of what you're doing and what the company is all about. Is it a speculative company? Does it have a good balance sheet? Does it have a track record? I think you want to get in touch with reality. The closer you are to reality, the better you'll be at making judgments about risk," Royce says.

According to John Goode, you also lower risk by buying decent businesses. "If you've got a good franchise with significant upside, that upside versus a constrained downside by definition produces a positive risk/reward ratio," he says.

GLOSSARY OF FREQUENTLY USED VALUE-INVESTING TERMS

alpha—Excess return provided by an investment that is uncorrelated with the general stock market.

asset allocation—Act of spreading investment funds across various asset categories, such as stocks, bonds, and cash.

behavioral finance—A field of study that combines finance and psychology in an effort to predict the behavior of markets or particular securities.

beta—A co-efficient measure of a stock's relative volatility in relation to the Standard & Poor's 500 index, which has a beta of 1.

bid price—The highest amount a buyer is willing to pay for shares of a stock.

book value—What a company would be worth if all assets were sold (assets minus liabilities). Also, the price at which an asset is carried on a balance sheet.

bottom-up investing—The search for outstanding individual stocks with little regard for overall economic trends.

cash ratio—Ratio of cash and marketable securities to current liabilities. Tells the extent to which liabilities could be immediately liquidated.

contrarian—Investor who does the opposite of the majority at any particular time.

convertible bond—Security that can be exchanged for other securities of the issuer (under certain conditions), usually from preferred stock or bonds into common stock.

cost of capital—The opportunity cost of an investment. In other words, the rate of return that a company or investor could earn at the same risk level as the investment being considered.

credit risk—Possibility that a bond issuer will default on the payment of interest and return of principal. Risk is minimized by investing in bonds issued by large blue-chip corporations or government agencies.

current assets—Balance sheet item equal to the sum of cash and cash equivalents, accounts receivable, inventory, marketable securities, prepaid expenses, and other assets that could be converted into cash in less than one year.

current ratio—Current assets divided by current liabilities. Shows a company's ability to pay current debts from current assets.

debt-to-equity ratio—Long-term debt divided by shareholders' equity. Indicates how highly leveraged a company is.

distribution—Dividends paid from net investment income plus realized capital gains.

diversification—Spreading risk by putting assets into several different investment categories, such as stocks, bonds, and cash.

dividend—Distribution of earnings to shareholders.

dividend yield—The cash dividend paid per share each year divided by the current share price.

dollar cost averaging—The process of accumulating positions in stocks and mutual funds by investing a set amount of money each month, thus buying more shares when prices are down, less when they are up.

fair market value—Price at which an asset is or can be passed on from a willing buyer to a willing seller.

institutional investor—Organization that trades a large volume of securities, like a mutual fund, bank, or insurance company.

intrinsic value—Estimated worth of a company; often as determined by a value manager's proprietary valuation models.

market capitalization or market value—Calculated by multiplying the number of shares outstanding by the per share price of a stock. One can also categorize equities into several different classes, including micro-cap, small-cap, mid-cap, and large-cap. The general guidelines for these classifications are as follows:

- micro-cap—market capitalizations of $0 to $500 million.
- small-cap—market capitalizations of $500 to $2 billion
- mid-cap—market capitalizations of $2 billion to $5 billion.
- large-cap—market capitalizations of $5 billion or more.

Nasdaq Composite—An index of the National Association of Securities Dealers weighted by market value and representing domestic companies that are sold over the counter.

net current assets—Assets calculated by taking current assets minus current liabilities. Also referred to as working capital.

price/earnings ratio (PE)—Price of a stock divided by its earnings per share.

price-to-book ratio (P/B)—Shareholders' equity divided by the number of outstanding shares. If under 1, it means a stock is selling for less than the price the company paid for its assets, though this is not necessarily indicative of a good value.

price-to-cash-flow ratio—A stock's capitalization divided by its cash flow for the latest fiscal year.

price-to-sales ratio—A stock's capitalization divided by its sales over the trailing 12 months.

private market value—The value of a company if each of its parts were owned and/or sold independently.

return on equity (ROE)—Measure of how well a company used reinvested earnings to generate additional earnings. Equal to a fiscal year's after-tax income divided by book value, expressed as a percentage.

Standard & Poor's Composite Index of 500 Stocks (S&P 500)—An index that tracks the performance of 500 stocks, mostly blue chips, and represents almost two-thirds of the U.S. stock market's total value. It is weighted by market value.

shareholders' equity—Total assets minus total liabilities of an individual company. Also known as net assets.

stock—Represents ownership in a corporation. Usually listed in terms of shares.

top-down—Investment strategy which first finds the best sectors or industries to invest in, and then searches for the best companies within those sectors or industries.

technical analysis—Method of analyzing securities by relying on the assumption that market data, such as price charts, volume, and open interest can help predict future—especially short-term—market trends.

turnover—For a company, the ratio of annual sales to inventory. For a mutual fund, the number of times a year that a manager turns over the securities in a portfolio.

ABOUT THE AUTHOR

Kirk Kazanjian is a nationally recognized investment expert, best-selling author, and lifelong entrepreneur. He spent several years as an award-winning television news anchor and business reporter, before moving into various roles within the investment industry. Among other things, Kazanjian is the former Director of Research and Investment Strategy for two leading investment firms, where he performed investment manager research and due diligence, oversaw the creation of new investment programs, and developed strategies for managing more than $1.6 billion in client assets.

In addition to *Value Investing with the Masters*, Kazanjian has written many other investment books, including *Wizards of Wall Street, Growing Rich with Growth Stocks,* and the annual *Mutual Fund Investor's Guide.*

Kazanjian regularly offers investment advice on CNBC, CNNfn, and Bloomberg, plus many other radio and television stations across the country. He has been featured in numerous publications, including *Barron's, Mutual Funds Magazine, Entrepreneur, The Christian Science Monitor,* and *USA Today,* and is a popular speaker and teacher on investment topics.

The author welcomes your comments and feedback. He can be reached through his website at www.kirkkazanjian.com.

INDEX